Anoth

MW01717406

A Life Spent Near the Edge

By: D. B. Waldman

David Waldman

dbwaldmanauthor@gmail.com

Another Bullet Dodged

A Life Spent Near the Edge

Contents

Another Bullet Dodged

A Life Spent Near the Edge

Contents

FOREWORD

One can't explain why a little boy bonds to his grandfather; it just happens. My son bonded to my father over the simple act of eating bagels together. He became Bagel Grandpa. I bonded with my dad's father, Morris, over trains. His nickname to me was Button-man.

Morris was born in 1899 in Belarus, in Eastern Europe. Around 1912, his family fled due to escalating attacks on Jewish towns that began in 1903 and spread across the Russian Empire. Jews were murdered in their homes in what became known as pogroms—state-tolerated violence intended to annihilate Jewish communities.

Because the United States imposed strict quotas on Jewish immigration, my Waldman family first fled to Argentina, then to Uruguay. My grandfather attended high school in South America and became fluent in Spanish—his third language, after Russian and Yiddish.

When his family finally won the lottery to immigrate to the United States, World War I was underway, creating a manpower shortage. American railroads needed laborers, including Spanish-speaking workers imported from Mexico. Because Morris spoke Spanish and some English, the Pennsylvania Railroad in Cleveland hired him to help manage Hispanic workers in the rail yards. Thus began his 45-year railroad career in 1919.

In the 1960s, every Friday night my family piled into our VW van and drove from Cleveland Heights down the hill to East Cleveland for Sabbath dinner at my grandparents' home. Those evenings with Button-man are among my earliest memories. After dinner, some of us grandchildren would walk with Grandpa to the end of the street, sit on a stone wall by the tracks, and wait for trains to pass. I remember holding his hand and feeling the ground tremble as the engines thundered by.

Somewhere in that ritual, a subtle message lodged itself in my young brain—connecting transportation with joy. At least, I like to believe that.

My grandfather retired after his fourth heart attack around his sixty-fifth birthday, having risen to the position of train conductor—the captain of the train. He died six months later, in 1965, when I was seven years old. The love of movement and machinery he planted in me never left. I carry that piece of him with me still.

With that transportation bug firmly embedded, forty-two years of my adult life were spent moving through the world as a professional aviator. I lived the gift of motion that began with Button-man's love of the rails and his love for his grandchildren.

As a captain for Northwest Airlines, I honored my grandfather before nearly every departure. On the public address system, I would welcome passengers aboard, blow a train whistle, and announce, "All aboard." It felt right. I suspect a few older passengers smiled, too.

Tradition connects people across time. That small ritual reminded me that I was the great-grandson of peasant farmers from Eastern Europe and the grandson of a railroad conductor in the New World.

A career in aviation gave me the opportunity to see cities across five continents. I crisscrossed the globe for decades, though the experience was less glamorous than it sounds. A crew hotel room is a lonely place compared to traveling with loved ones. Those who don't travel for work may not understand that distinction, but it is real—and at times, overpowering.

Crewmembers often try to substitute for family by doing things together on the road: sightseeing, meals, shared walks through unfamiliar cities. Those moments help. But at the end of the day, the road warrior still lays his head down alone. It is, after all, a business trip.

This is not a complaint. I chose this profession knowingly and loved it. Still, raising a family while flying internationally brought unique challenges—especially before the internet and modern communication tools existed.

Much of my career occurred before email, video calls, or affordable global phone service. International communication was unreliable and expensive. As a result, my family adopted a no-communication rule while I was overseas. Unless someone was seriously ill or injured, we would not speak during trips that often lasted twelve to fourteen days.

That reality segmented my life into two worlds: one at home as a husband and father, and another alone, moving through the world. Much of what happened to me on the road never made it back to my family. Likewise, much of their daily life passed without me.

My professional career spanned 1978-2020. The years of raising children overlapped heavily with that time. My kids missed large portions of my life, and I missed large portions of theirs.

Today, my children are adults in their mid-thirties. I am retired. This book is my attempt to connect those two lives at last—to share what happened during the years I was gone and to bring those stories home.

I have limited this book to thirty episodes that meaningfully shaped me. A life spent in motion is not constantly dramatic; most days are routine. But there are moments—moments that require bullets to be dodged—that stay with you forever.

While these stories were first written for my family, I hope they resonate beyond it. Aviators may recognize the technical truths within them. Travelers may recognize the pull of the road. And perhaps younger readers will see the value of perseverance, sacrifice, and humility in building a life.

My hope is that these pages offer a blend of travel, tension, humor, education, and honesty—and that the reader occasionally pauses, reflects, and feels they were there with me.

ACKNOWLEDGMENTS

This book would not exist without the tireless efforts of my good friend and next-door neighbor, Charles McLeskey, M.D.

Day after day, Charlie sat with me and read this manuscript aloud—line by line, page by page. In addition to correcting grammar and spelling, he helped organize a narrative that others could more easily follow, understand, and (I hope) enjoy.

While the stories are mine, Charlie's insight made them readable. He also observed that I am something of a "trouble magnet," and it was he who coined the title **ANOTHER BULLET DODGED**.

Without his patience and commitment, this book would not have been completed. He claims it is the first book he has ever read cover to cover—and out loud, no less. That level of dedication deserves more thanks than words can provide.

Charlie, thank you for being my friend, my teacher, my sounding board, and my champion.

I also wish to thank my brother Lee, who created the cover artwork for this book. His love and support have been constant, and I am grateful for the care he brought to helping share my story with others.

A Note to the Reader

Throughout this book, you will occasionally see the words *See Inside the Story.* These references point to optional sections at the end of the chapter that explain technical terms, aviation procedures, or background information in greater detail.

You may skip them and continue with the story, or read them at the end of the chapter for additional context.

Also, photos referenced in the story are located in the middle of the book.

Chapter 1

IN THE CROSSHAIRS

Part 1

"Good judgement comes from experience, and a lot of that comes from bad judgement."
—Will Rogers

Age 38 · 1996

We were still circling in a holding pattern over the narrowest part of the Persian Gulf, only miles from Iranian airspace, when the cockpit speakers exploded to life with an external voice.

"Northwest Flight 9827, you have strayed into Iranian airspace. Iranian Air Force fighters have been scrambled to intercept you. Immediately turn heading one-eight-zero, accelerate to maximum speed, and get the hell out of there. They are going supersonic."

The blood drained from our faces.

The voice didn't come from God—but it might as well have.

I stared at the captain flying the airplane.

"What the hell happened?" I said.

"Turn. Dive. Now."

He looked over with an expression I'll never forget—caught, unmoored, suddenly small.

"I was hand-flying," he said. "Got a little disoriented."

"In the Persian Gulf?" I snapped. "In 1996? With Iran twenty-one miles away?"

He shrugged. "Sorry."

The captain rolled into a hard turn toward the south and shoved the power levers forward until they hit the stops. The engines surged as we pitched into a steep descent, trading altitude for speed.

It felt like digging spurs into a horse's ribs.

Giddy up, old girl.

Our DC-10 was a four-hundred-thousand-pound giant, optimized for efficiency, not escape. We needed to get from a slow holding speed to maximum speed immediately, and gravity was the only ally available.

I reached forward and switched the weather radar into map mode—using it not for storm recognition, but for coastline identification. The picture sharpened.

We were thirteen miles beyond the Iranian coastline—twenty-five miles from international airspace.

The cockpit went quiet—not calm, but focused.

Eyes fixed on the airspeed indicator as it crept upward, tenth by tenth, toward the redline. Once we reached it and stabilized on the escape heading, there would be nothing left to do.

No tactics.

No maneuvering.

No leverage.

For every mile we clawed back toward international airspace, they could cover three.

We couldn't outrun them.

We couldn't outclimb them.

We couldn't outmaneuver them.

And we couldn't shoot missiles at them.

At Mach 0.87—roughly 620 miles per hour—we were fast by airline standards. Glacial compared to Iranian fighters that could exceed Mach 2.

The Mach needle hunted between 0.86 and 0.88. We were already at redline. Any faster risked structural failure—tearing the airplane apart long before a missile ever reached us.

Prudence demanded restraint even while survival demanded speed.

So, we waited.

Time and distance were the only variables left in a deadly equation.

Twenty-five miles.

At their speed, that was nothing.

At ours, it was everything.

The Iranian coastline seemed frozen in place, as if distance itself had decided to punish us.

I felt completely helpless.

Whoever had warned us could see what we could not. They could track the fighters. They could calculate closure rates. They could tell us when the math turned in our favor—or against it.

But they couldn't protect us.

Sending U.S. fighters into Iranian airspace would be an act of war, and no airline crew was worth that.

Time slowed.

Not dramatically—clinically.

The danger hadn't passed. There was simply nothing left to do but wait. *(See Inside the Story: Why we believed Iran would shoot us out of the sky rather than forcing us to land.)*

My mind replayed the last half hour, searching for the moment we'd fallen off the rails and ended up in Iran, fleeing for our lives. Twenty-five minutes earlier, our flying day had been progressing normally—boringly—after completing our mission.

We had delivered U.S. troops to Prince Sultan Air Base in Saudi Arabia and departed for Dubai.

Saudi ATC handed us off to the UAE controller.

Everything had been routine.

Until it wasn't.

Because of regional tensions, the UAE required a discreet five-digit security code for airspace entry. We had it—printed clearly on our flight paperwork.

On first contact, I gave the code.

"Entry denied," the controller replied.

I tried again.

Denied.

A third time.

Denied.

With only ten miles to the UAE boundary and no clearance, we were ordered into a holding pattern over the Strait of Hormuz—international airspace but pressed tight against Iran's edge.

Close enough to feel the gravity of it.

The only way out was to resolve the clearance problem, and as Pilot Monitoring, that responsibility fell to me. I assumed it was a simple error—a daily mismatch, a clerical problem. But in

1996, airline crews flying a 1972 airplane didn't have satellite radios. To reach my company in Minneapolis, I had to use HF—World War II–era technology that sounded like two kids shouting through tin cans tied together with string.

In red: the approximate location of our holding pattern near the northern tip of the United Arab Emirates, over the Strait of Hormuz.

Baghdad Radio finally answered. After repeated phonetic spellings and garbled exchanges, they patched me through to Northwest Dispatch in Minnesota.

I explained our predicament: denied entry, low fuel state, and holding over the Gulf.

The dispatcher read me the correct code.

It matched ours exactly.

He asked us to stand by while he called the UAE directly.

While we waited, fuel burned.

We were holding in the low twenties—an inefficient altitude for a heavy jet, burning roughly four thousand gallons per hour. The second officer announced we were approaching bingo fuel: the point where a decision must be made—land or divert immediately.

Every minute mattered now.

Dispatch finally came back on the HF radio. He had personally spoken with the UAE general responsible for airspace access. The code was correct. We were assured everything would be fine.

I switched back to VHF and called UAE ATC again, referencing the general by name and the verified code.

The response was immediate.

"Entry denied."

I stared at the microphone, words forming but refusing to assemble.

The second officer leaned forward.

"We're at bingo fuel."

Decision time.

The captain exhaled sharply.

"Let's divert."

I opened the divert paperwork and felt my stomach drop.

"Abu Dhabi," I said. "Our alternate airfield is Abu Dhabi—also in the UAE."

We stared at each other in silence.

Calling dispatch again wasn't an option. Too slow. Too much fuel was already gone.

"Declare an emergency," the captain said. "Request direct to Abu Dhabi."

I keyed the mic.

"UAE Control, Northwest 9827 declaring a fuel emergency. Request immediate vectors to Abu Dhabi."

"Denied," the controller replied. "No entry without the proper code."

We were now burning into reserves.

Margins shrinking by the minute.

The second officer handled the math—fuel flows and distances.

I handled the radios.

Riyadh was out of range. Kuwait was also too far. Qatar refused us. Oman might work—barely—if nothing went wrong. Iran wasn't an option worth speaking aloud.

The captain pulled the power back to minimum holding speed to conserve fuel further. The second officer buried himself in calculations.

We needed to find a place to land—and soon.

Every minute was sixty-six fewer gallons of fuel.

I spread charts across my lap and worked the radios nonstop. Each of us was doing exactly what we were trained to do.

Yet no one was watching the big picture.

Finally, a country had accepted us.

Bahrain.

Only one hundred miles away.

Immediate entry granted.

I had lifted my head to tell the crew the good news.

And that was when our world fell apart. The words *Bahrain has accepted us* had just rolled off my lips when the speakers had crackled to life…

The replay in my head stopped. I was right back in the cockpit, in the present.

My eyes were still locked on the airspeed indicator.

Mach 0.87—that's all we could do.

Finally, the Iranian coastline slid past the windshield.

Twelve more miles—roughly a hundred seconds at our current speed—stood between us and international airspace.

Until safety.

Fuel starvation was still a real concern, but it had dropped off the top of the list, even though our Pratt & Whitney engines were gulping fuel at a gargantuan rate. Airspace and missiles were still the primary danger.

Seven miles a minute felt impossibly slow when you were the prey.

Then the cockpit speakers came alive a second time.

"Fighters have broken off pursuit. You are clear."

Then the savior voice gave us a heading to Bahrain.

That voice that had warned us—and now released us—came from an AWACS: an Airborne Warning and Control System aircraft orbiting high above the Persian Gulf, a flying command center. They could see what we could not—radar tracks, closure rates, and Iranian fighters. *(See Inside the Story: Why a U.S. Passenger Airliner Was Flying in the Persian Gulf in 1996.)*

Photo #1. USAF AWACS in the Saudi desert

The entire escape lasted less than four minutes.

It felt like hours.

But as the tension in my body relaxed and I took a deep restorative breath, the reality struck back—we were not out of the woods.

The missile threat was gone.

The fuel problem wasn't. In fact, it was worse.

We had paid for survival with fuel we didn't have to spend.

The power levers were still nearly firewalled. The fuel gauges told the story without emotion.

The second officer spoke definitively.

"We don't have fuel for a go-around."

No drama. Just facts.

I slumped back in my seat.

The sprint had cost us dearly. We no longer had any buffer fuel for an error. The approach into Bahrain had to be perfect.

And of course—none of us had ever been there.

If we had to execute a missed approach into Bahrain, there would be no second try—just a smokin' hole.

Land—or run out of fuel.

Those were the stakes, and we all knew it.

The captain flew the approach precisely. No wavering from standards. There was no room for anything else.

The wheels touched down in Bahrain with the lowest fuel state I would ever see on a DC-10—or any large transport airplane after.

ANOTHER BULLET DODGED

Learning Points:

- *A crew is only as good as the weakest link in the chain.*
- *Competence must never be assumed simply because someone is experienced, respected, or likeable.*

Inside the Story *(Optional Reading)*

Why we believed Iran would shoot us out of the sky rather than forcing us to land

History wasn't on our side. In 1988, the *USS Vincennes* shot down Iran Air Flight 655 after mistaking it for a military aircraft. Two hundred ninety civilians were killed.

That event mattered.

We were an American military charter, now inside Iranian airspace. If fighters intercepted us, there was no reason to expect a measured response or a routine escort to landing.

We were not part of any conflict—but in that moment, that distinction might not have mattered.

We were in the crosshairs.

Why a U.S. Passenger Airliner Was Flying in the Persian Gulf in 1996

Northwest Flight 9827 was not a normal passenger flight. It was a military charter operating during a tense period in the Middle East following the first Gulf War.

In August 1990, Iraq's leader Saddam Hussein invaded neighboring Kuwait, seizing its vast oil reserves. The United States quickly assembled a coalition of more than forty countries to expel Iraqi forces. After months of military buildup, Operation Desert Storm began in January 1991 and liberated Kuwait in just over a month.

The war officially ended, but the region did not become peaceful overnight. Large numbers of American forces remained in Saudi Arabia to enforce a no-fly zone over Iraq and maintain stability in the region.

In June 1996, a terrorist truck bomb destroyed part of the Khobar Towers housing complex in Dhahran, Saudi Arabia, killing nineteen U.S. servicemen and injuring hundreds more. In response, the U.S. military moved thousands of personnel away from vulnerable urban housing and relocated them to Prince Sultan Air Base, located deep in the desert south of Riyadh.

Moving that many people and supplies required far more airlift capacity than the U.S. military alone possessed. Commercial airlines—including Northwest Airlines—were contracted to assist with the transportation of troops and equipment throughout the region.

That is why a civilian DC-10 carrying American troops was operating in the Persian Gulf that day—and why U.S. AWACS aircraft were already in the sky watching everything that moved.

CHAPTER 1

IN THE CROSSHAIRS

PART 2

AGE 38 · 1996

We rolled to a stop and set the brakes. For a moment, nobody spoke. No checklists followed. No radio calls. No debrief. The engines spooled down one by one, their whine tapering into silence, and the cockpit suddenly felt too big—too quiet—for three men who had just spent the last hour living to stay alive.

The silence was deafening.

No one moved.

The adrenaline drained all at once—like a car thrown into neutral at a hundred miles an hour.

Then the cockpit door banged open, and the flight attendants poured in—still operating under the assumption that this had been a routine flight, because from their side of the cockpit door, nothing had seemed abnormal.

"Where are we?" one of them demanded, half amused, half irritated.

No one answered.

They looked at each other, then back at us.

We hadn't briefed the cabin. We hadn't said a word. There hadn't been time—or bandwidth—to widen the circle beyond the three of us up front.

"Guys. Where are we?"

I was aware of the question, but the words wouldn't assemble. My mouth felt disconnected from my brain, like the language part of me had gone offline. I could hear them waiting, but I couldn't meet the moment with anything human.

They stared at us, waiting for more. It didn't come.

From their perspective, we had landed at some unexpected airport after a routine military charter. They'd been watching a movie. Maybe dozing. They hadn't felt the turn, the dive, the acceleration. They hadn't heard the AWACS call on Guard. They hadn't watched fuel numbers bleed downward or imagined Iranian fighter jets closing from behind waiting for missile lock.

They just saw us—three pilots sitting stiff as mannequins. Catatonic. Uncommunicative. Weird pilots doing weird pilot things.

Finally, without turning around, one of us managed, "Bahrain." That single word didn't solve the problem. It only made it stranger.

The flight attendants waited another beat, expecting the rest of the story. But the rest of the story wasn't available. Not to them, not yet—and if I'm honest, not fully to us either.

We were still trapped in that cockpit state where emotion is a luxury and speaking feels optional.

They backed out, muttering to each other, and the door closed again.

Eventually we completed the shutdown checklist mechanically, switches and levers falling into place on muscle memory alone. Only then did I notice my hands were shaking—not violently, just enough to be undeniable. My pulse thudded in my ears, a pressure building behind my eyes that I didn't yet understand. The airplane was shut down, and we were safe. My body clearly hadn't gotten the message.

Twenty-five miles. Four minutes. At a fighter's speed, the difference between survival and disaster. Measured in seconds on a watch face. The math that had almost not worked in our favor now began to haunt me. How close we had come—not in theory, not abstractly, but physically.

I thought about my wife.

My kids.

How none of them had any idea what had almost erased me from their lives.

The jet bridge thumped into place.

The cockpit door opened again, this time with purpose.

"Captain," the handler said politely, "welcome to Bahrain."

Welcome. The word felt oddly out of place in our current state of mind.

I unstrapped and stood, my legs feeling strangely weak. We gathered our headsets and flight bags in silence, the small, automatic rituals of leaving the cockpit after a flight.

The airplane smelled different now—not fuel or electronics or air-conditioning, but something harder to define. The scent of fear born of survival.

As we stepped off the plane and onto the jet bridge, the desert heat pressed in immediately—thick, dry, foreign.

The day hadn't changed. The world hadn't noticed.

But we had.

And only then—walking slowly toward the terminal—did the weight of it finally settle in.

After clearing immigration and customs, the handler showed us how to call our company in Minneapolis. Northwest Dispatch had no idea we weren't in the UAE. As far as they knew, we were in Dubai—mission complete, another routine charter—without the slightest awareness of how thin the line between normal and catastrophic had been.

With Northwest's approval, the handler arranged hotels, transportation, overnight parking for the airplane, and fuel for the morning.

We trailed the handler through the terminal, flight bags dragging, harness marks still visible on our shirts. The flight attendants' voices filled the space behind us—questions, jokes, fragments of speculation—but none of it seemed meant for us. We walked in silence, eyes forward, still somewhere else.

It settled in slowly.

Not fear.

Not relief.

Weight.

The delayed recognition of what had just happened.

For the final stretch of the flight, we had been pure function—task-oriented, emotionally flat, cognitively narrow. There had been no room for fear. Fear would have been inefficient.

Now the job was done.

And the bill came due.

On the bus ride to the hotel, the captain finally spoke to the cabin crew.

"I'm buying dinner for everyone tonight," he said. "And I'll explain what happened over a meal."

Dinner sounded impossible. All I wanted was a locked hotel room door and silence.

In my room, I dropped my bags, turned on the shower, and stepped under the water like it was a decontamination chamber. I stood there and let the water run over my face until breathing felt normal again.

And then the human part caught up.

The shame came first.

Not from the mistake—but from the helplessness.

Three professional pilots, reduced to waiting for someone else to tell us if we lived or died.

I stayed in the shower a long time. Long enough that the steam softened the image in the mirror and the world blurred at the edges.

When I finally turned the water off, I didn't feel clean.

I felt wrung out.

Standing there afterward, towel around my waist, the pieces began to fall into place.

What happened over Iran didn't start over Iran.

Two days earlier, at check-in in Minneapolis, I had met the captain and second officer for the first time. I'd been a DC-10 copilot for four years by then. I knew the airplane. I knew these military charters. I had flown plenty of similar trips. Nothing about this one had looked special on paper.

Day three had started in Germany at Ramstein Air Base—another military launch point, another load of young Americans carrying duffels and nervous energy. By the time we lifted off for Prince Sultan Air Base in the Saudi desert, our DC-10 held 290 U.S. airmen, eight flight attendants, and the three of us up front.

We landed in brutal heat—still daylight, around 108 degrees. The troops filed off into the shimmering distance, and I remember thinking how quickly their world had changed. Air-conditioning to sand and sun, in one step.

From Prince Sultan we departed for Dubai. Because of a Saudi–UAE dispute at the time, we couldn't simply cross the border the obvious way. We had to exit Saudi airspace out over the Persian Gulf and enter the UAE from international waters. It added distance—but not much. Just another reminder that politics reaches into cockpits whether you want it to or not.

Then it all replayed in a blur: the UAE entry code issue, the holding pattern over the Strait of Hormuz pressed tight against Iran's edge, Baghdad Radio, Minneapolis Dispatch, the UAE general, bingo fuel, the frantic search for an alternate, the fuel emergency declaration, and being chased by fighter jets—each decision stacking on the last until the weight became more than the system could carry.

I considered skipping dinner.

But I knew I shouldn't. The cabin crew deserved to understand what they'd unknowingly lived through, and we owed them that explanation—spoken aloud, together, outside the cockpit—like a ritual that marks an event as real.

Down in the lobby, the crew gathered in a tight cluster. Nobody was their normal self. The flight attendants were quieter now, watching us.

We walked into the warm night on the streets of Manama and found a Middle Eastern restaurant. Menus opened and closed without anyone really reading. Water glasses clinked. A waiter smiled politely, unaware he was serving people who hours ago had been seconds from dying.

The captain finally spoke.

He didn't perform the story. He delivered it.

Piece by piece, he explained the denial, the holding, the emergency, the search for a place to land, the AWACS call, the fighters. As he spoke, the flight attendants' faces changed—confusion giving way to disbelief, then anger.

One of them whispered, "We had no idea."

That was the point.

They hadn't known because we hadn't told them—because cockpit logic allows information to move only as needed to keep the machine safe.

The cost of that professionalism was visible now. They were shaken by a reality they rarely had to face—the risks that exist on every flight, normally hidden, now suddenly undeniable.

The tension between widebody pilots and flight attendants isn't exactly hostility. It's proximity without full shared context—two crews doing different jobs inside the same metal tube. In moments like this, that gap becomes painfully clear.

Dinner ended early. We were exhausted. And in 1996, in a Muslim country, the night didn't have the usual social lubricant to soften the edges. We returned to the hotel quieter than we'd left.

Sleep came fast for me—and it came ugly.

I woke repeatedly to fragments: the AWACS controller's voice, the Mach needle, the imagined sound of "missile lock" in the fighter pilot's helmet. What wasn't imagined was the mosque loudspeakers calling people to prayer at dusk and dawn—and every time the sound rose, I jerked awake as if someone had keyed the Guard frequency again.

The next day, we flew from Bahrain to Germany without incident. The airplane behaved. The clearances worked. The world returned to normal as if the day before had been a fever dream.

But none of us were normal.

When we finally returned to Minneapolis on day six, the captain didn't linger. He didn't joke at shutdown. He didn't rehash the trip.

He marched straight into the Chief Pilot's office and retired that day.

The events over the Persian Gulf had shaken him badly.

I never saw him again.

The mistake that day wasn't just navigational. It was organizational. We were three capable pilots working in parallel instead of one crew working together.

I made mistakes, too. I didn't see it at the time. That's on me.

I stayed in my silo too long. I worked the entry code issue and the radios in search of a country to accept us so single-mindedly that I stopped scanning the larger picture—and stopped scanning my crewmates. We were professionals doing our jobs, yet for stretches we weren't a team.

I carried that lesson for decades, especially once I became a captain: no matter how deep you are inside a task, you never stop scanning the humans around you. Not when the situation turns abnormal. Not when stress spikes. Not when time compresses.

ANOTHER BULLET DODGED

Learning Points:

- *Lucky aviators survive to become better aviators.*
- *Somewhere there is an AWACS crew to whom I owe a case of Scotch. Thank you.*

CHAPTER 2

THE HOOK IS SET

"Once you have tasted flight, you will forever walk the earth with your eyes turned skyward..."
—Leonardo da Vinci

AGE 5 · 1963

Some moments arrive before we have the words to understand them. One of mine came early.

In 1963, at the age of five, my parents loaded their growing brood—four boys and a girl—onto an airplane bound for Miami to visit my mother's parents, who had recently retired to Florida.

In a time before jetways, boarding an airplane meant walking outside. There was no insulation from the elements, no separation from the machine itself. You crossed open concrete and climbed metal stairs, close enough to feel the airplane before you ever boarded.

On that December morning, the tarmac lights glowed through an early-day freezing fog, illuminating the metallic beast in a way that felt almost unreal. Moist air clung to the cold metal skin. The DC-7 sat motionless, enormous, and patient. She had straight, thick wings and four massive propellers, and to me she felt less like a machine than a waiting animal—powerful, quiet, and alive.

Painted white with bold black stripes, her name read Eastern Air Lines.

She commanded attention.

She had mine.

I had never been to an airport before. Never seen an airplane up close. Never smelled the sweet, acrid scent of burned aviation gasoline or felt that heavy thump in my chest when large engines came alive across the ramp.

Like a gaggle of geese, the Waldman family traipsed across the tarmac at Cleveland Hopkins Airport toward a waiting

Douglas DC-7. My mother held the hand of my youngest brother, Wayne, then three. My father guided my next youngest brother, Lee, four years old. My older sister, Gwenn, and older brother, Alan, bounded ahead.

I lagged behind, already pulled toward something I couldn't name.

That morning, every sense I had switched on at once. Something settled over me—a quiet, focused trance that made the rest of the world feel very far away.

As I stepped onboard, the captain happened to glance back over his right shoulder. Our eyes met.

I was dressed neatly in slacks, a white shirt, a striped tie, and a small blue sport coat. He smiled and motioned me forward into the cockpit.

There was no hesitation. No looking back for permission. No conscious decision at all. My body simply moved forward—into the airplane, into the front room full of lights and levers, into a space occupied by four adult men I had never seen before.

The cockpit smelled of gasoline and cigarettes, heavy, human in a way that made me want to wrinkle my nose. It wasn't pleasant—yet I couldn't leave.

The moment held me transfixed.

I stood speechless, surrounded by oversized controls and glowing dials that, to me, looked like clocks.

It felt as if I was being transported into a different world.

Someone placed a pilot's hat on my head and propped me on pillows in an extra seat just behind them. Bells rang. Colored lights flashed. They smiled and carried on as if this were all perfectly normal.

They asked if I wanted to stay.

I nodded. Still unable to speak in my hypnotic state. Perhaps they recognized that look. Maybe they too had worn it once themselves.

I don't know if my parents ever came looking for the missing middle duckling. My eyes never left the instruments. I watched as the men moved with easy confidence, explaining things I couldn't possibly understand.

One of them reached overhead and moved a row of switches. The airplane shook violently as an engine roared to life. A thick plume of whitish-gray smoke rolled past the windows, briefly blocking everything outside. A new smell filled the cockpit, sweet and burnt. The machine felt awake.

With the engines running, the airplane began to creep forward, slowly leaving the terminal behind. After a long, deliberate crawl, it stopped again. Hands flew across panels. Levers moved. Once again, the airplane got very, very loud and lurched like a horse ready to leap from the starting gate. I know now they were testing systems. Then, it was just fascinating motion and sound.

Someone buckled me in and told me it was time to take off.

I didn't know what that meant—but I nodded anyway.

The cockpit grew loud again, louder than before, and the airplane surged forward. It was rough and almost frightening at first, and then suddenly it wasn't. The roar softened into wind rushing past the cockpit, and the ground fell away.

We were flying.

Houses shrank. Cars became toys. The earth slipped beneath us as we rose higher and higher, suspended in a way nothing else in life prepares you for. It wasn't falling or floating. It was lifting—clean and deliberate—away from everything I knew—leaving everything familiar behind.

I sat in quiet bliss, smiling from somewhere deep inside. It's a smile only aviators know. One that never really goes away.

Years later, I would come across a line by Ernest Gann that felt uncomfortably accurate: "Fate is the hunter." I didn't know it that morning on the tarmac, but I had already been hunted by fate.

The course of my life quietly shifted that morning.

From that day on, the five-year-old version of me spoke of only one thing.

Someday, I would be a pilot.

The hook was set.

Learning Points:

- *A stranger can profoundly affect another life without ever knowing it.*
- *Sometimes luck—something science can't measure—matters more than planning.*
- *Early exposure matters—what captures a child's attention can shape a lifetime.*

Photo #2. Eastern Air Lines DC-7 on the tarmac.

CHAPTER 3

THE FOLD OF THE PAPER

"The secret of getting ahead is getting started."
—Mark Twain

AGE 12-15 · 1970-1973

Hours before the first hint of light crept above the eastern horizon, I was out alone, navigating the streets of Cleveland Heights, Ohio.

I was twelve years old and terrified.

At four in the morning, the city is dead. Every sound carries in the cool, still air—branches rustling, a sudden movement in the dark. The smallest nocturnal animals scurrying through dried leaves made just enough noise to stop me cold—jaw clenched, body rigid, listening hard, frightened by what I couldn't see.

And on the rare mornings I crossed paths with another human being—that was far worse.

By today's standards, a child walking city streets alone at four in the morning would be unthinkable. Parents no longer trust the world that way. In 1970, they still did. My parents weren't taking a leap of faith with me; they were accepting the social contract of the time—one in which neighborhoods were presumed safe and adults looked out for one another's kids.

I didn't analyze any of that back then. I wasn't afraid of society. I was afraid of the dark—the quiet, the way imagination fills empty streets before daylight has a chance to erase it.

Cleveland Heights sat just east of the city, a relatively safe place to grow up. It held both extremes—large, stately mansions from the 1910s and blocks of modest blue-collar homes—we lived in the modest section by design. My father, a medical doctor, didn't want us growing up overly indulged.

Those first months delivering *The Plain Dealer* scared the hell out of me. Every morning at 4:00 a.m., my alarm sounded. Minutes later, I slipped out the side door, careful not to wake anyone, leaving the family asleep. By 4:04, I was walking Hyde Park toward the paper drop-off location at the corner of Hyde Park and Minor Park—the world quiet enough that my own footsteps felt loud.

Ralph, the delivery-truck driver, was usually there when I arrived. He wasn't friendly or unfriendly—just efficient. Brief. Indifferent. Maybe dealing with kids at o-dark-hundred had worn him down.

He was average height and slender, with a cigarette perpetually hanging from his mouth. His teeth were yellowed. His skin looked tough and worn, deeply creased. To me, he seemed ancient, though he was probably only in his mid-thirties.

What mattered to me wasn't whether Ralph was friendly. It was that he was always there. He never left me standing alone on a dark corner waiting. He ran on schedule every morning, without fail. He also never tried to pad my count. He treated the work seriously—and by extension, he treated me seriously too.

He didn't talk like my dad or his friends. His English was rougher, his grammar different. I noticed it immediately, though I didn't yet understand why.

What I did understand was how he handled that truck.

He drove it skillfully, like a musician plays an instrument, powering the old 1950s rig through dark, empty streets with both front doors wide open—winter or summer. He was half seated, half standing, steering with one hand while grabbing bundles with the other.

The truck barely slowed as he worked. Using a hooked tool he'd made himself, he snagged the steel strapping and flung fifty-paper bundles through the open doorway, landing them perfectly on the curb. I stood on the corner as seven massive bundles sailed out in quick succession. Occasionally, he peeled a few papers from the middle to match route counts.

Some mornings he'd toss me one full bundle and another missing two.

"Two on vacation… right?"

"Yeah. Only need ninety-eight today."

That mattered. Extra papers cost me money.

Paperboys bought the papers we delivered. We weren't employees. We weren't paid hourly. We made our money on the spread between what we paid the publisher and what customers paid us. If I miscounted, I paid for it. If I hustled, I earned more. It was business—plain and simple.

Delivering newspapers didn't require a seventh-grade education. Anyone could throw a newspaper onto a lawn.

Doing it well was another matter.

Papers had to arrive on time and dry. Customers had to be treated politely. Vacation holds had to be remembered. Money had to be collected.

Each week, I collected cash door to door, knocking on houses night after night. I was responsible for paying for every paper I delivered, and once a week the district manager came to our house to collect what I owed. What I had left after that was mine to manage. Running a route was a small business.

My father, shaped by the Great Depression, made sure I saved part of my income for college. The rest funded my passions—balsa-wood model airplanes, then radio-controlled aircraft, and eventually hockey camps in Canada. If I wanted more, I worked more.

In 1970, I paid seven cents for each daily paper and sold them for ten. Sundays were monsters—thick, heavy, and worth more. By week's end, I cleared about twenty-eight dollars—which felt like a fortune to a kid. That worked out to almost double minimum wage—set at about $1.20 an hour back then.

More than the money, it was the freedom that came with it. Money meant options. Money meant independence. For the most part, I was my own boss, and I liked most of my customers, so the work didn't feel like punishment; it gave me purpose. That was enough to keep me there for three years.

When the weather cooperated, I walked the route, folding and tossing as I went. I never rode a bike—the distance from sidewalk to front door demanded precision. With a tight fold and a clean throw, I could be back in bed an hour after waking, usually asleep again shortly after five.

For all the rewards of that first job, one unavoidable truth remained.

I was afraid of the dark.

And the halfway point of my route made sure I faced that fear head on.

On South Taylor Road lived the two things that frightened me more than anything else at that age.

Taylor Road was a four-lane artery, dark and empty most mornings between Blanche Avenue and Superior Park Drive. Only one dim streetlight glowed across the road from my side of the street. The block was lined with three-story, dark brick, 1920s Old English Tudor-style buildings, with small mom-and-pop shops below and apartments stacked above.

Midway down the block, just past the variety store, after the beauty parlor, and just before a dank, smelly watering hole called the Druid Arms, stood my number-one nemesis—the local three-chair barbershop.

Its bright fluorescent lights glowed through the full-length glass storefront, giving the place an unnatural feel in the darkness. I tried not to look as I approached, but like a moth to a flame, I always did.

All three barber chairs faced the street. Each was wrapped in white robes and towels shaped to resemble figures of the Ku Klux Klan, in full regalia, staring back at the sidewalk.

I didn't need an explanation. I knew exactly what I was looking at.

Even after three years on the route, I never got used to it. My instincts told me to stay away—and I did.

And as if that weren't enough, some mornings brought a second encounter.

Hidden in the dark alcove of one apartment building's entrance was a woman who talked to herself. Heavyset and hunched, she appeared to be in her late thirties and troubled. She frightened me every time I saw her.

As I rounded the corner, still shaken from the barbershop, there she would be—five feet tall and nearly as wide—shouting at me in an agitated tone, in a language I didn't understand. She never stopped until I was well past her and out of sight, her voice following me down the street.

I didn't run. I never ran. I tried to be polite. But the urge to flee was always there, pulling hard. At that age, I had no framework for understanding loneliness, mental illness, or poverty. That understanding came much later.

Once past her building, I continued along Taylor Road toward Mike's Gulf Oil service station. It had two old-fashioned tallboy pumps and a two-bay garage. The owner kept the place immaculate. His shiny tow truck was always parked diagonally across the pumps, blocking access to the garage doors. Everything about the station suggested order and care.

But the real gold mine of my morning wasn't even part of my route.

Catty-corner from the gas station stood Unger's Kosher Bakery. The storefront windows stretched nearly the full width of the building. From across the street, I could see older, plump women working behind the counter, sliding long metal trays of fresh-baked goods into display cases.

I never went in through the front door.

I went to the back door—where we had an arrangement.

The bakers wanted something to read once the morning rush slowed. I wanted chocolate-glazed doughnuts, hot and fresh from the oven. One newspaper for three doughnuts. In the front of the store, those doughnuts sold for ten cents each. My paper retailed for ten cents.

I considered it an excellent trade.

I learned early that if you were willing to part with something of value, you could sometimes turn it into something of greater value.

With the bakery behind me, I headed down Blanche Avenue for the final leg of my route. Thirteen papers left. Then I could go home. But first, I had to pass the corner house at Blanche and Taylor—Michelle Riggerio's place.

Throughout junior high, she was my heartthrob. Tall and slender, olive skin, jet-black hair, big dark eyes, and a smile bright enough to light the street. From a distance, I was in love.

Every morning, I imagined her sitting on the front stoop at 4:50 a.m., waiting for me to pass so she could call me over.

I also knew that if it ever happened, I would instantly dissolve into a puddle at her feet.

We graduated from ninth grade without me ever holding her hand or asking her out. It took another ten years before I lost my shyness around girls—far too late for Michelle and me.

At the bottom of Blanche was my street, Hyde Park. With my delivery bags nearly empty—except for the bag of doughnuts—I had twelve more front lawns to cross. At 5:00 a.m., I slipped back into the house. Not a creature was stirring. I tiptoed upstairs and climbed back into bed for two more hours of sleep.

Over time, those early hours became my favorite part of the day—a quiet refuge from three loud brothers and a busy house.

Fear gave way to routine. The stillness grew familiar, and the streets began to feel like they belonged to me.

For all my fears, I came to love that job.

I have many fond memories from my years as a paperboy, but one morning stands above the rest.

It was winter of 1972, two years into my route. I woke at 4:00 a.m. as usual, pulled on old warm clothes, grabbed my delivery bags, and stepped outside.

I stopped dead.

The city was coated in clear ice—smooth, pristine, untouched. It looked as if the entire neighborhood had just been resurfaced by a Zamboni. Beautiful. Treacherous.

I assumed Ralph would be late. Lying back down in bed was tempting, but curiosity won.

Instead, I went to the basement, to the warm spot beside the massive old boiler that looked like a spider on steroids. I dug my hockey skates out of my moldy equipment bag, strapped on my size-ten Bauers, and headed back outside.

The streets became my rink. I skated hard—fast and free—up and down the road for twenty minutes. No cars. No lights. No people. Just the sound of steel blades cutting ice.

When Ralph finally arrived, he was clearly flustered, the ash hanging precariously from his cigarette. In a frenetic state, he dropped the papers and fishtailed away down Berkeley Road, somehow keeping the truck upright.

I loaded sixty pounds of newspapers into my bags, slung them over my shoulders like bandoliers, and pushed off.

The weight slowed me, but it didn't stop me. I found my balance, leaned into it, and let momentum take over. I finished the route faster than I ever had, then skated on until the sky lightened and the first brave drivers began testing their luck.

I got home just before eight, still buzzing. The neighborhood was waking up, erasing the private ice world I'd been given for a few stolen hours.

I sat at the kitchen table and tried to explain the morning to my father. He read the paper, sipped his instant Sanka, and listened while I talked too fast, trying to translate joy into words. I never got my post-route nap that day.

I didn't care.

That morning stayed with me—not because it was reckless or extraordinary, but because it was earned. I had done my job. I had faced what scared me. And in return, the world had briefly opened itself up and said, here—this is yours.

At that age, I didn't have language for independence or confidence or mastery. I just knew I had made it through another dark morning on my own.

ANOTHER BULLET DODGED

Learning Points:

- *Children grow when they are given real responsibility and allowed to meet it on their own terms.*
- *Confidence comes less from having money than from knowing how to earn it.*
- *Independence is not granted; it is built quietly through repetition, reliability, and follow-through.*
- *Punctuality and attention to detail become habits when they are demanded early and consistently.*

CHAPTER 4

THE GIFT OF FRIENDSHIP

"Not to know what happened before you were born, is to remain forever a child."
—Marcus Cicero

AGE 13-19 · 1971-1977

I was lucky to have two loving parents and a family that valued education—facts I barely appreciated at thirteen. At the time, I assumed that was just how life worked. Only later did I understand how fragile those givens really were, and how much they shaped everything that followed.

As you read this book, you may feel my parents took a somewhat hands-off approach to raising me. They did—but that was typical of the era. Kids were expected to figure things out on their own, with minimal supervision and a lot of trust. Their love was never in question, and I credit them with many of the qualities I possess. Still, I've come to believe that for children to truly flourish, they need adult input from people outside their immediate family. Often that role is filled by a coach, a teacher, or a distant relative. For me, it was the new neighbors who moved in next door just after my thirteenth birthday.

I had just completed my Bar Mitzvah, and like most adolescent boys, I gave little thought to the wider world. My life revolved around building model airplanes, playing hockey, hanging out with friends, and delivering my paper route. That all began to change when John and Kathy Gaubatz arrived.

They were older than me, obviously—they had bought a house—but from my perspective they weren't dinosaurs like my parents. John was a stately twenty-seven, Kathy a wise twenty-six. They were young and cool, though not in any conventional way. They were intellectual, slightly odd, and a bit square.

John was gangly—a six-foot-six law professor with a face that reminded me of Abraham Lincoln. His expression was usually serious, almost stern, revealing little of what he was thinking. Kathy, by contrast, was a firecracker. Barely five feet tall and thinly built, she smiled often and moved with energy and purpose.

When we first met, Kathy was nine months pregnant with what would become their only child. Under normal circumstances they were an unusual-looking couple, but with Kathy about to pop, they looked like a cartoon. She resembled an olive with toothpicks sticking out each end, and John looked like Lurch from The Addams Family.

John had just accepted a position at Case Western Reserve Law School, prompting their move from Chicago, where he trained at the University of Chicago Law School. Kathy had been a social worker and was on leave due to the pregnancy and relocation.

For reasons I didn't understand back then, I was immediately intrigued. Once the moving van pulled away, I alone knocked on their door. Despite being busy and surrounded by boxes, they invited me in and talked with me. What struck me most was that they didn't treat me like a kid. They asked questions, listened carefully, and shared their thoughts on whatever topic I raised. That afternoon marked the beginning of a lifelong friendship.

Over time, I spent countless hours at their home talking about everything imaginable. No subject was off-limits, and nothing felt hidden or awkward. Kathy would casually nurse baby Daniel right in front of me, which—at thirteen—was entirely new territory. Amazingly, it didn't feel sexual; it felt natural, exactly as it was meant to be. For an adolescent boy, that's saying a lot.

They expanded my understanding of the world, taught me how to think critically, and modeled respectful dialogue with opposing views. I spent as much time with John and Kathy as I did with kids my own age, absorbing how adults outside my family processed life. They were two of the smartest people I ever knew—so smart they never needed to show it. Their intelligence came wrapped in humility and sincerity.

In 1974, I sat with Kathy in her living room watching the Watergate hearings. When John came home from work, the three of us would discuss what had unfolded that day—often focusing on how our government had attempted to subvert justice. I was a kid swimming in adult waters, and I loved every minute of it.

Our friendship wasn't fleeting. No matter where we lived, we stayed connected. I left Cleveland in 1976 to attend college in Daytona Beach, Florida. Coincidentally, John and Kathy relocated to Coral Gables after John accepted a position as Assistant Dean at the University of Miami Law School. We were only four hours apart, so during school breaks I often hitchhiked down to Miami to spend time with them.

Time and distance never seemed to matter. Our relationship always picked right back up. They challenged my thinking gently but persistently, never allowing me to spout opinions without defending them. They were remarkable people and true friends.

Six years after Daniel's birth, in 1977, we shared one of our most memorable experiences when I came to Miami to sell my replica 1956 MG TD kit car.

Photo #3. Our kit car—Jim in the left seat, David in the right seat.

My good friend Jim McGrath and I had built the car during our senior year of high school as part of an elective called "Senior Project." It allowed us to leave school at noon each day to work on something we loved. We started with a 1968 VW Beetle chassis and engine and transformed it into a tan-and-chocolate-brown classic. We earned an A in the class and ownership in a great car—just not the right to keep it.

The money we used to build the car had been earmarked for college. Our parents agreed to let us tap our education savings, but only on one condition: the car had to be sold before sophomore year, with the proceeds returned to our college savings accounts.

The car was never meant to be a permanent trophy—just a temporary privilege with a firm expiration date.

Miami seemed like a much better market than Daytona or Cleveland, so I asked John and Kathy if I could sell the car from their home. They graciously agreed.

On the drive south from Daytona during spring break, disaster struck. Thirty-five miles out of Daytona, I blew the engine—not because of how I drove it, but because of how we built it. Jim and I had made several rookie mistakes during the engine assembly, mistakes born of enthusiasm, limited experience, and teenage confidence. That spring day, they finally caught up with me.

My roommates rescued me, towed the car home, and together Lance and I rebuilt the air-cooled VW engine as quickly as we could.

I had already placed a seven-day classified ad in the Miami Herald, and time was ticking. Amazon did not exist, and parts were not easy to come by. The clock kept running.

By the time I arrived in Coral Gables, the ad had generated exactly zero interest. Each morning I waited, hoping the phone would ring. By the second day in Miami, with the classified ad about to expire and my rebuilt engine still an unanswered question mark, I assumed the entire trip had been a waste.

Then, on the last possible day, the phone finally rang. By then, I was ready to sell my car to anyone.

Or so I thought.

When the buyer arrived, we were all alarmed. A chauffeur-driven black stretch Lincoln pulled up with fully tinted windows. The driver was a tall, fit Latino man in a tight black uniform. When he stepped out to open the rear door, I noticed the unmistakable bulge of a handgun pressed against his lower back.

The passenger emerged wearing a tailored light-colored suit, dark sunglasses, and a white fedora. If you had a mental image of what a South American "businessman" looked like, this was it—bodyguard included.

When the buyers approached the front door, Kathy made it clear she didn't want them inside the house. I swiftly maneuvered them to the side yard to show them the car. The boss admired it, then immediately shut down any suggestion that I be involved in the test drive.

"Only my assistant drives me," he said firmly, making it clear this was not negotiable.

He told me the car would be a birthday gift for his sixteen-year-old daughter and that if he liked it, he would ship it to her in Colombia. I gulped—sixteen years old, Colombia—and suddenly every bolt in that engine felt suspect.

I knew the engine was garbage. All I could think about was when—not if—it would fail.

After a short test drive, they returned. The man retrieved an attaché case from the limo and walked toward the house. This time, Kathy hesitated briefly before stepping aside and letting him in. In that pause, I sensed her calculation—whether it was safer to keep whatever came next contained inside or risk the neighbors witnessing something none of us could explain.

We sat at the kitchen table. The room felt smaller than it had moments before. El Jefe placed the case between us on the table and adjusted it carefully, as if its position mattered. He did not hurry. He released the latches one at a time, each metallic click landing louder than it should have in the quiet.

No one spoke. No one moved.

I glanced at John and Kathy. They exchanged a look I had never seen before—tight, uncertain. They were the calmest people I knew, unflappable in every setting. Seeing even a flicker of unease on their faces made my stomach drop.

He lifted the lid just enough to block our view and leaned forward over the case. My attention tunneled onto his hands. I stopped breathing without realizing it. I remember thinking—not dramatically, just plainly—that if a weapon appeared, there was nothing I could do. I was a college kid, sitting at a kitchen table in Miami, scared and completely out of my depth.

The seconds stretched. The silence pressed in. I became acutely aware of the ordinary things—the hum of the refrigerator, the faint traffic outside—and how surreal it felt that life was continuing normally while my world had narrowed to the space between his hands and the open case.

Then his hands emerged… holding thirty-four one-hundred-dollar bills.

He smiled broadly. "You asked thirty-five hundred," he said evenly. "I think thirty-four hundred is fair."

As he leaned back, no longer shielding the case, I stole a glance inside. It was packed top to bottom with hundred-dollar bills—hundreds of thousands, easily.

Thirty-four hundred dollars wasn't a negotiation. It was pocket change.

I nodded. I don't remember what I said, if anything. In my mind, the deal was already done. The engine might last a week or a year—it didn't matter. All I could feel was the slow return of air to my lungs. No weapons. No shouting. No sudden turns. Just money on the table and a way out.

John and Kathy had barely moved the entire time. When I looked at them again, I saw the same thing I felt—relief, edged with disbelief. The tension didn't vanish; it loosened, as if someone had finally eased their grip.

I signed the title, took the money, and a few hours later the car was on its way to South America.

For years afterward, John and Kathy referred to it simply as "The Visit." They would bring it up casually, usually with a smile that arrived a beat late, and joke about the Colombian drug lord coming back when the engine inevitably failed.

We laughed every time. But the laughter always carried an edge.

Beneath the humor was the shared memory of how close that afternoon had felt to something else entirely—something none of us wanted to name. The joke wasn't bravado. It was relief, revisited over and over again.

Thankfully, he never visited again.

ANOTHER BULLET DODGED

In 1994, a few months after their son Daniel's death, John and Kathy visited my family in Hawaii. Despite unimaginable loss, they were as loving and stoic as ever.

Photo #4. John, Kathy, me, Ayla, Fran and Aaron in Hawaii.

I loved them like older siblings. Sadly, they are all gone now. John died in his sixties from throat cancer. Kathy passed a few years later from complications of type 1 diabetes she had managed since childhood. Daniel, whose death preceded theirs, was only twenty when he died in his sleep at college.

No parent should have to bury a child.

I still miss them.

Learning Points:

- *Friends come in all ages and often appear when least expected.*
- *Exposing children to adults beyond their parents broadens perspective.*

CHAPTER 5

GO WEST, YOUNG MAN

PART 1

"Change is inevitable. Growth is optional."
—John C. Maxwell

AGE 16-18 · 1974-1976

In high school, I had two very good friends—best friends, in fact. The kind of friends you count on without thinking, then realize decades later, you're still doing exactly that.

Andy Magar and Buddy Goodman were those guys for me. The three of us spent most of our high school years together, stumbling our way toward manhood with far more confidence than skill.

Some friendships fade with distance and time.

These didn't.

Photo #5. Left to right: Buddy, Andy and David in 2023.

My friendship with Andy began in third grade—61 years ago. We met when Andy's family emigrated from Egypt to the U.S. Andy was just eight. Because of language issues, he was held back a year and landed in my class. Not knowing English never slowed Andy down—not for a single day. We became instant best friends.

Andy possessed a superpower—he was never shy or insecure. Watching him interact with anyone, anywhere was impressive. He didn't hesitate, didn't overthink, and never seemed worried about how things might turn out. He even talked to the prettiest girls at high school as if that were the most natural thing in the world.

Watching Andy in action quietly exposed the folly of my own shyness and insecurity around girls—traits I would unfortunately carry well into my mid-twenties.

My friendship with Buddy doesn't go back to grade school the way Andy and I do. Buddy and I didn't meet until tenth grade. We met in driver's training class when we randomly sat next to each other on day one. We quickly discovered that we both loved cars—and by coincidence, we both knew Andy Magar.

During that eight-week class, our friendship formed—with a twist. We both had our eyes on the same young lady. Somehow, I channeled my inner Andy and asked her out. The Andy Magar technique worked. She said yes. The relationship didn't last, but Buddy and I built a friendship that has stood every test since.

Andy, Buddy, and I all have April birthdays, but since Andy was a year older, he could drive before either Buddy or I. And since a fifteen-year-old boy's brain is occupied roughly 95 percent of the time thinking about girls or cars, Andy was steps ahead of us in both categories. He had the confidence to talk to any girl—and by 1973, he had a driver's license.

Andy's parents let him buy a car after his sixteenth birthday. He wasn't allowed to drive it on city streets; instead, it was to be a project car in the high school auto shop. They believed he wasn't yet responsible enough to drive his own car, so they wouldn't register it.

They were right—especially with his two knucklehead friends at his side.

Andy's parents believed that without plates, the car would stay at school.

Oh, how naïve parents can be.

One of the many impressive abilities of an adolescent male brain is its capacity to normalize ideas that, to any adult observer, are clearly terrible.

Andy and I decided we'd acquire license plates regardless. We both worked after school at a local car wash. The big spinning brushes regularly knocked license plates clean off customers' cars. Those plates sat in a bin in the manager's office.

You can probably see where this is headed. We helped ourselves to two plates. Not two from the same car—that would have required forethought—but two completely different plates that shared only one thing: both were from Ohio.

Geniuses.

We bolted them onto Andy's 1967 Dodge Dart and immediately started cruising around town. We now had wheels and total freedom. We were certain that we'd outsmarted Andy's parents and equally certain the cops would never notice mismatched front and rear plates.

For weeks, Andy and his various fifteen-year-old friends enjoyed cruising the streets of Cleveland in his unregistered automobile. Eventually, that run came to an end when Buddy and Andy were pulled over.

When Andy could produce only a driver's license, the rear plate was run through the system. It didn't match a white 1967 Dodge Dart owned by Andy Magar. The front plate didn't match the back plate—and neither plate belonged on the car.

The encounter ended exactly as you'd expect. Another carefully engineered teenage plan collapsed under even the lightest scrutiny.

A tow truck arrived, Andy's car was hauled off to the impound lot, and Buddy and Andy were instructed to hitchhike home.

It's hard not to admire how confidently we believed we were smarter than everyone else. Foolish, but very confident.

The summer between junior and senior year, Buddy and I opened our own exterior house-painting business. We needed to make some money to put toward college—now only a year away and already feeling very real and very expensive.

To equip the business, we bought a $500 VW Beetle from John and Kathy Gaubatz and $200 worth of used ladders and scaffolding. Then we started canvassing neighborhoods.

Buying a Beetle for an exterior painting business should immediately signal that this is a story about teenagers—not adults.

We couldn't have chosen a more inappropriate vehicle for hauling ladders and scaffolding across town. Yet that's exactly what two adolescent males did.

Three ladders—about 150 pounds of them—were strapped to the roof, extending five feet past both the front and rear bumpers. Nothing looked sillier than the two of us driving around the east side of Cleveland with massive ladders perched on that tiny car. We looked like a traveling circus act—two jesters in the front seats, trusting gravity and optimism to do the rest.

By stupid luck, it worked. The Beetle survived a summer of heat and hard labor, and better yet, it gave us notoriety. That ridiculous little car became our calling card—marketing you couldn't have purchased.

As if the Beetle itself weren't enough, we painted it to look like a ladybug. In hindsight, we absolutely should have named the business Lady Bug Painting, but that would have required forethought and business sense—two traits still very much under development.

Customers didn't question our youth, our experience, or our bizarre choice of transportation. The shtick worked. We stayed busy all summer, and when it was over, we'd each earned about $2,000—a lot of money in 1975 for two seventeen-year-olds.

The next summer, after high school graduation, Buddy and I came up with another brilliant idea. By then, we'd survived enough bad ones together to believe we were invincible—or at least compatible in our stupidity. This time, the plan was bigger. We'd take the $4,000 we'd earned the year before and buy a brand-new, bare-bones Ford Econoline van. We'd build it into a proper hippie van—beds, stereo, coolers—and take a two-month trip around the western United States.

In our minds, the math was simple. We'd put about 10,000 miles on it, return two months later, and sell it for roughly what we paid. Adventure and fiscal responsibility—two concepts we believed could comfortably coexist.

My parents were fine with it. Buddy's dad was not.

He couldn't get comfortable spending a large chunk of Buddy's college money on a trip with an uncertain financial outcome. The adventure was approved. The transportation plan was not.

With the safe option off the table, we did what any two rational eighteen-year-olds would do—we bought a 1965 Dodge Dart with 102,000 miles on it for $215.

It was a Cleveland rust bucket: loud, tired, and held together by corrosion and optimism.

Somehow, the reliable option was too risky, while the questionable one passed parental scrutiny.

It's hard to say who showed poorer judgment in that decision—the two teenagers heading west in a rusted old Dodge Dart, or the adult who thought this was the safer choice.

June was spent painting houses to build travel cash, and by mid-July of '76, we were ready. We had no itinerary—just a plan to backpack, drive, and see where the road took us. That kind of aimless travel was still possible then. These were the days before reservations were required at national parks, when you could walk into a ranger station, fill out a backcountry permit, and head into the hills.

The day before departure, we upgraded the Dodge's stereo. The car might have been a rolling rust experiment, but we weren't going to suffer in silence. We pulled out the original AM radio and installed a new stereo with a fancy reversible cassette deck. If nothing else, we'd have music.

We'd never backpacked in western mountains before. More accurately, we'd never backpacked at all. It was the blind leading the blind.

That became obvious when the two knuckleheads went grocery shopping. This was long before REI, outdoor outfitters, or the internet. Without experience, there was no obvious way to know what food belonged on a five-day backpacking trip. So, we guessed.

Freeze-dried food. Fresh food. Snacks. Everything went in together. We called it preparation.

We stuffed our gear in the car wherever it fit, hid our pot stash, slammed the trunk shut, and admired our work. As far as we were concerned, we were ready.

The next morning, we blasted out of Cleveland on I-80. The Dodge rattled, summer air poured through the open windows, and Joe Walsh's *Rocky Mountain Way* blared through the speakers. We were eighteen, heading west, and convinced we had it all figured out.

After a grueling 800-mile day, we pulled into a bland, roadside campground somewhere in Nebraska. The sun was going down, we were exhausted, and the Dodge had started doing something new and unsettling.

It would run fine for a while, then suddenly lose power, hesitate, and feel like it was going to die—only to come back to life just as abruptly. We knew that if we couldn't get the car running better, we'd have no choice but to cancel the trip and head back to Ohio.

After setting up camp, Buddy and I lifted the hood and stared into the engine compartment like two people hoping the problem might fix itself if we looked serious and long enough. We talked, guessed, poked at things, and generally accomplished nothing.

We were deep into what passed for a productive troubleshooting session when I noticed a guy walking toward our campsite from a distance. I had no idea why he was headed our way, but something about him immediately got my attention.

He was huge. Not just tall—huge. I had known tall people. This was different. The man had the proportions of a mature oak tree. His arms looked like branches that had been growing for decades. His shoulders were as wide as a doorway, and his head sat on a neck that could have doubled as a fire hydrant. Easily the largest, most muscular human being I had ever seen.

He kept walking straight toward us, saying nothing, giving no indication of his intentions. I nudged Buddy and told him to look. When Buddy turned, he nearly cracked his head on the raised hood.

The man was carrying something in his hands. I couldn't tell what it was, and in our slightly altered state, that uncertainty mattered. His face gave nothing away. No smile. No frown. No signal at all. We froze and watched him close the distance, every step feeling heavier than the last.

When he reached our campsite, he finally broke into a wide smile, swung a pack off his shoulder, and said, "You guys want a beer? Need any help?"

The immediate relief was humbling. We climbed out from under the hood, made introductions, and accepted the beers. Buddy promptly nicknamed him "Animal," which seemed appropriate. He had the build of a grizzly bear and the demeanor of a Labrador.

As it turned out, Animal was a professional auto mechanic on a month-long wander around the country in his truck. He also just happened to have a fully stocked toolbox bolted into the truck bed. After a couple of beers and some stories, he asked to look at our car and search for the trouble.

I said, "Sure—do you know Dodge crap?"

He laughed and said, "I've owned some crap in my day. I think I can handle it."

Within minutes, he spotted the issue. Someone had replaced a section of the fuel line to the carburetor and routed it directly over the exhaust manifold. Every so often, the heat would vaporize the fuel in the line, starving the carburetor of liquid gasoline.

Animal rerouted the line, wiped his hands, and told us we wouldn't have that problem anymore. He was right.

Then he looked at us, the car, and our gear and asked the most reasonable question: "Why are you guys doing this long trip in such a piece of junk?"

I looked at Buddy and let him answer.

We traveled with Animal for a few more days, enjoying his company and his competence, before he eventually headed south, and we continued west toward Colorado and Rocky Mountain National Park (RMNP).

This would not be my first time in Colorado, but it would be my first time experiencing it as an adult—and my first visit to Rocky Mountain National Park.

I'd first seen the Mountain West in 1966, when I was eight years old and the entire Waldman clan headed west in a forty-four-foot Ford motorhome. That twelve-thousand-mile trip was a revelation for a Midwest kid. Wide-open spaces. Big sky. Mountains that didn't end. Somewhere along the way, it planted a love for the west that never quite went away.

But that trip didn't end well. My mother refused to drive on the highway, leaving my father behind the wheel day after day. *(See Inside the Story: Why My Mother Would Not Drive at Highway Speeds.)*

Five kids packed into a rolling argument didn't help. Weeks in, somewhere in the mountains, my father finally reached his limit. Without warning, he turned the rig around and pointed it east.

Rocky Mountain National Park—one of the trip's highlights—never happened. So, in 1976, Buddy and I made RMNP our first national park stop. It felt overdue.

We drove into the small mountain town of Estes Park just outside the park gates. It was exactly what you'd expect—souvenir shops, restaurants, outdoor stores, and that quiet mountain-town energy of people heading in and out of the wilderness. We picked up a few supplies, pointed the Dodge toward the entrance, and soon found ourselves standing at a ranger station getting a backcountry permit. The ranger took a few extra minutes to talk about bear safety and backcountry etiquette. I'm not sure if everyone received the same briefing or if Buddy and I simply screamed inexperience, but it was helpful—and reassuring.

With the permit secured, we found a trailhead, loaded our packs from the trunk, and stepped into the mountains.

The hiking itself wasn't technical, but it was hard. Mostly, we struggled with the altitude. Neither of us had ever carried a fifty-pound pack in the mountains before, and it showed. Every step felt heavier than it should have, and our confidence faded quickly as our lungs tried to catch up.

Over the next few days, almost without noticing, we got stronger. Our pace improved. The packs settled in, and breathing came a little easier. Every night we camped beside an alpine lake, alone, surrounded by peaks and silence. The place felt vast and untouched—easily the most beautiful environment I had ever experienced.

By the third day, Buddy nicknamed me "the goat" because I kept cutting switchbacks and charging straight up the hillsides. It felt liberating. I was buzzing with energy, eager for the next climb and whatever waited beyond it. The mountains no longer felt intimidating. They felt inviting, and I had never felt more alive—or freer.

We saw almost no one during the entire hike—maybe five people total. Whether backcountry hiking simply was not very popular then, or the park was big enough to swallow everyone whole, we were starting to enjoy the solitude.

That last evening, we camped high in the park at around 10,300 feet. We had no bear encounters, but after four days in the wilderness, we did have one very questionable episode.

In a move that made perfect sense to us at the time, we had eaten most of our freeze-dried meals early in the hike and saved our prized fresh salami for the final night. It felt like a reward—one of those small victories you convince yourself you have earned.

We drank a little whiskey and polished off the salami.

I fell asleep content, unaware of how brief that feeling would be.

Sometime after midnight, hours after we'd gone to sleep, I woke with a low rumble in my stomach that immediately felt wrong. It deepened, sharpened, and began to demand attention.

I barely made it out of the tent before the first wave hit. I didn't have time to pull on clothes. I was crouched on the cold ground, convulsing in pain.

Earlier that night, the air had been comfortable. Now it was around thirty-eight degrees, with a stiff breeze cutting through the pines. I shook uncontrollably as the cold worked its way into my bones.

The contractions came every thirty minutes. Each time I crawled back into my sleeping bag and drifted toward sleep, my body betrayed me again. Every spasm felt like a hydraulic ram slamming into my abdomen, determined to empty whatever was left inside me. There was no rhythm to fight—only endurance.

I spent most of the night outside the tent, collapsed in a bed of pine needles, too sick to care. By the time the dry heaves started, I was covered in pine litter, vomit, and worse, shivering uncontrollably. It felt like I'd gone ten rounds with a prizefighter who only aimed for my gut.

Buddy did what he could. He brought me water, a cloth, and eventually a tarp to throw over me. There wasn't much else he could do. I was too sick to even ask how he was holding up.

By dawn, I was a shell of myself—and Buddy was starting to go down too. He slipped quickly into the same miserable pattern I'd lived through all night.

Between bouts, we broke camp in a hurry. We yanked our packs from the trees, stuffed everything inside with no order, and started running down the mountain—no plan, no pacing, just the need to get lower and get out.

We ran with toilet paper and matches in our hands, ready for the next inevitable stop. Every twenty minutes, one of us doubled over just off the trail. It was relentless—run, stop, suffer, run again.

We made it to the car in just over two hours, a descent that had taken us days to climb.

We smelled like goats and looked like hell had run us over.

Everything we were wearing went straight into trash bags. We moved the car to the nearest campground with a latrine and parked as close as possible. For hours, we took turns sprinting back and forth to the toilet until the spasms finally eased.

Sitting there, dehydrated, and exhausted, it didn't take long to identify the culprit.

The salami.

In full disclosure, we had bought it a week earlier in Cleveland from a well-respected butcher shop. Our logic had been simple. Salamis hang in shops for months. Being in our pack for 4 days—no big deal!

What we had neglected to factor in was that the salami had spent five days in the trunk of a Dodge Dart, in July, in hundred-degree heat.

It's hard to comprehend how neither of us considered this a problem. We had carried unrefrigerated meat across the western United States in midsummer and treated it like a delicacy.

We had failed basic backpacking, basic food safety, and arguably basic common sense.

At eighteen, Buddy and I were capable of remarkable optimism and astonishing blind spots too.

Sometimes we paid dearly for them.

This was one of those times.

By midafternoon, we were finally functional again. Weak, dehydrated, and completely wrung out—but upright. We decided to drive out of Rocky Mountain National Park and head back toward Estes Park to restock supplies (no salami) and regroup before the next leg of the trip.

When we started the engine that afternoon, we had no idea that the food poisoning would turn out to be the least remarkable event of the day.

We had entered the park on July 30th and were now driving out on August 2nd.

This was long before cell phones. While we'd been up in the backcountry, we were completely cut off from the outside world. No news. No updates. No sense of what had happened beyond the circle of mountains we'd been living inside.

As we descended toward Estes Park, something felt off almost immediately. Familiar landmarks were gone. Roads looked wrong. Trees were missing. Entire sections of the landscape had been stripped bare. It felt less like driving into a town and more like stumbling into the remains of one.

When we reached what had been downtown, we were in shock. The place we had walked through just days earlier no longer existed in any meaningful way. Buildings were flattened.

Bridges were gone. Mud and debris covered everything. There were no people.

The best comparison I can offer is a moonscape—as if some massive force had passed through and erased the town without warning. We walked in silence, trying to reconcile what we were seeing with the place we remembered.

Nothing lined up. It felt like stepping into the aftermath of something we should have heard coming—but hadn't.

In the face of that kind of devastating destruction, our own digestive distress suddenly felt small.

We later learned that while we'd been high in the mountains, a storm had parked itself over the Big Thompson Canyon. In just a few hours, it dumped an unimaginable amount of rain. By the next morning, a wall of water and mud tore through the canyon and into Estes Park, destroying nearly everything in its path. When it finally passed, 90 percent of the homes and businesses in Estes Park were destroyed.

Standing there, trying to understand what we were seeing, it finally hit us how close we'd come—not through anything we'd done, but through where we hadn't been. We had missed disaster by nothing more than unintentional timing.

In all, the flood destroyed 418 homes and businesses in the canyon and killed 148 people.

ANOTHER BULLET DODGED

Learning Points:

- *One's digestive system is not a metal trash receptacle that can take any assault levied.*
- *Being disconnected from one's modern world can be wonderful, transformative, and restorative. However, being disconnected does carry consequences.*

Inside the Story *(Optional Reading)*

Why My Mother Would Not Drive at Highway Speeds

The trip was supposed to last two months. It ended after six weeks.

My mother refused to do any driving, so my father was behind the wheel every day. In fact, the only driving she would ever do was around Cleveland in our family's 1963 Volkswagen microbus. The last time she had driven at highway speeds was during my parents' honeymoon in 1952 in the Poconos. It didn't go well.

She crossed the center line and hit another car head-on at 55 miles per hour. Both of my parents nearly died. They survived—but my mother's driving confidence did not. From that day forward she imposed a permanent ban on herself: no more highway driving.

Which meant that on our cross-country adventure, my father was stuck with every mile.

Our 1975 Cleveland house-painting business flyer. Simple, earnest, and wildly confident for two seventeen-year-olds.

CHAPTER 5

GO WEST, YOUNG MAN

PART 2

AGE 18 · 1976

After Estes Park, we kept moving—because that's what eighteen-year-olds do when they don't know what to do with what they've just seen.

The subsequent weeks of backpacking went much better for the two boys from Cleveland. We made better food choices and hiked with more determination and strength, as if effort might somehow balance the luck we'd just been handed.

After hiking the Grand Canyon, we met a couple we considered "older"—they were twenty-four—who invited us to their home in Tucson if we ever made it that far south.

Following a trek around northern Arizona, we decided to head south.

I was asleep in the right seat—stoned enough that my dreams were still louder than the engine—when Buddy started yelling.

"Chico! Chico! Wake the hell up!

I've got no brakes!"

The words didn't land all at once. I came up foggy and disoriented, desert flashing past the windshield.

"What do you mean?" I said.

Buddy glanced over, eyes wide, his voice flat in a way that cut through the panic.

"Man, the pedal just goes to the floor.

No brakes.

Nada. No emergency brake either."

That last part didn't need explaining. We both knew it. The emergency brake pedal had been useless for weeks—the control cable snapped underneath the car, likely rusted through from age and neglect.

It had felt like a small problem when it happened.

It wasn't small now.

The road ahead was straight and flat, stretching through open desert with a few cars scattered far ahead and behind us.

Sixty-five miles per hour.

The windows were down—no air-conditioning—and heat and grit poured into the car while Pink Floyd's *Dark Side of the Moon* played on, indifferent and relentless.

My chest tightened as my brain caught up with the math.

No hydraulic brakes.

No emergency brake.

No hazard flashers, either—nothing to warn anyone around us that we were in trouble.

Buddy lifted his foot off the accelerator. The car barely noticed.

Fifty-five miles per hour, still free rolling, helped along by a slight downhill grade.

Adrenaline hit hard—fear first, then something uglier underneath it. A stupid, reckless flicker of excitement, as if some impulsive part of my teenage brain wanted to treat this like a dare instead of a problem that could kill us.

A few miles ahead, the road began to rise.

Just a little.

Enough to matter.

"If we downshift," one of us said—maybe him, maybe me—"use the hill."

It was the only idea we had.

Buddy worked the transmission, dropping gears carefully, feeling for resistance. The engine screamed in protest, fighting the music.

The car shuddered.

I sat up straighter, alert, and pulled the lap belt tight across my hips—no shoulder harnesses in that car, nothing extra to save us.

The problem was the road. Two lanes. A few cars out there. If we came up on slower traffic with oncoming cars at the same time, there would be no place to go. No graceful exit. No alternative plan.

Mile after mile, Buddy eased the right wheels into the dirt whenever the edge allowed it. Dust exploded up through the open windows, coating our arms and faces. The car bucked and wobbled. Each time he brought it back onto the pavement, my stomach clenched, waiting for the speed to build again.

Slowly—painfully—the Dart began to lose momentum.

Forty.

Thirty.

Twenty.

The car shuddered once more and finally rolled to a stop.

For a moment, neither of us moved. The engine ticked as it cooled. Pink Floyd kept playing.

Then we were out of the car, shaking, furious, our hearts pounding in our chests.

We kicked the rear fenders like the Dodge could feel shame.

I picked up a rock, fully intending to throw it through a window, then thought better of it and wedged it behind the right rear tire instead.

We stood there in the heat, staring at each other.

And then—suddenly very sober—we started laughing.

We had stopped the speeding Dart.

We had won.

Our Dodge had tried to kill us, and once again we had somehow managed our way out of it.

Only afterward did the bigger thought land. Just a day earlier, we had been driving mountain roads—steep, winding, narrow, with no shoulders and no guardrails.

If the brakes had failed the day before, gravity would likely have finished Buddy and me.

Call it luck.

Call it fate.

Call it timing.

Whatever it was, it wasn't skill.

Afterward, displaying a level of judgment that had clearly not caught up with our newfound sobriety, we cautiously limped the brakeless Dodge into the next town. Once there, we resolved the brake issue—along with a long list of other small mechanical problems that seemed to materialize daily—and kept going.

We hiked and camped all over the western United States, saw national parks that made Ohio feel like a different planet, and met people who were generous, curious, and kind to two sunburned teenagers from Cleveland who looked like they'd been living out of the trunk—because we had.

We grew up out there, but not all at once and not because we suddenly became wise. We grew up because the pattern kept repeating: problem, panic, improvisation, relief, laughter. The confidence we carried home didn't come from competence. It came from surviving our own mistakes often enough to believe we might survive the next one too.

We eventually made it safely back to Cleveland a week before college began. The Dodge Dart—the same one that had tried to kill us more than once—limped home too. Somehow, we sold it for $120.

Buddy left for the University of Toledo and went on to become a mechanical engineer, eventually spending his career with Volvo heavy equipment. Andy built his own business and, to this day, still says hello to anyone, anywhere, all the time.

The trip bonded Buddy and me for life. The ordeals we faced—random, avoidable, and mostly self-inflicted—turned us into brothers.

We thought we were chasing the West.

Mostly, we were being carried—by luck and generosity in disguises we were too young to recognize.

ANOTHER BULLET DODGED

Thank you, Andy, Buddy, and Jim, for being my friends!

Learning Points:

- *Adolescence has a remarkable ability to confuse survival with competence.*
- *Real friendships aren't proven by shared success, but by who's still standing next to you when the plan collapses.*
- *Mechanical failures, bad decisions, and natural forces don't announce themselves in advance.*
- *Timing often matters more than skill.*
- *Confidence earned young is often borrowed from luck and mistaken for ability.*
- *Many early victories aren't earned—they're granted.*

A FINAL NOTE

One last detail belongs to that time. In the years before cell phones, this is how we stayed in touch with parents during our ten-week odyssey.

About once a week, we'd call our parents' landline collect using a bogus, pre-planned name. They would reject the call, which told them everything they needed to know—we were alive, we were okay.

A collect call using our real name meant we needed help.

That call never came.

Photo #6. Buddy and David in the Utah mountains, 2023.

CHAPTER 6

FLIGHT SCHOOL

"The greater danger for most of us lies not in setting our goals too high and failing; but rather in setting our aim too low and achieving our mark."
—Michelangelo

AGE 18-21 · 1976-1979

On my first unsupervised solo flight, I learned how quickly confidence can be tested when no one else is in the airplane.

Shortly after takeoff from Daytona, a violent metallic banging erupted from the right side of the airplane. It was loud, constant, and impossible to ignore—a sharp, irregular pounding that felt dangerous in a way my training hadn't prepared me for. The noise started the moment the wheels left the runway and showed no sign of abating.

I remember gripping the yoke and staring straight ahead, afraid to turn back toward the airport. I only had nine hours as a pilot, so my mind leapt immediately to the worst explanation—the airplane was breaking up. I didn't want to bank, I didn't want to change pitch attitude, I didn't want to add any stress to a machine I suddenly no longer trusted.

I asked Air Traffic Control for a straight-out departure and flew west, making very minor pitch and bank changes. West, twelve long miles to a small airport in DeLand, Florida. All the while listening to a sound I was certain meant the airplane was slowly coming apart around me.

During that flight, other thoughts crept in uninvited. I'd spent years insisting being a pilot was what I wanted, but not everyone back home had shared my certainty. I'd been the kid who got airsick on airplanes—the teen who struggled in school—the one people quietly encouraged while wondering if he was aiming too high.

My grandmother never missed a chance to suggest a more sensible path.

Until that moment, while flying an airplane I was convinced would crash at any moment, those voices had been easy to dismiss. Now, alone in the air, with something clearly wrong, those voices were harder to ignore. It wasn't flying I doubted. It was whether I was equal to it.

The moment I touched down in DeLand and began slowing, the noise stopped. The airplane rolled quietly now, intact, ordinary. I remember realizing—almost with surprise—that I was still alive.

I taxied clear and shut down, letting the silence settle before climbing out. Walking around the airplane, I found the problem immediately. The passenger-side shoulder harness was hanging outside the door. The metal buckle having beaten itself against the fuselage the entire flight.

I'd missed it on preflight.

My fault.

A small oversight with an outsized lesson.

That flight didn't make me question whether I wanted to fly.

It reminded me that wanting it wasn't enough. Attention mattered. Discipline mattered. And mistakes—especially simple ones—could feel enormous when you were alone with them.

I didn't drift toward aviation. I declared it early. From early childhood, I knew I would be a pilot. My father chose his path. Flying was mine. It felt simple, clear, and unquestioned.

What I couldn't explain—then or now—was why that certainty came so early.

The hook had been set at five years old on a Cleveland Hopkins tarmac. That much I understood.

What I never understood was why it took hold so completely.

I spent my youth building model airplanes, hanging out at airports, begging my parents for airplane rides every birthday, and flying radio-controlled airplanes until the batteries ran dry and the sun went down.

Other interests came and went.

Flying didn't.

As I got older, that focus set me apart. While friends experimented with possibilities, I committed early. What I didn't yet understand was how that certainty would quietly narrow my social world as well as my options.

At the time, certainty felt like clarity. Only later would I recognize how much it also raised the stakes.

By most conventional measures, I did not do well in high school. My grades were mediocre, and my transcript gave little hint of what would come later. It wasn't a lack of effort so much as a poor fit. I struggled in rigid classroom settings that rewarded conformity and punished deviation, and I had no language yet for why some kinds of learning came easily while others did not.

Dyslexia would be identified years later. At the time, I simply knew that school felt like friction—constant, unproductive, and disconnected from how my mind worked.

Aviation, by contrast, made immediate sense. It was structured, practical, and unforgiving in ways that felt honest. You either understood it or you didn't.

Colleges in that era were still willing to take chances on students like me, and I was lucky they did. Kent State and Purdue both accepted me into their aviation programs. I chose Kent State at first—mostly for proximity and in-state tuition—without visiting either campus or giving the decision much thought.

That plan didn't last. Almost by accident, I learned that Embry-Riddle Aeronautical University existed in Daytona Beach, Florida. I applied very late, was accepted, and changed course again.

My parents didn't push me in any direction. My father and I made a simple deal: he would cover tuition and flight training, and I would pay my living expenses. It was generous. I didn't yet understand how much responsibility it carried.

When the summer of 1976 ended, my father dropped me at a stranger's house, watched me load two bags into another kid's aging Toyota station wagon, and sent me south.

The drive blurred by in exhaustion and talk of the future. When we arrived in Daytona twenty-four hours later, my ride headed for the dorms. I didn't have that option. Because of my late enrollment, there was no room for me on campus.

I was dropped at a hotel across from the Daytona International Speedway.

That was when it hit.

I was in a town I didn't know, without a car, without friends, without any college experience—and without a place to live. There was no safety net, no orientation period, no gradual transition. I had committed fully. Now I had to make it work.

The next morning, in the hotel parking lot, I met Tim, another freshman. We talked cars. I asked for a ride to campus. He said yes. The first problem was solved.

The days that followed became a crash course in independence. I registered for classes, learned the city buses, hunted for housing, and figured out how alone I really was. Armed with a map, a notebook, and a roll of quarters for pay phones, I took on Daytona on foot and by bus.

Within days, I found half of a duplex six miles from campus.

Rent was $265 a month. Utilities included.

College flipped a switch that high school never had. For the first time, the material mattered to me—not because of grades or expectations, but because it was connected to something real. Flying gave context to everything else. Physics, weather, aircraft systems, procedures—it all pointed toward a purpose I understood.

Just as important, I learned how I learned. I wasn't broken. I had simply never been taught how to read in a way my brain could process. The breakthrough came quietly and entirely on my own: colored highlighters. Not one—several. I marked every textbook, every page, every paragraph, layering colors until patterns emerged. Information that had once blurred together finally separated and clicked into place.

Once that switch flipped, I pushed hard. I rewrote notes, recorded lectures, studied late into the night when the house was quiet, and created systems that worked for me instead of against me. Effort finally translated into results. Somehow, it even landed me on the Dean's List.

That success didn't slow me down—it did the opposite. I began stacking course loads, carrying as many as twenty-three credit hours at a time, determined to finish both school and flight training in three years instead of four. The pressure was self-imposed. I wasn't chasing accolades or even fully aware of how airline seniority would someday work. I only knew that time felt precious, and that momentum mattered.

My days were full, my sleep negotiable, and my pace relentless. It felt productive. It felt controlled. I didn't yet recognize the cost of running that hard for that long—only that it was working.

To support myself, I initially worked as a line boy pumping Avgas, then later started restoring cars out of the carport at our rental house. I didn't have the money to buy cars outright, so I improvised. I used university deferment loans as temporary capital, restored classic cars, sold them, paid the loans back, and lived off the profits. At the time, it felt like problem-solving. In hindsight, it was also a system that worked only as long as nothing went wrong.

Photo #7. David with the engine he just pulled from a 1966 Corvette.

That vulnerability became clear during my sophomore year. I had spent the entire semester restoring my 1966 Corvette convertible, counting on its sale to repay the loan I'd deferred through the university. The numbers were tight but workable. The plan depended on timing—and on the assumption that the car would remain intact.

It didn't.

On an ordinary drive, another car ran a red light and hit me hard. The Corvette was badly damaged. Overnight, the asset I was relying on became something else entirely. The school still wanted its money. I didn't have it.

What made it worse was knowing exactly who I couldn't call.

My father had trusted me to manage my end of the arrangement. He had covered tuition and flight training without hovering or conditions. Admitting that I might have lost part of that trust felt worse than the financial problem itself. So, I didn't tell him. I watched the calendar instead.

The cutoff date was fixed. I knew exactly when the university would shut me out if the balance wasn't cleared. Just before that happened, I found a buyer willing to take the Corvette in damaged condition. The insurance settlement followed soon after and covered the rest of the balance.

I made no profit on the deal. I also didn't get kicked out of school. I remember signing the paperwork, thinking less about the money than about how close I'd come to disappointing my father with a risk he never agreed to take.

The system held—but narrowly.

The Corvette scare wasn't the only thing happening during those first few years. My academic pace had already put me on a different track. During my second year, I was selected for the Embry-Riddle Fellowship program. It was limited and competitive, and earning a spot felt less like recognition than confirmation that the workload I'd chosen was producing results.

The fellowship accelerated flight training dramatically. By the end of what should have been my sophomore year—already compressed into something closer to a junior year—I had completed ratings most students wouldn't reach until late in their senior year.

The program solved a practical problem as well: flight time costs money, and money was always tight. Becoming a fellow changed the math. By senior year, I was instructing—teaching in the afternoons, flying constantly, and logging hours while carrying a full academic load. Instead of paying for flight hours, I was accumulating them and being paid to be flying, as a certified flight instructor.

The structure worked for both sides. The university gained instructors already trained in its system. I gained flight time at a pace that simply wasn't available to most students, and free tuition. When I graduated, I had nearly 1,200 flight hours. Most of my peers had around 300.

Those extra hours didn't come easily. They came from long days, constant repetition, and a schedule that left little room for anything else.

In that era at Embry-Riddle, instructors wore no headsets and had no boom microphones. We sat shoulder to shoulder with students and shouted over the engine all day, the propeller only a few feet in front of us. After hours in the airplane, my voice went first. Then my patience. Fatigue followed quietly.

One afternoon, after five and a half hours of working with one student after another, I was flying with a student practicing stall entry and recovery. I knew the exercise well. I let it develop slightly longer than I should have—watching, waiting, trusting that I had time.

When the wing stalled and the nose dropped, the student pressed hard on the wrong rudder pedal. The stall tightened immediately into a spin. I expected the possibility—but not the force of it. I intervened late—not incorrectly, just late—and had to physically overpower his input on the pedals to reassert control. Once authority was clear, the recovery was textbook.

We recovered below the school's minimum allowed altitude—the hard floor meant to keep training mistakes survivable.

I wasn't frightened. I knew how to recover from spins, and the airplane had done exactly what aerodynamics said it would. What stayed with me was something else entirely. Fatigue had narrowed my margin. Authority had been momentarily diluted. A student's confusion, combined with my hesitation, had pushed us closer to the edge than good judgment allows.

The lesson wasn't about skill. It was about vigilance—how quietly control can be surrendered, and how decisively it must be reclaimed.

It was a quiet correction, but a permanent one.

Photo #8. David the instructor, with a Cessna 172 in 1979.

Being a college senior didn't ensure immunity from male stupidity. Mine was still very much alive and well.

I lived near the beach with three other students who knew how to party. All of us drove restored muscle cars. Mine was a Corvette—loud and unmistakable.

One December night in 1978, bored and restless, we drove out to rural Flagler County to watch—and possibly join—an illegal street race. Three full-sized adult men squeezed into Sam's two-seat 1963 split-window Stingray and headed north, convinced this was a reasonable way to spend a Friday night.

It was almost midnight when we arrived at a deserted four-mile stretch of county road—straight, flat, and far from anything resembling civilization. To us, it looked organized. Cars lined up two by two, each driver paired off against an opponent with comparable machinery. No one had raced yet. We were frozen in that brief pause before bad judgment turns into action.

Then red lights appeared out of the darkness.

Sheriff's vehicles rolled in from both ends of the road, lights flashing hard enough to erase every idea we'd been entertaining. We were ordered back into our cars and told to follow them to the jailhouse. No sirens. No urgency. Just a line of young men driving themselves toward consequences we hadn't thought through.

Inside the jail, more than twenty of us were packed into several small cells. Privacy vanished immediately. When one person used the lone porcelain fixture, the rest of us stared at the wall, pretending not to notice. Sitting there, I made a quiet promise to myself that whatever direction my life was headed, it wouldn't include places like this.

Time stretched.

Eventually, raised voices erupted somewhere beyond the cell block. We couldn't hear every word, but we didn't need to. It became clear that the deputies who had broken up the gathering had acted ahead of whatever plan the sheriff himself had intended. He was angry—not at us, but at them.

They had wanted to charge us with drag racing and reckless driving—serious offenses that carried large fines, license suspensions, and the kind of record that doesn't fade easily. The problem was simple: no one had raced yet. Engines had idled. Cars had lined up. But nothing illegal enough to support the charge had happened.

We listened as doors opened and closed, voices rising and falling. The uncertainty did the work fear usually does. Whatever case the sheriff had hoped to build wasn't holding together.

By the time the noise subsided, the charge had collapsed into something smaller: illegal assembly.

It wasn't what he wanted, but it was all he had.

Sam convinced the sheriff that he had cash at home and could post bail for all of us—if only he were allowed to go get it. This was before ATMs, and none of us had family nearby. The implication was obvious. If Sam wasn't released, they'd be housing and feeding us all weekend.

Against logic, it worked.

After three in the morning, Sam returned and posted bail for Lance and me. As we stepped outside, he waved the remaining cash in front of us. Somewhere along the way, the deputies had taken bail money from Sam for us—but never for Sam himself.

Packed into the Corvette, we pulled away. And because we were young and still hadn't learned when to stop, Sam burned rubber leaving the jail.

Three months later, twenty-eight of us stood sweating in an old southern courthouse, dressed in cheap suits and badly knotted ties. Ceiling fans turned lazily overhead, doing little to move the heavy air. One by one, we were called forward. Some pleaded guilty. When it was my turn, I entered a plea of nolo contendere—no contest. Different words, same result.

We were all convicted and fined $234 each. That amount included the $134 bail already taken from us and another $100 paid to the clerk on the way out. Years later, when I ran a background check, there was no record of the arrest or the conviction.

ANOTHER BULLET DODGED

A childhood fantasy could have collapsed under ordinary pressure. Embry-Riddle didn't test the dream with spectacle. It tested it quietly—through money that had to arrive on time, the fear that my lifelong airsickness might end my flying career before it began, fatigue that dulled attention, and judgment that didn't always keep pace with momentum.

Instead of breaking, the dream refined itself. The airsickness faded. The effort intensified. I learned where skill carried weight, where luck occasionally intervened, and how unforgiving simple oversights could feel when no one else was there to catch them.

I graduated—and prepared to join the Navy.

CHAPTER 7

RESURRECTION—HEAVY METAL

PART 1 — BILL WHITESELL

"Aviation is the branch of engineering that is least forgiving of mistakes."
—Freeman Dyson

AGE 21-22 · 1979-1980

I raised my right hand and swore an oath to the United States Navy.

Moments later, I walked out of the room. I drove to the home of a fifty-two-year-old former airline pilot named Bill Whitesell and accepted his offer to fly DC-7 cargo airplanes from Miami to the Caribbean as a copilot and flight engineer.

It felt like the adventure of a lifetime.

Years later, I would wonder whether it was bravery, stupidity, or simply the power of believing what I desperately wanted to be true. Whatever it was, the Bill Whitesell saga began in early 1979, when an Embry-Riddle Aviation Law class led to a chance meeting in a campus parking lot, just three months before graduation.

I was a newly minted, cocky Certified Flight Instructor with a Fu Manchu mustache and a freshly restored Corvette—external proof, I thought, that I had arrived. Bill stood six-foot-three, weighed about 250 pounds, and carried himself like a man accustomed to being listened to. With his full white beard, thick white hair, and booming voice, he didn't enter rooms so much as claim them.

When I shook his massive bear paw, I felt the weight of his presence immediately. That day, a friendship began—rooted in a shared love of machines: airplanes, cars, trains, anything powerful and reciprocating.

To me, he didn't just sound confident—he sounded finished. Like a man who had already lived the life I was trying to imagine. At twenty, I didn't yet know how dangerous that feeling could be: mistaking certainty for wisdom, and volume for truth.

His professional life had started much earlier. At seventeen, near the end of World War II, he lied about his age to join the Marine Corps. He flew F4U Corsair fighters, then transitioned into airline flying shortly after the war with Eastern Air Lines. By the time I met him in 1979, Bill had been an airline pilot, entrepreneur, and a recognizable figure in general aviation.

Hired by Eastern in the late forties, his career spanned the golden age of large, piston-engine airliners—before jets erased both the unique sound and the romance. After leaving Eastern, he flew heavy reciprocating airplanes around the world for small airlines, becoming indispensable precisely because few others wanted—or knew how—to fly them. Bill built a reputation as a check airman and an unapologetic lover of old, heavy metal.

For my generation, a college degree was mandatory. For Bill's, experience was king. Still, not having a degree gnawed at him. It was the one credential he didn't possess, and by the late seventies it had become something he could no longer ignore. Like the Tin Man in The Wizard of Oz, he already had everything inside him; all he needed was the piece of paper. With Embry-Riddle—arguably the world's premier aviation university—just ten miles from his Ormond Beach home, earning a degree became his late-career quest.

At fifty-two, Bill was by far the oldest student in our 250-member graduating class receiving a Bachelor of Science in Aeronautics. In truth, he already had plenty of BS. His stories alone guaranteed that. On campus, he was a novelty—an elder statesman surrounded by a thousand young aviation bucks. I'd occasionally see him holding court, spinning one of his legendary yarns while students leaned in, half-aware they were being entertained and half-aware they were being instructed.

Bill told stories in the style of Mark Twain, and he seemed to embrace Twain's advice that *one should never let the truth get in the way of a good story.* At the time, I thought his embellishments were harmless—entertainment.

More importantly, I had no older pilots in my life to guide me in my new profession. I'm not sure Bill specifically signed up for it, but I needed an aviation mentor, and I latched on to him.

With graduation two weeks away, I believed my résumé would open doors: a 3.6 GPA, 1,200 flight hours, and a degree from a prestigious aviation university. I even wrote Juan Trippe, the legendary president of Pan Am World Airways, announcing my graduation and asking for a job.

I received neither an interview nor a reply.

Reality hit hard. No airline courted me. None even responded. I had the certificates, the logbook entries, the confidence of someone who had done everything "right." I was ready to move forward. The industry, it turned out, was not.

The year 1979 was brutal economically, especially for commercial aviation. Beyond continuing as a flight instructor in Daytona Beach, my prospects were bleak. Regional airlines barely existed. Entry-level flying jobs were scarce. Pilot positions were largely confined to major airlines—far smaller than today—or a handful of commuter carriers flying nineteen-seat airplanes. Corporate flight departments existed, but they wanted older, experienced pilots.

I had already spent thirteen months instructing at Embry-Riddle, and I was mentally done with it. Something had to change.

Fortunately—or so it seemed—the U.S. Navy had a place for me. A recruiter pulled some strings and secured a guaranteed slot in Naval Flight School. Not because I was special, but because I had a degree and flight hours. The plan was Officer Candidate School in the summer of '79, followed by fourteen months of flight training starting in Pensacola. Flying for the Navy felt like momentum.

At night, though, doubt crept in.

I was not considering the Navy simply to become a pilot. I wanted to be a fighter pilot. But as I learned how naval aviation assignments actually worked, one phrase surfaced again and again: *needs of the service.* It meant that even after entering flight training, I could be assigned wherever the Navy needed pilots—helicopters, patrol aircraft, transports—rather than the fighters I had imagined.

Seven years was a long time to surrender that much control. The fear wasn't really about airplanes. It was about committing my future to a system that might never ask what I wanted.

As my May swear-in date approached, the pressure mounted. I had to leave Daytona. I had to move beyond flight instructing. Becoming a "real pilot" felt urgent. Bill—the only professional aviator I knew and trusted—listened as I wrestled with the decision. He understood the appeal of lighting the sky on fire at Mach 2. He also warned me about surrendering seven years of my youth.

Then, out of nowhere, Bill threw me a curveball. He offered me a job.

Bill spoke about the plan with easy confidence, as if timelines were suggestions and obstacles merely details. He claimed he had acquired three out-of-service DC-7 freighters and planned to haul cargo—legal cargo—from Miami to the Caribbean by mid-summer. (Foolishly, I didn't ask which summer.)

It wasn't flying Tomcats, but it was heavy metal—transport-category airplanes, the big leagues, and no seven-year military commitment. Still, I didn't accept immediately. DC-7 time was intoxicating, but it didn't quite match flying F-14s.

Bill was persuasive without pressing. He didn't argue; he simply kept the idea alive, repeating it casually, confidently, until it felt less like a gamble and more like an opportunity waiting to be claimed.

In mid-May, I stood in a room with twenty-two other men, arms raised, reciting an oath I barely understood. The words felt final in a way I hadn't expected.

Then, without warning, a voice in the back of my head said: Get out of here. Now.

There was no debate. No analysis. Just instinct.

I walked out, drove straight to Bill's house, and accepted his offer on the spot.

Weeks later, the truth began to seep out—not all at once, and never in a way that forced a clean decision. Each new detail arrived small enough to excuse, easy enough to explain away.

What I'd been sold wasn't a job—it was a business plan. There were no airworthy airplanes. The three DC-7s Bill owned were derelict hulks. Two sat abandoned on a closed airfield in Wakeman, Ohio, grounded for seven years. The third languished in Sebring, Florida, having not flown in a decade.

The idea of building one flyable airplane from the remains of all three by late summer of '79 now seemed absurd.

As reality emerged piece by piece, disappointment followed. Miami would have to wait. Heavy flying would have to wait. First, I was moving to rural Ohio to resurrect a machine that might—maybe—someday fly.

I knew, abstractly, what wisdom would recommend. I just couldn't make it apply to me.

I had already walked out on the Navy, alienated the recruiter, quit my job, sold my car, and terminated my apartment lease. I was cornered. I wanted desperately to believe the fairy tale. So, I buried my head in the sand and let myself be carried by a vision untethered from reality.

Bill had two sons, Bruce and Joe (name changed). Both were pilots. Both signed on to the DC-7 scheme. Bruce, in particular, was the kind of guy people gravitated toward without quite knowing why. Rooms felt lighter when he entered them. Conversations flowed more easily. His presence kept situations from tipping.

Flying also came naturally to him—stick and rudder as instinctive as breathing. He had none of my formal training yet possessed a man-machine connection most pilots only ever chase.

Bruce moved through uncertainty with an ease I envied, or at least that's how it appeared from the outside.

For all the admiration Bruce received, there was still something he never quite claimed. He never complained about it or spoke directly about it. If anything, he joked—deflecting attention with humor whenever the subject drifted too close. I didn't yet understand what that was about. I only knew it mattered.

We were the same age, loved fast cars and airplanes, and shared the same ambition. We bonded instantly.

Each of us had different reasons for being on this quest.

I wanted to become a professional pilot.

Bruce wanted something harder to name.

Bill needed a win in business aviation after earlier failures.

We were pulling on the same rope toward the same destination—but for different reasons.

None of us yet understood how much that mattered.

CHAPTER 7

RESURRECTION—HEAVY METAL

PART 2 · ARRIVING IN WAKEMAN

AGE 21-22 · 1979-1980

The day after completing my last flight lesson as a paid instructor, I loaded everything I owned into Bruce's hippie VW van, hugged my college friends goodbye, and turned the page to the next chapter of my life.

Bruce treated departures like festivals. I treated them like contracts. In the months ahead, those differences would balance us well.

Just prior to leaving, a few other young aviators joined our loose caravan—guys riding on Bill's coattails, chasing the same improbable dream.

Bill led the way in his Dodge dually, towing a thirty-foot fifth-wheel camper. Bruce and I followed behind, the van rattling, incense and old vinyl fighting for airspace inside.

We drove straight through the night—twenty-four hours of bad coffee, shared optimism, and road-trip bravado—arriving at Wakeman Airport late the next day.

We were exhausted.

We were ready.

What greeted us didn't match the picture any of us had been carrying.

Photo #9. Ortner Airport in 2023 cleaned up and reopened.

Wakeman/Ortner Airport was a 3,300-foot strip of asphalt slowly losing a war with Ohio farmland. Corn pressed in from all sides. If not for a single, out-of-place blue hangar rising above the fields, you could have driven past and never known an airport existed at all.

Wakeman itself was barely a town—951 people, a gas station, a restaurant, a motel, and one stop sign holding the whole thing together. A place you didn't so much arrive at as run out of road into.

The airport had been built by the Ortner brothers, whose boom-and-bust operation in the '60s and '70s flew auto parts between Cleveland and Detroit. They needed distance—from competitors, from regulators, from scrutiny. Wakeman offered all three. It was the boonies by design.

None of us spoke as we turned off the road and rolled directly onto the old tarmac.

The ramp was cracked, weed-choked, and disturbingly empty. No airplanes. No signs of life. This was wrong. We had been told Ortner Air Service once operated a fleet that included DC-7s, DC-3s, Curtiss C-46 Commandos, a Convair 240, twenty Beech 18s, and even WWII warbirds used for airshows.

We expected abundance. We got absence.

We parked the fifth-wheel behind the hangar, out of sight from the road, unhitched it, then piled back into the truck to explore the property.

Our day went downhill from there.

Aircraft hulks lay scattered through the surrounding fields, half-swallowed by earth and neglect. It looked less like aircraft storage and more like the remains of a Luftwaffe airfield in 1945 after an Allied bombing run.

We came upon a DC-7 sitting tail-down in the mud, axles submerged, engines gone. Every door and panel stood wide open.

Without any doubt, birds owned it now.

It quickly became obvious what had happened here. The Ortners had stripped these airplanes clean, harvesting parts and abandoning the shells where they fell.

None of us got out of the truck to look closely. Denial is powerful—not dramatic, not loud, just quietly efficient. I told myself this had to be a parts plane. This wreck was not ours. It couldn't be.

Bruce stared out the windshield, jaw set—but his foot bounced lightly on the floor mat to a rhythm playing in his head, like motion alone might keep the day from tipping completely sideways. Bill said nothing, staring straight ahead, already replaying numbers that could no longer add up.

We continued our slow reconnaissance, hunting for our promised airplanes. We passed a T-hangar being reclaimed by nature. Beech 18 fuselages sat half-buried, looking more like abandoned old farm implements than aircraft. Engine stands, propellers, and random aviation debris lay scattered everywhere, quietly corroding.

Still—where were our DC-7s?

Eventually we found a Curtiss Commando in the weeds. Then an A-26 WWII bomber. Then two DC-7s—one a C model, the other a B.

Bill clarified that he had not purchased the C.

But the B?

Registration N750Z.

That one was ours.

Relief flickered—briefly.

We kept searching. There should have been another. There had to be another.

There wasn't.

Then reality landed, hard.

The first hulk we had dismissed—the one sitting tail-deep in the mud—was also one of ours.

N751Z.

The thought flashed through my head uninvited: I could be in Pensacola right now, preparing to fly Tomcats.

Instead, I was standing in Ohio cornfields, about to clean up after tomcats that had been hunting birds in my airplanes for years.

"Goose—we have a problem."

Bruce and I felt physically sick. Even Bill—usually unshakable—went quiet. I could see the math running behind his eyes, the weight of the deal settling into his gut.

Bill had paid Ortner nineteen thousand dollars in cash, sight unseen for these planes. Standing there that June day, it felt like Ortner should have paid him nineteen grand just to haul the aluminum carcasses away.

By the time darkness fell, we were empty—physically and emotionally. We left the airport to find food and, hopefully, alcohol.

We needed a drink. All of us.

That night Bill and the others stayed at the motel. Bruce and I moved into the fifth-wheel camper—our new home. The night passed without ceremony.

Photo #10. Our home for over a year next to the blue hangar.

Morning arrived violently.

A furious pounding rattled the camper screen door. A wild-eyed man stood outside, looking ready to drag us out bodily for trespassing.

Only after we began talking did we realize he was Ortner Jr.—the same man who had sold Bill the airplanes.

Somewhere in the fine print, it hadn't been made clear that Bill intended to house his crew on the field.

Bill had a way of charming snakes.

Bruce had a way of calming them.

Within minutes, the three of us sat beneath the camper awning, drinking coffee and trading stories about great old airplanes. Bruce listened more than he talked, nodding, smiling, absorbing—giving Ortner room to feel heard, and all of us room to breathe. It was his gift—he could lower blood pressure without seeming to try.

Once Bill arrived, the tone shifted.

If we were going to resurrect anything here, we needed access—hangar space, tools, electricity, ground equipment, ramp privileges, and power for the camper. I won't say these details were overlooked, but from the body language alone, both sides were clearly disappointed in each other.

Eventually, a deal emerged. Keys were handed over. Permissions granted. We received a briefing on the quirks—and dangers—of operating WWII-era ground equipment.

Then came the real work.

We had to decide which airplane might fly again—and which would die so the other could live.

We dragged a ladder across 500 feet of tall grass to N751Z, the closest airplane.

Photo #11. N751Z, one of the Whitesells' purchased planes.

Without engines as counterweight, she sat tail-low in the mud.

Bill climbed up first.

The sounds he made inside told us everything.

Bruce went next. Then me.

As I reached the top rung, time slowed. I flashed back to being five years old, invited into the cockpit of this same airplane type at Cleveland Hopkins in 1963. I smiled—until the smell hit.

Bird piss. Rot. Decay.

This wasn't an airplane. It was a biological hazard.

The instrument panel had become a nesting site. Instruments gone; holes filled with debris. Seats shredded. The E&E rack behind the captain's seat housed animals instead of avionics.

Walking aft revealed missing floors, shifted bulkheads, and nature fully in control. Bill hadn't bought an airplane. He had bought an artificial avian habitat.

Outside wasn't any better. Tires were rotted. Axles buried. Compartments alive with squawking birds who clearly believed we were the intruders.

At the tail, the verdict became unavoidable. Years sunk in mud had compromised the structure beyond trust.

"This will be the parts plane," Bill said.

We all hoped the other would be better.

But standing there, ankle-deep in mud and bird droppings, I understood something I hadn't yet put into words: optimism alone may not carry us.

The second DC-7 sat farther out in the field. Her tires were only eight inches into the mud. The axles were intact.

She had no engines on the right wing and two dead ones on the left—but the weight kept her upright.

She smelled and looked just as bad as N751Z.

But her structure was not sunken in the mud.

She became the chosen one.

This was the airplane I would live and breathe for the next sixteen months of my life.

Her name would be Dulcinea.

Learning Point:

- *Sometimes the first test of professionalism isn't skill—it's whether you stay when every instinct tells you to run.*

CHAPTER 7

RESURRECTION—HEAVY METAL

PART 3 · THE WORK BEGINS

AGE 21-22 · 1979-1980

Dulcinea was a retired American Airlines (AA) passenger plane, originally certified as N381AA in 1956. When the jet age arrived in the early 1960s, American sent her back to Douglas Aircraft to be converted into a freighter. That decision bought her a second life and five more years in the AA fleet. By the mid-sixties, however, major U.S. airlines had transitioned to all-jet fleets, and her time at American came to an end.

She was sold and eventually passed through a series of second- and third-tier freight operators—California Airmotive, Zantop Air Transport, and Universal Airlines—before finally ending up at Ortner Air Service. There, her existence as a commercial aircraft would almost certainly have ended if not for the Whitesells.

Being sold to the Ortners usually meant a death sentence for any queen of the sky. Rather than spending money on large, required inspections, they rode airplanes hard, stripped them bare, and parked them in the field once heavy maintenance came due. That's where they died.

By the time we met her, Dulcinea was no longer an airplane so much as a suggestion of one.

The hulk she had become had been cannibalized for an unknown length of time after being parked in the fields of Wakeman. She sat abandoned in an Ohio cornfield—forgotten and forlorn—for at least seven years following the demise of Ortner Air Service. Now we were here to breathe new life into this neglected old girl.

Her future home was intended to be Miami, where she would serve as the initial workhorse for Whitesells' newly formed company, La Mancha Aire. The name was fitting. We were about to attempt the Impossible Dream, and Bill—whether he realized it or not—was Don Quixote charging windmills. The name would prove prophetic.

Digging In

The first week was dominated by digging—literal digging. We excavated a septic field beside our camper trailer, then turned to the bigger problem: freeing Dulcinea from the mud. Before any restoration could begin, we had to engineer, build, and execute a way to move her to a workable location.

We dug trenches from the sunken landing gear to solid ground, then built wooden ramps and laid them into the trenches to create a stable rolling surface. After days of struggle—and with the help of local farm tractors—we finally moved her to a semi-hard surface next to the hangar.

From that day forward, she was never more than forty feet from Bruce and me.

The following days were spent stripping every piece of instrumentation and electronics from the two hulks so Bill could take them back to Miami for refurbishment. Countless hours went into assessing parts and materials he would need to procure. Work schedules were compiled, checklists assembled, and a plan of action laid out for the overall project.

Ten days after we arrived at that desolate place called Ortner Airport, the entire crew departed—except for Bruce and me.

Predictably, the young aviators who had piggybacked on Bill's momentum scattered once the work became dirty, repetitive, and lonely.

Bill returned to Florida to focus on obtaining the FAA operating certificate, sourcing parts, and searching for investors or bankers willing to help turn his dream into reality.

It all sounded reasonable—necessary, even—but none of it brought structure or help to the Wakeman project.

That left Bruce and me alone with Dulcinea: a plane, a hangar, a camper, and acres of cornfields stretching to the horizon.

First Night Alone

The first night after everyone left, the silence felt different. Heavy. The kind of quiet that settles in once you realize there's no one coming back tomorrow.

The weight of the project bore down on us. Bruce didn't sit with it for long. He started moving, looking for something—anything—that might break the stillness. We discovered the first of what seemed like a thousand wooden freight pallets scattered across the airfield.

When darkness fell, the Wakeman bonfire tradition was born.

This wasn't a campfire—it was a statement.

We lit pallet fires that announced to anyone living nearby that Wakeman Airport was no longer abandoned, that we were there, and that Dulcinea would rise again. Night after night, flames climbed six feet into the air. We burned oil-soaked pallet after pallet yet never seemed to make a dent in the supply.

Those fires weren't just for warmth. They pushed back the darkness. They made the place feel claimed.

Bruce coped by staying light—moving between tasks, keeping things from feeling heavy. But living in close quarters has a way of revealing what doesn't get said. Beneath the humor, there were moments when his ease felt practiced, like something carefully maintained rather than automatic. I didn't know what sat underneath it yet. I just knew it was there.

By nature, I filled the void and carried the weight of what this endeavor was supposed to accomplish.

Neither of us was a certified mechanic, and aside from Bill's task list, we had little direction. The project was overwhelming, and we both knew it. But with Bruce on site, the Whitesells had a son watching over the operation. With me, they had a young workaholic—someone who would keep grinding long after a wiser person might have walked away.

What could possibly go wrong?

We were too young and too invested to spend much time asking.

So, we pressed on anyway.

It's often said that a blind squirrel gets a nut every now and then. In our case, it was more like the blind leading the blind—probably all nuts—but somehow making progress anyway.

Within days, we settled into a monotonous, all-consuming rhythm—working on Dulcinea from sunup to sundown, seven days a week. For the first month, we did nothing but clean.

We removed bird nests, droppings, filth, grime, grease, and dirt from an aircraft that had been ridden hard and put away wet.

That month alone, we went through an entire 55-gallon drum of MEK—methyl ethyl ketone. Not a single glove or respirator was used. In 1979, that didn't raise eyebrows. Today, it should.

Our hands were submerged in that chemical day after day, scrubbing every nook and cranny. The smell never left.

To say we became intimate with Dulcinea is an understatement. Our lives—and hers—became intertwined.

Even our downtime was spent with her.

We sat in her cockpit or sprawled across her wings, reading manuals, talking systems, dissecting design details, learning her quirks.

She hung over us—literally and figuratively.

What Bruce and I accomplished as unskilled laborers with minimal supervision borders on the miraculous. The volume of work we completed still amazes me. Maybe it was because the project sat right outside our front door in the middle of nowhere. Or maybe it was simply the power of shared purpose.

Either way, we pressed on day after day.

It was an extraordinary summer.

Firelight and Gravity

Most evenings ended around the campfire. We swapped Daytona stories, quizzed each other on DC-7 systems, and listened to Bruce play guitar. He played whatever came to him in the moment—songs that drifted in and out without structure, like the summer itself.

The isolation stripped life down to its basics—work, food, fire, sleep. It brought me closer than I've ever been to a cowboy existence: that singular, tranquil life that draws young men to wide-open spaces and solitary work.

We loved it.

But I'd be lying if I said two 21-year-old studs were content living alone on the "ranch."

Something was missing.

Girls.

By the second month, we had started talking—half-joking, half-serious—about how to fix that.

Before we ever made it to a local watering hole, Phyllis and Shelley found us.

Like manna from heaven, they simply appeared.

Both worked at the Elyria Ford assembly plant about forty miles away and were on a road trip when they spotted the big airplane beside the hangar. Curious, they turned onto the tarmac and found us deep in the belly of the beast.

Somehow, they saw past the grease-covered bare chests and the eau de parfum of industrial solvents. The four of us clicked immediately, and our lives shifted that day.

As summer wore on, we adjusted our routines to make life at an abandoned rural airfield more livable.

We even bought my brother Wayne's Honda 175 dirt bike for recreation.

Then Bruce brought home a dog from the pound—a black lab he named Rasta, short for Rastafarian. Bruce said it casually, like it wasn't a decision at all.

Rasta fit him perfectly—unplanned, loyal, happy to roam if someone whistled him home.

Before long, Rasta had become part of the operation, stretched out in the shade beneath Dulcinea's wing while Bruce and I worked, or lounging under the canopy of the fifth-wheel.

For the first time since arriving in Wakeman, the place was beginning to feel like home.

Old Farmers, New Lessons

That summer, we also befriended two old-timers who stored their airplanes in the crumbling T-hangars. One owned a 1950s Cessna 172, the other a 1961 Aircoupe.

Against all logic, they flew regularly from that decaying runway—and soon trusted us with keys to their airplanes.

Free use of someone else's airplane was an unimaginable gift to two young pilots.

One afternoon during a lunch break, I was flying the Aircoupe with the old farmer when we began talking about how we had each learned to fly. I launched into my Embry-Riddle pedigree and credentials as a CFI.

The conversation stalled.

Then he asked quietly, "What is a CFI?"

Perplexed, I explained—a certified flight instructor, like the person who taught you to fly.

He turned his head, looked me straight in the eyes, and with a big, warm grin said, "I ain't never had no flying instruction."

I didn't bother trying to hide my surprise.

It was written all over my face.

"It was for sale in the newspaper about ten years ago," he continued. "I liked it. I bought it. I flew it home."

My by-the-book instincts kicked in hard. "So, you don't have a pilot's license?"

"Hell no. Don't have a driver's license either. They all just machines. Been drivin' tractors all my life. I know how machines work."

That day, I was the one getting schooled.

We flew together more that fall. I taught him stalls, weight and balance, and engine-out landings. He had no interest in books, regulations, or logbooks.

Eventually, I learned he didn't even keep the required maintenance records.

That ended our flying together. I had too much at stake.

Still, the experience cracked something open in me. It showed me how differently people relate to flight—and how aviation once relied less on permission and more on personal responsibility and innate skills.

Sweat Equity

Despite the growing comfort, the work never let up. In August heat, Bruce and I crawled on our bellies through narrow access tunnels in the aircraft's underside, lubricating nearly fifty control cables that ran from the cockpit to the engines and tail.

It was brutal, sweaty work.

In hindsight, it should have waited for fall, when temperatures dropped into the fifties. But we were certain we wouldn't be in Wakeman by then.

We still believed our future was just around the corner.

We expected to be flying Dulcinea daily out of Miami, so we sweated through the job in ninety-five-degree heat.

When the cleaning was finished, painting began.
During college, I had run a small business restoring classic automobiles, which included painting. I liked to spray paint. With only a handful of refurbished parts arriving from Bill—and months of unsupervised freedom—we went all in.

We painted everything.

The wheel wells went blinding glossy white.

Photo #12. Me in a polyester suit in the painted nose wheelwell.

Every access panel and crawlspace got attention. The fuselage became silver and white with a yellow racing stripe. The wings turned silver metallic. The engine nacelles received intricate designs, including detailed inlet accents.

Photo #13. Engines #3 and 4 with the new striping.

Then I convinced Bruce that instrument panels in aviation gray were beneath our girl. The cockpit became cream with chocolate-brown accents.

We never lived that decision down.

Photo #14. The cockpit painted cream waiting for instruments.

Dulcinea once again looked like the queen of the ball. All she needed now were Wright R-3350 Cyclone engines, props, and electronics—her dancing shoes.

The Slow Fade

As fall approached, the DC-7 parts promised from Miami still hadn't arrived. Neither had our pay, more than a month overdue.

Work on Dulcinea slowed to a crawl. She was ready—but the parts never came.

Photo #15. Painting nearly complete.

When cold lake winds made life in an unheated travel trailer unmanageable, we let Bill—Papa Bear, the man funding the dream—know we were locking everything up and driving to Florida.

Learning Points:

- *When the signs are clearly in front of you, trust your intuition.*
- *When the pay stops, you're working at your own risk.*

CHAPTER 7

RESURRECTION—HEAVY METAL

PART 4 · PLANE THREE – SEBRING

AGE 21-22 · 1979-1980

On our first day back in Daytona, Bill gathered Bruce and me and laid it out plainly. The third airplane—the one in Sebring—was never going to fly again. She existed now for one purpose only: to give up her engines and props so Dulcinea could live.

In a few days, Bill said, I would head down to Sebring to work with a new hire named Vic Hardy. Together, Vic and I would be tasked with getting the Sebring engines running by early spring. Once we proved they could breathe again, we would pull them from the wings, mount them on stands, and truck them north to Wakeman.

Dulcinea had waited long enough.

Then Bill did something unexpected.

He paid me the weeks of back pay he owed.

It bought him more time than it should have.

When I asked Bill how we were supposed to move four R-3350 engines, he smiled and pointed out the window to a used tractor-trailer he'd just purchased. Then, as if it were obvious, he told me I needed to go get my Florida commercial driver's license so I could drive it.

Seven months after being hired, I still hadn't flown a heavy airplane for Bill. Instead, I was about to become a heavy over-the-road 18-wheeler trucker.

I told myself it was temporary.

By then, the blinders were strapped on tightly.

Then over the next eight months, I drove that International Transtar ten-speed back and forth between Ohio and Florida four times. It remains one of the worst jobs I've ever had.

Instead of flying Navy fighters—or even hauling freight out of Miami—I was grinding up and down I-75, staring at taillights and mile markers, wondering how things had gone so sideways.

Bruce made the smarter choice. He declined the Sebring assignment and stayed in Daytona to knock out another semester at the community college. He would have brought humor to what became a grim operation, but I didn't blame him for choosing classrooms over corrosion.

A few days later, Bill drove me to Sebring to get things started.

The third DC-7 looked tired in a quieter way than our Wakeman birds. She hadn't been vandalized or stripped. She still had most of her parts. But ten years under the Florida sun had taken their toll. UV exposure, salt air, and humidity had eaten deep into her structure. The corrosion alone made her unflyable. She wasn't a derelict hulk—but she was finished as an airplane.

The following day Vic arrived from Miami. Bill put him in charge. The task list was simple enough on paper.

Break the rust binding pistons to cylinders.

Replace every hose.

Restore ignition systems.

Replace prop governors.

Bring enough instrumentation online to run engines safely. Make smoke—without making metal. *(See Inside the Story: What "making metal" means.)*

For six months in Wakeman, Bruce and I had worked alone. Two novices, equal parts determination, and ignorance, pushing a project that probably should have scared us more than it did.

Now I had a real boss.

Vic didn't know what I'd already endured.

I resented him on principle. Not because he was meticulous. By the book. Unapologetically disciplined. I respected those attributes. But if I'm being terribly honest, it was ego—he was now more important to the operation than I was.

And he was right about the way we'd been doing things in Wakeman. It was reckless—it wasn't how aviation maintenance was meant to be done. Bruce and I improvised because we had no choice.

Vic brought structure, and with it, a sense of calm.

To my surprise, we hit it off immediately. We discovered we liked each other—and nearly fifty years later, we're still good friends.

For the first time, someone was setting standards instead of making it up as we went along.

Once Bill left town, Vic handed me my marching orders: fabricate hoses. Hundreds of them.

I disappeared into a dark, cluttered little tool shed with bulk hose, fittings, mandrels, and a hacksaw. No windows. No radio. Just repetition.

And my thoughts, which had nowhere else to go.

They weren't kind.

I replayed every decision I'd made since graduation. I could be in Pensacola right now. I could be wearing a flight suit. Instead, I was cutting hose in Nowheresville, Florida, for a company that couldn't always make payroll.

Vic offered more than once to swap jobs. I declined every time.

I wanted the isolation. It felt deserved.

Day after day I cut, fitted, tightened, repeated—hose after hose, engine after engine. When I finished a batch, I'd walk out to the ramp carrying four perfect replica hoses and a wrench, hand them to Vic, pull the next rotting original as a template, and retreat into my hole.

Fifteen days passed that way.

When Bill hired a third mechanic, the rhythm finally changed.

Jerry Sims (name changed) showed up mid-winter. Twenty-two years old. He had cut his teeth as a mechanic in Miami, straight out of what everyone called Cockroach Corner—also known as Corrosion Corner—the part of the airport where old recip freighters flew from, patched together just well enough to keep flying. *(See Inside the Story: Reciprocating Aircraft Engines.)*

Where Vic was methodical, Jerry was instinctive. He worked like a WWII mechanic out of a black-and-white movie—gruff, efficient, unimpressed by theory. People used to say of old-timer mechanics that they had engine oil in their veins, and Jerry fit the type.

What mattered was this: he knew R-3350 engines. And we needed him.

Not long after Jerry arrived, two things happened that finally pulled me out of my emotional spiral.

The first came when Bill showed up unexpectedly and told me to pack a bag.

We were going to Miami.

Bill was scheduled to give a captain's checkride on a DC-6 to Antigua, and he said he'd do my Flight Engineer checkride on the same trip.

Finally.

I'd passed the written exam nearly a year earlier and had been studying manuals ever since. After months of wrench-turning and gofer work, this felt like proof that the suffering might amount to something.

In Miami, Bill marched me into a pilot supply shop.

"Get yourself a uniform shirt, some epaulets, and a flight bag."

For the first time, he was treating me like a crewmember instead of hired labor.

Back at his crash pad, he showed me what belonged in the bag: charts, a flashlight, a circular slide rule—and a bottle of Scotch.

"Now," he said, "you're a real pilot."

He was kidding.

Mostly.

The Scotch, however, was serious. Not for the cockpit, but for layovers, negotiations, and whatever customs situation might arise. It was Bill's version of preparation.

Something changed for me that week flying in the Caribbean. Bill repeated one lesson often: never let yourself get complacent. Watching him manage marginal equipment, weather, and system failures with calm authority taught me more about command than any manual ever could.

I didn't admire him as a businessman.

But as a captain, he was the real thing.

I don't know if that week made all the misery worthwhile. But I know some of what I learned there surfaced in me years later, in different airplanes, when it mattered.

Back in Sebring, the second mental shift came soon after. We got all four engines running.

After ten silent years, they roared back to life, belching thick gray smoke. It felt miraculous. It wasn't just the engines that were back to life.

I stopped replaying Navy Tomcats in my head.

Through Vic, I learned how much skill radial engine starts demanded. He showed me that starting those big recips was an art—one hand on the throttles, the other managing start paddles and primer. Too much—or too little fuel—meant a backfire loud enough to announce your mistake to the entire airport.

Clean starts—they earned respect. The reward was that of a deep, satisfying whirrrrr filling the air and the distinctive smell of burned high-octane avgas.

Mess one up and you bought drinks at dinner.

We ran the engines hard. Burned off ten years of rust and tested everything. Cycled the props. Ran compression checks across all seventy-two cylinders—shockingly good, given what those engines had been through.

Only one engine gave us reason to pause. It showed metal in the oil screen after each test run.

Vic warned Bill repeatedly.

Bill waved it off. Jerry joked that unless the metal had a part number, it wasn't worth worrying about.

Nobody laughed.

This disagreement, along with some other issues around safety and proper maintenance, ultimately led to Vic having a blow-up with Bill in late March.

Vic finally had enough.

He quit.

The place felt emptier afterward.

Jerry and I pressed on, retrieving engine stands from Wakeman, then pulling the Sebring engines off the wing and loading them onto the stands for the eventual drive north.

And then came the task neither of us was ready for.

Airport management made their position clear.

The airplane had to go.

There was only one way she was leaving Sebring Airport. In pieces. Destined to become future beer cans.

Jerry and I showed up with metal cutoff saws and a knot in our stomachs we both understood without saying a word. We had lived with these airplanes. Named some of them. Bled on them. Even brought dates to meet her. And now we were being asked to cut her apart with our own hands.

We didn't talk much that first day.

The two factory-installed main deck cargo doors were worth more than the entire purchase price of the airplane. So, we started there—carefully measuring, cutting, and easing them free. When they finally came loose, we meticulously craned them onto a crude frame mounted on the flatbed trailer.

We drove those doors to Miami and sold them for cash. None of it went directly into our pockets, but that wasn't the point. Cash flowing into La Mancha Aire meant payroll would be covered for another week or two. For Jerry and me, that was reason enough to celebrate.

When we returned to Sebring, the real work began.

We cut the airplane into sections small enough for a scrap hauler to carry away on city roads. Each cut sent vibrations through the airframe and up our arms. It was brutal work. One section after another, the old girl dropped to the tarmac with a heavy thud. Dust and odors long hidden in her crevices billowed out around us, invading our senses and reminding us of the sin we were committing.

It felt wrong—not intellectually, but viscerally.

I don't believe airplanes have souls, but there was something profoundly unsettling about destroying something so beautiful and purposeful.

By the time we were finished, she had been reduced to a pile of aluminum worth about $2,100 in 2026 dollars.

I was hollowed out by that experience. I couldn't talk about it for a long time.

The DC-7 was the airplane that made me fall in love with aviation as a child. I had climbed into one as a five-year-old boy at Cleveland Hopkins and never fully come back down.

Now I was cutting one up with a power saw.

Tearing one apart piece by piece felt like a betrayal.

Eventually, there was nothing left to do but leave it behind.

Sebring was finished.

Four engines sat on stands, strapped to the flatbed, ready for the long drive north.

Dulcinea was waiting.

Learning Point:

- *When one's own money is on the line, judgment can be clouded.*

Inside the Story *(Optional Reading)*

What "Making Metal" means

Radial-engine mechanics use the phrase *making metal* when internal engine parts begin shedding metal particles into the oil system. Those particles can come from bearings, pistons, cylinders, gears, or other critical components wearing or failing.

Mechanics often monitored the health of these engines by examining the oil system. Tiny metal particles found in oil screens could reveal that internal parts were beginning to fail.

When a recip started making metal, experienced mechanics knew trouble was coming, and it is rarely a minor issue. Often it signals expensive repairs—or an impending engine failure.

Reciprocating Aircraft Engines

Before jet engines took over aviation, most airplanes were powered by large piston engines called reciprocating engines, or simply "recips." They worked on the same basic principle as a car engine: pistons moving back and forth inside cylinders, converting exploding fuel into rotating power that turned a propeller.

The difference was scale. Engines like the Wright R-3350—used on aircraft such as the B-29 bomber and later on large cargo airplanes—were enormous radial engines with eighteen cylinders arranged in a circle around the crankshaft. When running properly they produced tremendous power. When they weren't happy, they produced noise, smoke, and mechanical drama.

Inside a recip engine, hundreds of parts are constantly accelerating, stopping, and reversing direction thousands of times per minute. It's a violent mechanical environment, and things wear out.

CHAPTER 7

RESURRECTION—HEAVY METAL

PART 5 · RETURN TO WAKEMAN – Year Two

AGE 21-22 · 1979-1980

With winter still howling off Lake Erie and forecasts predicting a late spring in northern Ohio, our four-month project—which had already stretched past the one-year mark—would be delayed yet again. Dulcinea was too large to fit inside the Wakeman hangar, so progress would remain limited until winter finally loosened its grip.

Still, Jerry, Bruce, Bill, and I hitched the International Transtar tractor to the flatbed loaded with four engines and headed north.

This time, when we turned off the county road and rolled onto the Ortner tarmac, it felt very different than it had eleven months earlier. Oddly, it felt like I had come home—an idea that should have unsettled me more than it did.

The old girl looked lonely. A spring snowstorm had left snow and icicles clinging to her wings and upper fuselage. But most importantly, she looked untouched. Sad—but not vandalized.

Not the wreck we had discovered a year earlier. And this time, we came bearing gifts: engines, tires, brakes, instruments, and electronics.

Even the camper trailer had survived the winter. Still, it was far too cold to sleep in an unheated camper, so for the next few weeks we stayed at the motel down the road.

The following day we towed Dulcinea out of the dirt and snow and back onto the tarmac in front of the hangar, next to the fifth-wheel camper.

That return to pavement was short-lived.

Once Ortner learned we were back—and that Bill had returned without the past-due rent—he promptly threw us off his ramp. He changed the hangar locks and sent all of us and Dulcinea back to the weeds, to work without power or equipment.

It wasn't my responsibility to pay Ortner or judge his actions. From where I stood, it just felt punitive—rules changing midstream, leverage being applied because it could be. From my inexperienced viewpoint, Ortner had come out far ahead. If he hadn't sold the airplanes, he likely would have paid someone to scrap them. But I was only twenty-two—what did I know about business or the deal those two had struck?

Working without a hard surface carried real safety consequences. Swinging engines onto wing mounts in the dirt would be difficult and dangerous. But that was our reality—the apparent modus operandi of La Mancha Aire.

So, we started by unloading the four engines from the flatbed and staging them in the grass beside Dulcinea. Then Bruce and Bill headed back to Miami with the truck to retrieve our overhauled props, leaving Jerry and me alone to push the project forward.

Daily, Ortner became more of a thorn, but that was Bill's battle. For us, the real enemy was the weather. Lake Erie still packed winter's punch, and without hangar shelter the wind made work miserable. The gusts poked at our faces like tiny needles. We could partially cover our faces, but wearing gloves limited our dexterity, making exterior work challenging. Bare hands meant cold metal radiating straight into bone.

Still, the clock was ticking. We needed Dulcinea in Florida before summer. So, Jerry and I pressed on.

Facing the cold head-on, we hung all four engines in a single day. Nothing went wrong. It wasn't Jerry's first rodeo—only mine.

Once the engines were mounted, another solid week of work followed: connecting lines, pumping forty-two gallons of oil into each engine's tank, and wrestling freshly painted cowling pieces back into place after eight years on the ground.

Behind the scenes, Bruce and I had been lobbying Vic to return. Thankfully for us, his California plans fell through. He came back to Corrosion Corner, Miami—and ultimately to La Mancha Aire.

A week later, Vic and Bruce arrived in Wakeman with four freshly overhauled props. Now we had a full crew and every part we needed to put Humpty Dumpty back together.

Photo #16. Truck and props just back from overhaul in Miami.

That week we installed props. For such a sophisticated machine, the procedure was almost comically simple: hand-tighten the sixteen-inch prop nut, then torque it by placing a 180-pound man at the end of an eight-foot bar and bouncing slightly.

We did that four times and called it a day.

Photo #17. First of four props to be installed on engine #2.

She looked impressive—no longer a derelict, but a complex, purpose-built machine, ready for action.

Winter finally loosened its grip. Unfortunately, spring delivered its own curse: mud. The ground turned to soup, complicating everything. Our boots stayed soaked, and jacking the landing gear to install new wheels and brakes became a genuine engineering problem.

Totally unnecessary—but from Ortner's perspective, perhaps fitting punishment.

Vic's return transformed our efficiency. His depth of knowledge—especially on Douglas systems—was extraordinary. Bruce and I were motivated and could read manuals. Jerry had extensive round-motor experience. But without someone enforcing standards, effort alone wasn't enough.

With Vic setting the pace, days of scattered work collapsed into a clear sequence. A few days later, Dulcinea was ready for fuel.

Wakeman had no fuel service, so 100-octane avgas was trucked in from twenty miles away. We needed enough fuel to test the integrity of the tanks and then run the engines—but not so much that we created a safety hazard if the tanks leaked.

As expected, the tanks leaked like sieves.

These were not rubber bladders. The wings themselves held fuel in cavities of the structure. Eight years with no fuel in the tanks had caused the sealant to dry out and crack. Fuel dripped steadily from beneath the wings for days, forcing us to remove hundreds of rusted screws holding dozens of access panels in place and begin the miserable work of resealing the tanks.

The process never seemed to end: scrape out the old sealant, clean the mess, apply new compound, close it up, wait a day, add fuel, check for leaks—then drain the tank dry to use the fuel in the next tank.

Day after day, we repeated the process.

It is difficult to describe what it is like to stick your face inside a fuel tank thick with high-octane fumes.

Today, no mechanic would be allowed inside a fuel tank like we were. The tanks would be purged with inert gas, respirators required, and safety protocols enforced.

In Wakeman, we had none of that—we soldiered on.

Weeks later, the leaks finally stopped. The mud dried. We were finally ready for engine runs and landing-gear tests.

Ortner, meanwhile, grew more cantankerous. His threats to restrict Dulcinea's ability to depart until his fees were paid became a daily occurrence.

That was above our pay grade. Our task was singular: turn this DC-7 back into a flying machine—before time, or Ortner, caught up with us.

With the cowlings removed and a couple hundred gallons of fuel aboard, we climbed into the cockpit to bring Dulcinea fully alive for the first time in eight years.

I felt giddy—like an expectant father. Fourteen months of my life. Eight years of her dormancy. The Whitesells' dreams converging in one moment.

Vic chose me to start the engines.

I focused hard, wanting those big radials to purr. No way would I be buying any beer that night. Sitting in the left seat, a smile filled me from deep inside. I felt that same five-year-old joy I'd carried all my life—now it was my hands flying around the cockpit as I brought the beast back to life.

One by one, they lit off smoothly. No bangs, burps, or booms. No drama. Just prop wash and the smell of burned avgas.

Magical.

We ran them hard in Sebring. And again, in Wakeman that day—because in aviation, you verify twice.

No fires. No serious leaks. No major surprises.

Relief washed over us all.

Vic compiled a list of squawks—nothing shocking, but enough to keep four mechanics busy for weeks.

Only after we shut down and secured the airplane did we notice the crowd. Perhaps half of Wakeman lined the road, watching the smoke drift away and feeling the noise roll back across their quiet farmland.

Once the engines were safe and the adrenaline ebbed, we climbed down, wiped our hands, and walked across the tarmac toward them. That's when the stories started—of the Ortner Air Service heyday, of round motors coming and going, of life once buzzing through this little patch of Ohio.

It wasn't just Dulcinea that had awakened that day. Wakeman had, too.

For the first time in fourteen months, we felt like we belonged.

What a shame it took so long to meet these nice people—especially since we were likely just weeks from leaving forever.

That night, tension returned. Vic raised concerns about the engine still making metal. Jerry disagreed. The argument exploded—two mechanics, two philosophies, but only one would prevail.

By morning, the friction still felt like 100-grit sandpaper.

A line was drawn.

Safety versus patch-and-go.

Ultimately, Bill would decide when he returned.

While we waited, weeks passed with fourteen-hour days clearing squawks and preparing for the next hurdle: taxi tests.

High-power taxi tests are where theory ends and consequences begin.

Before attempting high-speed runs, we positioned Dulcinea at the far end of the runway and ran each engine individually at maximum power while stationary. Engines one and two ran clean.

When we advanced power on number three—the inboard engine on the right wing—the cockpit filled with an unmistakable sound.

The fire warning bell.

A red light illuminated.

Fire.

Vic didn't react immediately. Radial engines are notorious for triggering false fire warnings caused by leaking exhaust gases—serious, but often manageable. His calm voice steadied us. Still, with the engine out of view from the cockpit, he sent Bruce aft through the cabin to check visually.

We expected Bruce to return with a thumbs-up.

Instead, he came running forward, shouting.

"It's on fire. Lots of big flames."

There was no hesitation.

We shut down all four engines, cutting fuel to the nacelles. Normally that would starve a fire within seconds.

But the warning light stayed illuminated.

With the cowlings removed, the built-in fire-extinguishing system would be nearly useless. Any suppressant would disperse into open air. Worse, with the engine mounted directly into the wing, the fire could spread aft into fuel-bearing structure.

We were out of time.

We moved fast—out of the cockpit, through the cabin, and onto the right wing through the access hatch.

Flames rolled around the powerplant and inside the engine compartment.

Jerry grabbed the portable extinguisher and stepped onto the wing first. Vic followed. I was right behind them, with Bruce last.

As Jerry rushed forward, his feet went out from under him. Fresh oil coated the top surface of the wing—an unavoidable byproduct of running radial engines.

I saw it happen in slow motion.

He fell hard and began sliding faster and faster toward the wing's edge—six feet from open flame.

I lunged and grabbed his left leg.

Then my own feet slipped on the oil.

We were sliding together now, dragging the only extinguisher with us.

Bruce, still standing on a dry patch, grabbed my foot just in time.

In the chaos, Jerry lost his grip on the extinguisher. It flew free, bounced once, and nearly disappeared over the edge—until he stopped it with his other boot.

Balanced on the brink, Vic reached forward, grabbed the extinguisher, and emptied it into the fire.

The flames fought back—then collapsed.

Dulcinea survived.

ANOTHER BULLET DODGED

Later we found the cause of the fire: oil ignited by an exhaust flame during a brief engine backfire. With the cowlings installed, the fire likely never would have happened. But we had kept them off to avoid drawing Ortner's attention.

The fire was the consequence.

The next day Bill arrived. The engines ran flawlessly for him. Then came the landing-gear test—the one event that mattered almost more than anything else.

En route, engines can be shut down. Fires can be fought. But an airplane that cannot raise or lower its gear is an accident waiting to happen.

Eight years of inactivity is brutal on hydraulics. Corrosion pits actuator shafts. Seals harden. Pressure lines weaken. A failure here wouldn't announce itself politely—it would wait for the worst possible moment.

With Bill overseeing the test, we raised Dulcinea on wing jacks and cycled the gear.

Once.

Twice.

Ten times in all.

Each extension and retraction felt like a held breath. Each time, the gear locked into place as if she remembered exactly who she was.

Photo #18. Landing gear moving up into the wheelwell.

When it was over, we didn't cheer.

We just stood there—quietly relieved.

She wasn't just running.

She was trustworthy again.

Learning Point:

- *When risk becomes familiar, it stops feeling like risk—and that's when it becomes most dangerous.*

For a sobering parallel, see the NOVA documentary *B-29 Frozen in Time*, which chronicles the restoration—and loss, by fire—of the *Kee Bird* in Greenland.

Chapter 7

RESURRECTION—HEAVY METAL

Part 6 · Prison Break

Age 21-22 · 1979-1980

The night Bill arrived in Wakeman, the mood at the dinner table lifted—but it wasn't celebration so much as a temporary suspension of dread. The tests were successful. The engines ran well. We were close enough to believe again, which is a dangerous place to be when the only thing holding you together is momentum.

Then Bill poured cold water on the mood.

Ortner, he said, was escalating the conflict. Storage fees. Tool rental. Camper hookup rent. Tarmac use. Hulk-removal bonds—for both airplanes. Charges for anything that could plausibly be written on an invoice. And if that didn't get paid, Ortner had hinted at stronger measures: blocking the runway, calling the Sheriff, stopping us outright.

The year before, Ortner had been cooperative—almost enthusiastic. Two airport hulks were finally leaving his property. This year, something had shifted. Indifference at best. Obstruction at worst. It felt less like negotiation and more like a waiting game—one he expected to win.

Bill had no intention of paying. Instead, he offered a plan that didn't feel like aviation at all—it felt like evasion. "Total subterfuge," he said, smiling. The smile didn't reach his eyes. This wasn't strategy for efficiency. It was strategy born of fear.

For weeks following, Dulcinea stayed on jacks. Cowls off. Tools scattered. Whenever we were seen in town, we talked loudly about new problems and fresh delays. Anyone curious was invited to inspect our frustrations up close. Bill understood small towns. He knew every word would find its way back to Ortner.

Quietly, we kept working. One engine run at a time. No crowds. No spectacle. Slowly parts vanished from view—hauled off the field or tucked inside Dulcinea like contraband. We built progress behind a performance of failure, and I performed it with a fluency that should have disturbed me. But I wanted her to fly—badly enough to cross a line I knew was there, then tell myself it didn't count because the goal felt noble.

When the moment came, it came quietly. A thousand gallons of fuel arrived under cover of darkness—enough, according to our calculations, to get clear of Wakeman and, if nothing went wrong, reach Lexington. The margin wasn't generous. It just felt survivable.

The next night, under a pale spring moon, cowls went back on. Jacks came out. Cargo was secured. Dulcinea stood on her own legs again.

It felt exactly like a prison break—built on misinformation, secrecy, and timing.

At first light, it was time.

Vic, Bill, and I sat in the cockpit. Bruce waited in the Dodge dually, camper in tow. Jerry stood by with the tractor-trailer and flatbed. The plan was simple: once we were airborne, they would disappear. If we aborted, they would disconnect, normalize the scene, and claim it had only been a high-speed taxi test.

The tension inside the cockpit was thick—almost physical. It felt like breathing through cloth. Excitement pulsed beneath it, but reality pressed harder.

We were about to fly an untested airplane.

That dictated everything that followed.

Vic took the engineer's seat. His experience with old radials made the decision obvious. Bill sat left seat—owner, captain, thousands of DC-7 hours behind a calm exterior. I took the right seat, painfully aware that I was the least experienced man in the cockpit.

Soon, Dulcinea would either rise from the ashes—or prove, in the most definitive way possible, that we had been building a story instead of an airplane.

None of us said it aloud, but we all shared the same private hope: we were never coming back to the grass beside the blue hangar at Ortner Field. Ever.

Before the farmers had climbed onto their tractors, all four engines were running. We taxied away from the camper. As we turned toward the runway, I glanced left—down toward the far end of the pavement—and saw something that shouldn't have been there.

It gave me pause.

I said nothing.

In that moment, I chose momentum over caution, and I didn't even have the decency to call it what it was.

Thirty-three hundred feet of cracked crumbling asphalt is not much runway for a transport-category airplane. But we were light—minimal fuel, no payload. On paper, it worked. We had checked and rechecked the numbers. Dulcinea was well below maximum balanced field weight. *(See Inside the Story: Takeoff Decision Speeds and Balanced Field Length.)*

Balanced field length matters because it is the line between options. At the most critical moment of the takeoff roll, lose an engine, and either have enough runway left to stop—or enough performance to fly.

We did a high-speed taxi test down the runway. Four engines. Smoke and a lot of noise. Enough to wake the township. We knew time was running out. Someone would be coming to investigate soon.

It was time to pour the coals to her and get the hell out of Wakeman.

Photo #19. The Wakeman runway and the start of our first takeoff.

At the far end of the runway, Bill turned her around and lined us up on centerline. Vic scanned the gauges.

"Temps are in the green. Indications look good. We're ready."

But his eyes lingered on number three—the engine that had been making metal every time we pulled the oil screen. As chief mechanic, Vic carried that weight more heavily than the rest of us.

"Close the cowl flaps and oil cooler doors," Bill said. "We're going for it."

Then he looked at me.

"Your girl had better do her job today."

"She'll get us home," I said, hoping my voice sounded steadier than I felt.

"I want to hear sixty knots from you," Bill said.

I nodded. And just for a heartbeat, I was five years old again—sitting in a DC-7 cockpit at Hopkins Airport, joy pounding in my chest.

Bill brought the power levers up, the engines straining as he held the airplane still with the wheel brakes. The beast was jumping and lurching, eager—alive—ready to be released from her pen. Then he released the brakes and advanced the power levers to METO—conservative, measured. These were old engines. Untested.

The roll began.

And immediately, something was wrong.

She didn't accelerate.

Not like she should have.

Light airplane. Cool morning.

She should have leapt forward.

She didn't.

Vic scanned the instruments rapidly. "All engines look good."

"I told you to call sixty knots," Bill snapped.

"I will—when we get there!" I shot back.

Half the runway was already behind us.

My stomach tightened. I wanted to say it. Abort. The word was right there.

Vic said it first.

"ABORT!"

But Bill was already past that decision point in his mind. This had become do or die. He fire-walled the power levers.

The engines screamed under the strain.

Vic worked feverishly, fine-tuning, trying to keep them from tearing themselves apart.

Acceleration came—but too late to be comforting.

"Sixty knots," I called.

It didn't help.

We passed the hangar. The camper. We should have been rotating the nose airborne by now.

Instead, the airspeed crept upward, mocking us.

And at the end of the runway stood three trees—twenty feet tall, grown quietly over the eight years the airport had been closed.

Three trees I should have cut down months earlier.

Four hundred feet of runway left.

I was certain Dulcinea was about to be destroyed.

Strangely, I didn't think about myself. Or Bill. Or Vic. Or Bruce watching from the ground. I thought only of her. After everything she had endured—this was how it would end?

With engines nearly melting from overboost, Bill coaxed her into the air. We slipped past two of the three trees. The landing gear tore through the third, ripping branches free.

Bill lowered the nose and held us in ground effect, skimming ten feet above the fields. Corn tassels blurred beneath us as airspeed finally built into something survivable.

Photo #20. Climbing away from the Ortner Airport after takeoff.

Later, Bruce told us he was certain he was about to watch us die. When the gear struck the tree, he said he closed his eyes and turned away. He couldn't watch the rest.

Vic and I admitted later that we believed the same.

Bill never did.

For me, there was no doubt.

ANOTHER BULLET DODGED

Once airborne, Bill's excitement snapped into bravado. "Boys," he said, "it's time to buzz Wakeman."

In any sane cockpit, that impulse would have been shut down. In ours, it was treated like a perk of survival.

Vic immediately pulled the power back, opening cowl flaps and oil cooler doors, saving engines that had just given us everything they had. Once stabilized, Bill circled the field. Below us, Bruce and Jerry were already rolling—escape plan in motion.

One pass wasn't enough.

On the second buzz, Ortner's truck appeared on the tarmac. Bill flew so low there was no mistaking who the pass was for.

Then we were gone.

Photo #21. Bill rejoices after a buzz of the Ortner airfield.

Today, with decades of experience behind me, I'm not proud of the risks we took that day. But in 1980, I was a young aviator with barely more than zero time in heavy airplanes, flying beside a man I regarded as an aviation god.

At twenty-two, challenging a man like Bill didn't feel like professionalism. It felt like heresy.

Learning Points:

- *Captain Edward Smith was widely quoted before the Titanic's final voyage as saying, "I cannot imagine any condition which would cause a ship to founder. I cannot conceive of any vital disaster happening to this vessel." History showed how dangerous that kind of certainty can be.*
- *An unbroken record can become a liability when we confuse "it hasn't happened" with "it can't happen,"*
- *Trading margin for comfort is a slippery slope.*
- *Past success does not grant future immunity.*

Inside the Story *(Optional Reading)*

Takeoff Decision Speeds and Balanced Field Length

Before every takeoff, pilots calculate whether the runway is long enough for the airplane's weight. One of the most important concepts in that calculation is balanced field length.

Balanced field length is the point where two possibilities require the same amount of runway. If an engine fails at the worst possible moment during the takeoff roll, the crew must either have enough runway remaining to stop the airplane—or enough performance to continue the takeoff and climb safely on the remaining engines.

The decision speed that divides those two options is called V1. Before reaching V1, the pilots can reject the takeoff and stop on the runway. After passing V1, there is no longer enough runway to stop safely, so the takeoff must continue—even if an engine fails.

When the airplane's weight is calculated correctly, both options—stop or fly—require essentially the same runway distance. That is why it is called a balanced field.

For crews operating heavy airplanes from short runways, those calculations are not theoretical. They determine whether the takeoff is possible at all.

CHAPTER 7

RESURRECTION—HEAVY METAL

PART 7 · REALITY CATCHES UP TO US

AGE 21-22 · 1979-1980

After we climbed away from Wakeman and received our ATC clearance, I let my shoulders drop a notch. Not much—just enough to breathe. The hard part, I told myself, was behind us. My mind drifted ahead—past Ohio cornfields and cold concrete—to Miami heat and cold drinks. I could already imagine telling the story later, sanding down the rough edges, pretending we'd known exactly what we were doing all along.

Vic was having none of that.

He stayed locked in, eyes moving constantly, listening to the engines the way a good mechanic listens—with suspicion. Like a mother goose, he tracked every gosling. He understood far better than I did how many ways this flight could still go sideways.

Bill was hand-flying, focused on how Dulcinea felt—her control pressures, her responses, her temperament. I wasn't flying or running systems, so I settled into the role of safety pilot, scanning the big picture and working the radios.

About fifteen minutes after takeoff, something caught my eye.

The #4 engine—the outboard engine on my side—was streaking oil.

I watched the streak crawl aft across the upper cowling. There was no mistaking it.

I tried to get Vic's attention without making a production of it. When that failed, I reached over, tugged his sleeve, and pointed out the window.

He leaned forward, took one look, and said, "This isn't normal."

We looped Bill in and talked it through. Nothing in the engine indications explained the oil streaking across the cowling, so the propeller governor quickly became the leading suspect.

Bill listened, nodding, absorbing, then said quietly, "Let's track it."

Ten minutes later, tracking turned into action.

The cowling was now coated in a thick caramel-to-dark-brown film, and the oil quantity gauge was dropping fast enough that no one needed to do mental math. Bill shut down the #4 engine and feathered the prop while we still had enough oil pressure to make sure everything behaved properly.

That decision preserved the option to restart her later if we absolutely had to.

If the governor was the problem, waiting any longer would have been gambling. We were already trusting four old engines and four newly overhauled, completely unproven propellers. There was no reason to tempt fate further.

When the prop finally slowed and the blades came to rest at 12, 3, 6, and 9 o'clock, something settled heavy in my chest.

No one said a word, but the silence in the cockpit carried its own message.

We weren't going to Miami.

At least not the one with palm trees.

Regulations didn't require us to divert, but regulations don't sit in the cockpit when consequences arrive. With three remaining engines that hadn't yet earned our trust, the decision felt obvious.

Vic and I leaned toward landing as soon as practical. Bill wanted to put as much distance between us and Wakeman as he could safely justify—maybe as far as Knoxville.

Before the debate could settle itself, Dulcinea spoke again.

The #1 engine fire warning erupted.

Red lights flashed. Bells rang.

Ring-a-ding-ding. Ring-a-ding-ding.

"Silence the bells!" Bill shouted.

He feathered the #1 engine immediately. Once it shut down and cooled for a moment, the warnings stopped. That suggested it might not have been a fire at all—just heat where heat didn't belong. Suggestion wasn't certainty, and certainty was in short supply, but that was all we had to go on.

The bad news was we now had two outboard engines shut down.

Both remaining engines were unproven, and one already had a history of making metal. The question had shifted. It was no longer whether we could fly. It was whether we could stay airborne if one more engine quit.

None of us wanted to answer that experimentally.

As we approached the Cincinnati area, Wilmington Airport slid into view—a decommissioned Air Force base with a long runway and acres of concrete.

"Wilmington, it is," Bill said, without hesitation.

I declared an emergency. Bill brought our crippled bird down smoothly. We stopped on the runway while Fire Rescue crawled over the airplane, looking for anything glowing or smoldering. When they gave us the all-clear, a fire truck escorted us to the ramp.

The base was now home to Airborne Express. We hadn't asked for help, but we didn't need to. The ramp crew was already in motion—waving us in, staging an airstair, catching oil before it hit the concrete.

Total strangers, acting like we belonged there.

I also noticed Bill hadn't broken a sweat. Not a drop around his collar. He'd flown old iron all over the world, and very little rattled him. Watching him that day, steady and unhurried, I learned something important about command under pressure.

And just as clearly, I learned something else: even the calmest hand on the yoke can't save you when the system just beneath the surface has quietly cracked.

Bill disappeared inside to find a phone. Vic and I stayed with the airplane. He called one of the preplanned payphones south of Wakeman. Bruce and Jerry would be waiting for a call for a pre-arranged amount of time. The news was simple: head for Wilmington.

Up close, the answer was embarrassingly simple. The oil leak traced back to a loose fitting on the prop-governor oil line. Basic. Something we should have caught. It was safety-wired, but not properly tightened.

There was no blaming age or bad luck this time. That shutdown was ours. We owned it.

Saying that out loud hurt more than the work.

Bruce and Jerry arrived just as we turned our attention to the #1 fire warning. Instead of finding something ugly, we found nothing at all—no scorched wiring, no cooked components. The most likely culprit was a fire detector routed too close to hot hardware, a known DC-7 quirk. We rerouted the loop, ran the engine hard, and waited.

The warning stayed dark.

By the time we finally buttoned everything up, my patience was thinner than the gaskets we'd just put our faith in.

It had been a long day.

Dinner that night started the way exhaustion often expresses itself—looser, louder, a little mean. Ortner became the easy target, not because he was present, but because he wasn't. At twenty-two, it didn't feel like business. It felt personal—and when things feel personal, mockery comes easier than honesty.

As the plates emptied, the tone shifted. We began replaying the day, this time without jokes to soften the edges. We had flown Dulcinea successfully—but not without drama.

Terrible acceleration.

An oil leak.

A fire warning.

An emergency landing with two engines shut down. For an airplane that had been abandoned for eight years, it was an impressive first flight. It just wasn't the one we'd imagined.

We'd already explained the fire warning and oil leak, and we chalked the poor acceleration up to tight new brakes. We all believed tomorrow would be better.

Later, alone in a cheap motel room, the noise finally stopped. The realization hadn't arrived in the cockpit. It came hours later, stretched out on a thin mattress, staring at a stained ceiling while the memories of the day were still fresh.

My mind wouldn't settle. My chest felt tight. I replayed the takeoff again and again—how short the runway had felt, how hard we'd worked just to get airborne, how close we might have come to not getting airborne at all.

We'd been too busy escaping Wakeman, managing failures in the air, and fixing problems on the ground to absorb the risk while it was happening.

Earlier that day, I had nearly lost my life—not for a mission, not for a cause, but for a struggling company that had quietly run out of runway.

In the silence of that room, the truth finally settled in.

I had been calling this experience "paying dues." Lying there, I couldn't avoid the harder truth: I wasn't just risking my time or my education anymore.

I was risking my life.

And for what?

If I wanted that level of exposure, I should have been flying fighters for the Navy.

Sleep came in fragments.

Morning arrived quietly.

By the time we stepped onto the ramp, sunlight was spilling across Dulcinea, making her look honest again.

A night's sleep made yesterday's failures feel more distant than they really were.

Bill suggested a maintenance test hop before we pointed the nose south. No one argued. We all needed proof that yesterday was behind us.

Prudence would have said we should have done this back in Wakeman.

But prudence hadn't been invited along on our escape.

Staying close to the runway, we watched the gauges, temperatures, and engines behave exactly as they should. The airplane wasn't fighting us anymore.

The test hop went beautifully.

After landing, the relief was obvious.

We fueled for Miami, thanked the Airborne crew, and climbed back aboard.

Four engines started cleanly. Like any good radial engine, they rewarded our ground crew with a thick cloud of gray smoke—a proper farewell.

We taxied out feeling more like a flight crew than survivors.

Wilmington gave us a long runway and nothing growing at the far end of it. We used a low takeoff power setting, treating the engines with respect instead of urgency. Dulcinea lifted off smoothly and settled into a shallow climb, as if she finally agreed to come along.

The cockpit loosened. Conversation returned. We joked about Miami, about who we might invite to see our old girl once she was home.

Yesterday began to feel less like a warning and more like a toll we'd already passed through.

Then, seventy miles south, the illusion cracked.

The #3 engine didn't fail dramatically. It complained first. Power response dulled. RPM sagged. A vibration crept in—subtle at first, then undeniable. The kind that makes everyone stop talking at the same time.

Vic scanned the engine analyzer/oscilloscope and then at Bill.

"We lost a jug," he said.

No one argued. No one hoped it was something else.

Bill shut the engine down and turned us back toward Wilmington. No one disagreed.

The repetition alone was enough to tell us this wasn't chance asserting itself.

The flight back to Wilmington was short and quiet. With one engine shut down and the adrenaline gone, the cockpit carried the discouragement of another setback. Bill flew with the same steady hands as before, but the optimism that had crept back in earlier was gone now, replaced by something heavier and harder to shake.

The landing was uneventful.

We taxied straight to the far end of the Airborne ramp, back to the spot where our oil stains had barely dried. It felt like returning to the scene of a crime. Without a word, we shut down the remaining engines and climbed out of the cockpit, each of us already knowing what we were about to find but hoping—quietly—that we'd be wrong.

Bill was angry this time. Not explosive. Just a bit loud. Tight around the edges.

Vic didn't waste words. Yesterday's oil leak, he said, was on us. But this wasn't. These engines were old, unknown, and unreliable. We had no business trying to run an operation like this on faith and optimism. Treating an airplane like a taxicab—hoping it would just keep showing up for work—was a formula for predictable failure.

I didn't argue. Not even Jerry disagreed.

The Airborne crew saw us coming and didn't ask questions. Again, equipment appeared. Stands were rolled over. Tools followed. Whatever embarrassment we felt, we swallowed it.

Pride wasn't helping anyone at this point.

We de-cowled the #3 engine.

The blown jug revealed itself exactly where Vic said it would—down low, on the bottom of the aft bank. The worst possible place on a Wright Cyclone.

Of course it did.

These engines had nine cylinders arranged in a circle called a bank, two banks per engine, and this one had chosen the single location that demanded the most effort and the least mercy.

We pulled the oil screen next.

I held my breath.

Fine metal glittered in the mesh—nothing large, nothing catastrophic. Not good news, but not terrible either. By shutting the engine down quickly, we might have saved the rest of it.

Might was doing a lot of work in that sentence.

There was only one way to find out. Run the engine after the jug change.

For anyone lucky enough never to have worked on round engines, each air-cooled cylinder and its piston can be replaced individually while the engine stays bolted to the wing. On paper, it sounds almost civilized.

In practice, the bottom cylinders are punishment.

The blown jug sat low on the aft bank, buried where gravity and geometry conspire against you. Every step of the job required arms raised high overhead, shoulders burning long before progress was visible. There was no comfortable position—only degrees of miserable.

We loosened the twenty-two hold-down nuts slowly, deliberately. When the last one broke free, gravity reclaimed its due. Hot, filthy engine oil ran down our arms, soaked our sleeves, and pooled in places no human should ever have motor oil—specifically our armpits. The smell was thick and unmistakable. We had been thoroughly fouled by Dulcinea.

At the same time, our hands paid their own tax. Razor-sharp cooling fins—designed to move air efficiently for cooling aft cylinders—were just as good at turning knuckles into hamburger. Every reach, every slip added another cut. There was no way to work cleanly. There was only working through it.

This was the worst job on the airplane. Everyone knew it. No one said it.

Bill arranged for a replacement jug to be shipped from Miami. While he worked the phones, we worked the ramp. By late afternoon the old cylinder was finally free. Whether that engine was still truly healthy—or hiding something worse—would have to wait till tomorrow.

Just before sunset, we stood back and looked at the empty space where it had lived. The new jug would arrive overnight—via Airborne Express, fittingly enough.

By the time we got to the hotel, it had been hours since dark, sticky engine oil followed gravity down my arms. After the first shower, I still smelled like an engine. After the second, most of the oil was finally gone. I scrubbed grime out of my callused hands and from fresh cuts that burned with every pass of the washcloth.

Finally, I almost looked human again.

Dinner that night was different.

No one was joking. The easy release that had followed our first night in Wilmington was gone, replaced by the kind of quiet that tells you everyone is doing the same math in their own head.

Vic broke it first.

He laid it out the way a mechanic does when he's done pretending. This engine had already told us who it was. It had shed bearing metal in Sebring. It had done it again in Wakeman. Replacing the jug wasn't a fix—it was a gamble.

Bill pushed back. Engines were expensive. Time mattered. Jerry agreed. Small operators survived by fixing what could be fixed and flying what could still fly.

I sat there listening, fork idle in my hand, realizing something uncomfortable: both sides were right, and that was the problem.

It wasn't really about the engine anymore. It was about how much risk was acceptable, and who got to decide.

Jerry kept pressing. At one point he waved off Vic entirely and turned to Bill.

"If we ground every airplane that has an engine making a little metal," he said, "we'd have nothing for you pilots to fly."

By the end of the meal, the debate had shifted to manpower—and someone would have to leave La Mancha Aire.

It wasn't going to be Vic. Losing him meant losing both a pilot and a mechanic. By the time the plates were cleared, Bill had made his decision.

Jerry would leave in the morning. The engine would stay on the wing.

Sleep came hard that night. We had become a family over sixteen months of shared misery, and families don't fracture cleanly.

Morning arrived without ceremony.

At the airplane, a box sat near the landing gear as if it had grown there overnight. The shipping tag read AOG—Aircraft on Ground. Blunt. Accurate.

Bruce, Vic, and I went back to work.

Installing the new jug wasn't elegant, but it was straightforward. No shortcuts, steps 1 through 23. By midafternoon, the engine was back together. We ran it hard—then harder. Shut it down. Pulled the oil screen.

Clean.

We ran it again. Shut it down again. Pulled the screen again.

Still clean.

No one celebrated. We'd learned better than that. But when we finally buttoned up the cowling and stepped back, filthy, and exhausted, the relief was real.

By late on the third day after leaving Wakeman—W+3—Dulcinea was once again ready to head south.

Learning Points:

- *Shortcuts rarely announce themselves as danger. They feel like momentum—right up until the margin disappears and the cost arrives all at once.*
- *Leadership isn't revealed when everything works. It shows itself quietly, under pressure, when decisions must be made with incomplete information and real consequences.*
- *Machines will always tell the truth. The question is whether humans choose to listen.*

CHAPTER 7

RESURRECTION—HEAVY METAL

PART 8 · GROUNDHOG DAY

AGE 21-22 · 1979-1980

The next morning (W+4), our fuel arrived. We offered heartfelt thank-yous again to the folks at Airborne and apologized once more for making an oily mess of their ramp.

Once again: a start-up that looked routine, an engine run-up that gave us no reason to pause, a clean takeoff, and an initial climb that offered nothing to argue with.

For a few minutes, Dulcinea behaved the way we wanted her to. Gauges stayed steady. Temperatures remained normal. Nothing rattled, nothing complained. She flew smoothly, almost gracefully—like she was reminding us why we had fallen for her in the first place.

I didn't let myself hope. Not fully. Not yet.

But the thought slipped in anyway: maybe this time.

It lingered just long enough to hurt when it disappeared.

Shortly after leveling off, Vic noticed that the #4 engine would sputter and nearly shut down whenever the electric fuel boost pumps were turned off. It wasn't dramatic—no bang, no smoke—just a quiet refusal to behave unless we propped her up. Leaving the electric pump on would keep the engine happy, but it reduced redundancy and added risk.

We left the pump on and pressed on forward.

Dulcinea wasn't broken. She was needy and growing more so with every mile.

She demanded accommodation the way a sick partner does—not asking for rescue, only constant attention.

Then, just as we began to settle in for the long flight to Miami, the #2 engine tore itself apart.

The roar was instant and violent. The airplane shook hard enough to make it feel like she was trying to throw us off her back. Vic stared at the oscilloscope, watching the engine destroy itself in real time. We moved on instinct—feathering the prop, minimizing drag—doing everything we were trained to do.

Smoke poured from beneath the cowling. The engine seized and stopped dead.

It happened so fast there was nothing we could have done to save it.

Dulcinea was no longer negotiating.

We declared another emergency and turned back toward Wilmington.

The cockpit went quiet.

No one spoke beyond what was required to fly the airplane. When the en route controller handed us off to Wilmington Tower, the new controller couldn't resist welcoming the boomerang back home.

The comment landed because it was true.

On the ground, there was no ambiguity.

After de-cowling the #2 engine, the damage told the full story: huge chunks of metal in the oil screen, a gaping hole in the engine case, and a piece of connecting rod protruding through the hole like a broken bone. The powerplant was completely roached. Only the accessories were salvageable.

The rest was scrap metal and souvenirs.

When we told Bill what we'd found, he listened, nodded—and then casually mentioned he had new engines sitting in cans back in Florida.

The words didn't make me angry right away. They did something worse. They drained the room.

All the risks we'd justified. All the nights spent convincing ourselves this was the only way forward. In an instant, they weren't necessities anymore.

They were choices.

Choices we had never been given.

Vic finally said what we were all thinking. Why had we risked a thousand-mile flight on unknown engines when new ones were sitting in storage? Why not build the Sebring accessories onto new powerplants in Wakeman and do it right?

The answer was obvious. Bill had chosen the cheaper path and asked the rest of us to absorb the risk.

We were furious.

Not just at Bill, but at ourselves for trusting him.

We argued hard for him to bring four new engines so we could change them all on the ramp in Wilmington.

It was three against one.

Papa Bear overruled us all.

He agreed to bring only one engine. The other three, he said, would wait until we reached Florida and our maintenance facility in Flagler County. (Yes—the same Flagler County where I'd been arrested two years earlier.)

Bruce and Bill left right away to retrieve the engine—twenty hours each way by truck. Best case, three days before we could begin the build-up.

As soon as they departed, Vic and I went back to work.

Pulling a failed radial engine off a wing is not subtle labor. It's heavy, awkward, and unforgiving—the kind of work that forces you to focus whether you want to or not.

That first afternoon, the physical effort was almost a relief.

By the end of the day, the prop was off, an engine stand had been unloaded from Dulcinea's cargo bay, and the dead engine hung free of the wing.

The second day (W+6) was quieter. We stripped accessories from the failed powerplant and prepared them for transfer to the replacement engine.

That's when the thinking returned.

We talked about the money. About Bill. About whether any of this still made sense. After all, we hadn't been paid in over a month.

By evening, the work was done. The questions weren't.

Day three (W+7) gave us nothing to hide behind. We wandered Wilmington, killing time while waiting for Bill and Bruce to return.

We talked seriously about walking away.

What kept pulling us back was the same image: Dulcinea taxiing onto the Miami ramp under her own power—finished, useful, legitimate.

We both knew how much weight that vision was carrying. We hadn't been paid in six weeks. The money was likely gone, and we knew it.

We had already accomplished the Impossible Dream. Against all odds, we had taken a derelict DC-7 and made her fly again.

But flying wasn't the destination.

Miami was.

We needed to know whether Dulcinea could finish the journey and become the freight airplane we had imagined from the beginning. The odds no longer mattered as much as the question.

So, we stayed.

At dawn on day four (W+8), Vic and I arrived at the field to find a fresh engine in a can waiting on the ramp. Bill and Bruce were still asleep. We didn't wake them.

I had never done an engine change before. What felt familiar was the mood. Prying open the crate revealed a clean core—a chance—bringing with it a round of hope we didn't quite trust anymore.

We went to work without ceremony, falling into the same quiet rhythm that had carried us through the previous days. Tools out. Parts lay in order. Hands moving faster than the conversation ever could.

By the time Bill and Bruce showed up, the old powerplant was already off the engine stand and the new one was hanging in place. No one congratulated anyone. There was nothing to celebrate yet. We'd learned that lesson.

Day five (W+9) ended with the #2 engine mounted on the wing and running clean. No metal in the oil screen. Power exactly where it should have been. On paper, it was a success—the kind of in-the-field engine change that should have felt like a victory.

It didn't.

We ran all four engines and pulled all four oil screens. Everything checked out. Again. We stood there looking at the results, knowing how many times we'd said that before, knowing how little comfort it brought now.

Still, we made plans to leave in the morning, again.

There was nowhere else to go but forward.

Strapping into the cockpit on day six—our third departure from Wilmington (W+10)—the realization settled in slowly: nothing had changed except the calendar. Same field. Same airplane. Same promises. Different engine, the same possible outcome waiting somewhere downrange.

I thought of the movie Groundhog Day, the feeling of being trapped inside a loop you couldn't break.

When I called for clearance to Miami, I felt exposed saying the words out loud. Miami. As if naming it made us look foolish.

Maybe the controller sounded amused as he read our clearance to us. Maybe he didn't. But I heard something in his voice.

We always heard it now.

Taxiing out under gray skies and a light drizzle, the mood in the cockpit felt heavy. Not physically—emotionally. Dulcinea demanded constant attention, constant accommodation, and offered nothing but conditional cooperation. *(See Inside the Story: Why Dulcinea Was Not an All-Weather Airplane.)*

Again, takeoff and climb were uneventful.

Fly her gently enough, babysit her long enough, and maybe she'd allow us to keep going.

For a while.

None of us commented on how she was running. Not because we were superstitious—but because we were tired of being wrong.

Vic adjusted cowl flaps. Bill leaned mixtures. I scanned instruments and stayed busy, afraid that if I stopped moving my mind would catch up with the situation faster than I wanted it to.

We were thirty minutes out, nearing Knoxville, when the #3 engine began to bang again.

There was no shock this time. No spike of adrenaline. Just the familiar tightening in my chest. On the oscilloscope Vic identified that the replaced cylinder was fine. Two others weren't. We pulled the power back, let her cool for a moment, then shut her down and feathered the prop.

Another decision made for us.

We declared our fourth emergency in five flights, already knowing where we were going to land. Turning back toward Ohio felt less like failure and more like surrender.

Again.

Returning to Wilmington no longer felt dramatic.

It felt procedural. Familiar.

As we descended, the airport came back into view exactly as before—same runway, same taxiways, the same ending waiting for us yet again.

The tower and fire crews did their jobs professionally, but there was no hiding the tone now. Concern had given way to recognition. They knew us. They knew the airplane. I had the uneasy sense that they were watching us the way you watch something you expect to fail—not if, but when.

When we parked and shut down, the engines ticked and cooled around us. No one rushed to speak. There was nothing left to say that hadn't already been said in smaller pieces over the last ten days.

Bill finally broke the silence.

"Let's go see what's wrong and make a plan."

The words landed flat. Not because they were unreasonable—but because they were empty. We had been making plans the entire time. Plans to get one more engine to behave. Plans to get one more flight completed. Plans that assumed the next fix would be the one that held.

Standing there on the ramp, it became painfully clear to me that Bill wasn't planning anymore. He was reacting. Buying time. Hoping reality would bend if we leaned on it hard enough.

I felt something let go.

It wasn't anger at first. It was fear—clean and unmistakable. The kind that finally drowns out loyalty, gratitude, and habit.

Dulcinea wasn't a challenge anymore. She wasn't even a disappointment.

She was dangerous.

And Bill—the mentor I'd trusted, the man who had taught me so much—was no longer protecting us from that danger. He was asking us to accept it.

The words had been building for months.

Every missed paycheck.

Every promise.

Every compromise.

Every engine failure.

The words came out before I could soften them.

"Make your own damn plan.

I'm done with you and this shit show."

The moment hung there, heavier than any engine we'd pulled off the wing.

Vic didn't say anything. He didn't need to. I could feel him next to me, understanding exactly what had just happened—not as a tantrum, not as a betrayal, but as a line finally drawn.

I was still young. Still eager. Still wanted badly to be part of something that made a difference.

But I wasn't willing to trade my life for it.

Even at twenty-two, I could see what Bill could not: judgment under financial pressure doesn't flex—it distorts. And staying any longer meant pretending that wasn't true.

I had already given sixteen months to this dream. I wasn't giving it anything else.

Learning Points:

- *Experience informs judgment—but it does not suspend consequences.*
- *Risk does not disappear just because it has been avoided so far.*
- *"There is a time for departure even when there's no certain place to go." — Tennessee Williams*

Inside the Story *(Optional Reading)*

Why Dulcinea Was Not an All-Weather Airplane

When Dulcinea rolled out of the factory as a DC-7 in the 1950s, she was built for true all-weather airline service. But by the time she reached the world of third-tier cargo operators, many of the systems that made that possible had been removed.

Weight is the enemy of payload. Over the years, operators stripped out equipment that was expensive to maintain or reduced the amount of cargo the airplane could carry. One of the first things to go was the wing anti-ice system. Without it, ice forming on the leading edge of the wings could not be melted in flight, which severely limited operations in clouds or winter weather.

Other systems disappeared as well. The cabin pressurization compressors had long since been removed, meaning the airplane could not safely operate at higher altitudes where weather and turbulence are often avoided.

Fuel was another limitation. The DC-7's engines were originally designed to run on extremely high-octane aviation gasoline that was no longer available at most airports by the late 1970s. Without that fuel, the engines could not produce their full rated power at altitude.

By the time we inherited Dulcinea, she could still fly—but only within a narrow set of conditions. Weather, altitude, and engine performance all demanded constant attention.

Which is why every flight felt like a negotiation.

CHAPTER 7

RESURRECTION— HEAVY METAL

PART 9 — THE END OF THE ROAD

"There exists a wide gap between being right and getting others to recognize you are right."
—Pieter Bouw

AGE 21-22 · 1979-1980

I walked off the job in Wilmington and hitchhiked the 205 miles back to Cleveland. I reconnected with a woman I had loved since high school and made a quiet decision to start over without Dulcinea. A few weeks later, Tamara and I moved to Washington, D.C., and within a year we were married.

On the surface, life was moving forward. Internally, I was still sorting through what I had walked away from—parts of myself that had been bound up in that airplane.

Dulcinea's story, however, did not end with my departure. She eventually made it to Miami and successfully reentered the world of commercial airfreight hauling as the pride of Bill's fleet.

La Mancha Aire prospered for a time, growing to operate three DC-7s.

For a while, Bill was proven right.

Eventually, though, the company failed, and Dulcinea—N750Z—was sold yet again.

I was glad to hear that Dulcinea had survived, even if the feelings were complicated. She was doing what we had rebuilt her to do, and La Mancha Aire was proving, at least for a while, the dream hadn't been foolish. But knowing that didn't erase the loss of what I had walked away from—or how much it had taken with it.

N750Z continued hauling heavy freight for other small operators until she was placed in long-term storage at Turks Air in 1996. Years later, I learned she had avoided being cut up for scrap. Instead, she is being prepared to become a restaurant at New Smyrna Beach Airport in Florida.

The paint scheme Bruce and I lovingly applied in Wakeman is long gone. She now proudly wears her original American Airlines colors once more, and her original registration: N381AA.

Photo #22. Dulcinea in storage, New Smyrna, Florida, 2022.

Vic quit in Wilmington as well and never got to fly his girl from Ohio to Miami—the sense of accomplishment we all wanted and felt we'd earned. However, he did return to La Mancha Aire a third time and flew Dulcinea on commercial trips in and out of Miami, but that, too, was temporary. His career eventually carried him away from Corrosion Corner and into a better flying job. Vic went on to a thirty-five-year career with American Airlines, mostly based in Phoenix. The success didn't undo what Wilmington had cost—but it did give him the career he deserved.

Photo #23. Vic flying a Boeing 737 for America West in the 1990s before the merger with American.

Bruce stayed on at La Mancha Aire and spent years trying to earn his father's trust, respect, and acknowledgment—not just as a son, but as a professional. Every long night, every filthy job, every risk taken mattered to him in a way it didn't to anyone else.

On that maiden flight out of Wakeman, we all knew Bill had chosen me for the copilot seat—not his own son.

Bruce had earned that seat as much as I had. Whatever that moment cost him, he absorbed it without protest. He never complained.

Bruce was my best friend. When I left Dulcinea and Bill, I left him too. At twenty-two, I believed friendships, like airplanes, could always be repaired later.

I was wrong.

Bruce was tragically killed as a passenger in a Zantop Air Freight Lockheed Electra crash in Pennsylvania in 1983. The loss was sudden, violent, and absolute. Only later did I learn that an inexperienced captain overstressed the airframe, tearing the wings off in mid-flight.

His death taught me something I hadn't yet learned: sometimes the opportunity to repair a friendship disappears before you realize it's needed. The loss wasn't only that Bruce was gone—it was that the chance to repair what I had broken was gone with him.

To this day, I think of Bruce often and miss his easygoing joy for life.

Photo #24. Bruce in front of Dulcinea after a flight in 1981.

After Bruce's death—and the collapse of La Mancha Aire—Bill was never the same. The big presence that once filled a room thinned, as if something essential had been spent. He died of brain cancer in 1990.

I saw him once before he died. We said what needed to be said. When I left, I knew it was the last time. Some men are taken suddenly. Others are slowly emptied until there is nothing left to fight with.

Photo #25. Bill flying Dulcinea in 1982.

After leaving La Mancha Aire in 1980, I never again flew round motors or worked on large reciprocating-engine airplanes.

Photo #26. David in 1979 on Dulcinea's #3 engine before a night on the town.

Still, my connection to that unique sound—the chest-thumping rhythm, the smell of burned avgas, the drama of classic aircraft—lives on in memory:

Eastern Air Lines in '63.

La Mancha Aire.

Dulcinea.

Bill.

And my dear friend Bruce.

A boy who fell in love with airplanes.

A young man who learned that dreams can both build you and break you.

And an old airplane that taught me the difference between perseverance and wisdom.

Some dreams are worth chasing.

Some are worth walking away from.

Learning the difference is part of growing up.

My life was shaped by two old, salty dogs who flew Douglas DC-7s.

I owe a career, a life of joyful work, and a professional discipline to two men who gave the gift of aviation to a five-year-old boy and then, years later, to a young man.

Thank you both—wherever you now sit in the skies.

Learning Points:

- *Life will bring you what you need when you need it—if your door is open.*

CHAPTER 8
JETS AT LAST

"The sky is no longer the limit"
—Richard Branson

AGE 22-25 · 1980-1983

In D.C. everyone I spoke to wanted thousands of hours and jet time—two things I could only dream about then.

At twenty-two, I was broke, newly in love, and carrying the wreckage of La Mancha Aire around in my head.

I had spent sixteen months rebuilding airplanes and watching dreams leak oil. Now I was back to knocking on doors, hoping someone would take a chance on me.

La Mancha Aire had missed payroll week after week toward the end of my employment. By the time I finally quit, I hadn't been paid in six weeks. I had burned through what little savings I had left just to survive, and when I arrived in Washington, I was broke—financially and emotionally.

Professionally, I was starting over too. I didn't dwell on it. I licked my wounds, packed them away, and moved on—because stopping to examine the damage felt more dangerous than pretending it wasn't there.

The La Mancha Aire fiasco cost me more than money. It consumed over a year of my life and added almost no flight time to my logbook. That loss weighed on me daily. I had once leapfrogged my classmates by graduating early; now that advantage had evaporated. I didn't just feel behind—I was behind, convincing myself I'd catch up if I could just get one real break.

To be fair, the months at La Mancha Aire were not a total loss. I earned my flight engineer certificate and my Airframe and Powerplant (A&P) mechanic license. I also learned lessons about trust, optimism, and misplaced loyalty.

But I paid dearly for that education, and at the time it didn't feel like much of a consolation prize.

The broader world wasn't helping either. The national economy in 1980 was still reeling from the '79 recession. Aviation jobs were scarce, and desperation doesn't look good on a résumé.

Still, I had to resurrect my flying career somehow. I walked the ramp at National Airport in Washington, D.C., knocking on doors and shaking hands, trying to sound confident while quietly doing the math in my head.

Regrettably, I presented as a low-time pilot whose background was mostly in single-engine airplanes. The corporate flight departments wanted experience. I wanted a chance.

As weeks passed without progress, the pressure mounted. My savings thinned. My confidence followed. After a discouraging first month, I accepted a job as a flight instructor at Montgomery County Airport in Gaithersburg, Maryland—not because it was what I wanted, but because it was what I could get, and pride doesn't pay rent.

I didn't own a car, so getting to work became an endurance test. National Airport was a fifteen-minute bike ride from our house; Gaithersburg was a two-hour commute. I rode my bike to Dupont Circle, locked it to a tree, took the Metro with one transfer, exited at Silver Spring, waited for the Montgomery County bus to the mall, and then walked two miles to the airport—rehearsing quiet promises to myself that this was temporary.

Some days I did all that for a single student—who occasionally didn't show up. Then I reversed the entire trip home, unpaid. Those first six months in D.C. were brutal. I hated the commute, and I no longer enjoyed instructing. It was honest work, but it felt like treading water while time marched on. Something had to change. The commute was unsustainable. So was my morale.

That change came through a friend. Jeff Rubin worked as a pilot for the U.S. government at National Airport and knew many of the corporate pilots on the field. Before I ever arrived in Washington, Jeff had worked closely for two years with Chip Burton; although that assignment had ended a year earlier, they remained close friends.

Jeff didn't just introduce me—he advocated for me. He spoke about me the way you do when you're quietly staking your own reputation on someone else. His credibility opened doors that would have remained firmly shut otherwise.

One of those doors led to an introduction to Chip Burton. He was the chief pilot of a Jet Commander flown for a local land developer. When we met, something finally clicked. I'd like to believe Chip saw raw talent and drive in me. More likely: pilots were plentiful, and a low-cost pilot who also held an A&P—someone who could legally fix the jet on the road—was not.

It was a win-win for us both.

For the first time since La Mancha Aire, I felt like something good had come from that ordeal. Bill Whitesell's recommendation for my A&P certificate—earned during those painful months with Dulcinea—was the key that unlocked my first jet job. I still carried wounds from that year-and-a-half diversion from flying, but now I had proof it hadn't all been for nothing.

Flying the Jet Commander—and later a Gulfstream-1 based at National—was a massive leap forward. I went from a four-seat, 100-knot Cessna 172 to an eight-passenger jet cruising near 500 knots. Chip, with two decades more experience than I had, became my mentor. I watched how he moved through the job—quietly, methodically, without shortcuts.

Chip was demanding in ways most twenty-three-year-old pilots never consider. He taught me to taxi so smoothly that passengers couldn't tell when we slowed, turned, or accelerated. The same standard carried into the air. He seemed to measure success by what wasn't felt in the cabin.

"The customer should never feel the pilot's actions," he told me. "If they do, you're not doing your job."

That insistence on precision reshaped me. Praise from Chip was rare, but when it came, it stuck. I was still a sponge, and he filled it with habits that would quietly define the rest of my career.

He didn't have the formal aviation pedigree I did, but he was careful, thoughtful, and disciplined. He cared deeply about how the airplane looked, how it was flown, and how it was presented. His attention to detail wasn't flashy—but it was professional and fair. Working alongside him taught me what professionalism looked like when it didn't need to announce itself.

For two years, it was just Chip and me. Every weekend we flew from DCA to Charleston, South Carolina, so the boss and his wife could escape to Kiawah Island.

On one of those trips, after the boss had departed the airport, Chip and I were walking the wing while an FBO tug operator pushed our airplane to overnight parking. (Walking a wing means acting as a wingtip spotter while carrying a chock—a triangular wooden block used to prevent parked aircraft from rolling.)

As the jet reached a ninety-degree angle from its parking spot, the tow bar snapped. With the ramp sloping downhill, the Jet Commander began to roll free.

Chip sprinted behind the airplane and jammed a chock behind the right main gear. We expected the plane to stop.

It didn't. The wheel hopped the chock as if it weren't there.

Now the jet was accelerating. A hangar door loomed two hundred feet behind us.

I ran to the left main gear, threw my chock at the base of the wheel, and grabbed the landing gear strut—trying, foolishly, to slow twelve-and-a-half thousand pounds of airplane with my own body. Strength meant nothing. The airplane never slowed. The wheel bounced my chock aside without hesitation.

A light rain earlier had left a thin film of moisture on the ramp. My feet slipped. I went down—directly in the path of the rolling landing gear. With no time to escape, I twisted onto my side as the left main wheel crushed my ankle.

Chip watched in horror as the plane rolled over my leg and continued toward the hangar.

Lying on the pavement, clutching my ankle, I watched helplessly as the jet slammed tail-first into the hangar door. By sheer luck, the horizontal stabilizer struck the bi-fold door exactly at its hinge. The door partially collapsed inward, absorbing the impact, and stopping the airplane.

It could have been catastrophic.

Instead, the damage was limited to the elevator trim tab. The airplane was repairable. My ankle was swollen—but not broken.

ANOTHER BULLET DODGED

I repaired the damage myself. A week later, once the swelling subsided enough to fit into a dress shoe, Chip and I flew the jet home to DCA. We went back to work as if nothing unusual had happened, because in aviation that's often how you know you're doing your job.

Shortly after that, the real fracture appeared.

The owner of the airplane was miserable to work for—a man who confused wealth with authority and obedience with respect. He used to call mandatory "staff meetings" on Sunday mornings at his house. Those meetings consisted of escorting us through his twelve-car garage and assigning us to polish his antique car collection while he watched and talked. It wasn't subtle. The message was clear: we weren't employees—we were props.

A few months later, I was fired because I hadn't bought him a Christmas gift—on a twelve-thousand-dollar-a-year salary.

I couldn't afford an expensive gift.

So, I baked banana bread instead. I wrapped it, labeled it, and left it under the office Christmas tree, following the rules as they were explained to me.

He didn't see it. Or didn't look.

What he did see was an absence he interpreted as defiance.

His reaction at the office Christmas party was public and unmistakable.

I was fired on the spot, in front of everyone.

For reasons never fully explained, his wife had already taken the banana bread home to eat while it was still fresh.

By then, it didn't matter.

I was done.

The experience had shaped me. Chip had shaped me. But I'd lost all respect for the boss—and I wasn't willing to trade dignity for jet time anymore.

Professionalism also meant knowing when to walk away.

It had been two productive years. I was grateful to Chip.

I was ready to move on.

Learning Points:

- *True professionalism is often defined by what your passengers never notice you doing.*
- *Professional growth sometimes means recognizing when access to opportunity comes at the cost of dignity—and refusing the trade.*
- *Wealth does not automatically confer leadership, judgment, or respect for others.*

Chapter 9

LAST WILL AND TESTAMENT

Part 1

"Politics makes strange bedfellows"
—Harper's Weekly Magazine

Age 25-26 · 1983-1984

Even though Chip fought to get my job back, I ended up in a better flying position with Union Pacific Railroad.

For a young corporate pilot, it felt like a quiet step up rather than a leap forward. Nothing flashy. Nothing announced. Just an airplane that was always ready and a job that didn't advertise itself.

Photo #27. Me in the right seat of the Westwind cockpit.

I thought I was accepting a corporate flying job.

Instead, I became a witness with a front-row seat to a world of wealth, privilege, politics—and one bizarre legal episode that I still struggle to explain.

Union Pacific was building a small corporate flight department at National Airport (DCA) to serve the Harriman family, whose name and influence had been intertwined with the railroad for generations. They had just purchased a twin-engine, eight-passenger Israeli-built jet called a Westwind. Jim Tanner (name changed) was the captain and Director of Operations. He hired me as his copilot and Director of Maintenance.

A few months later, once I had enough time in the airplane to be proficient rather than just enthusiastic, Jim promoted me to co-captain. From then on, we switched off in the left seat every other flight.

There was no one else helping us. No dispatcher. No scheduler. No layers. For three years, Jim and I ran the entire operation—flying, maintenance, logistics, and whatever else was required. The airplane was always immediately available and the effort to make it so stayed invisible, by intention. That was the standard.

This was as far from La Mancha Aire as one could imagine, and at twenty-five, it felt like I had landed firmly back on my feet. My career was back where it was supposed to be.

The pay was solid for the time—$36,000 a year. The schedule wasn't punishing. The airplane was enjoyable to fly. Destinations varied. Most importantly, Jim and I controlled how the job was done. For a young aviator, it felt like winning without having to explain why.

The Harrimans were old money in the way that doesn't announce itself. They didn't explain who they were or why they mattered. That knowledge simply arrived ahead of them, clearing paths and opening doors.

Jim and I rarely saw it happen directly. We just noticed the absence of resistance—no delays, no explanations, no excuses. Things happened smoothly because they were expected to.

Averell Harriman had lived a life that intersected with history at its highest levels—railroads, war, diplomacy, politics. By the time I met him, he was officially retired, but retirement didn't seem to apply in the usual sense. He remained connected, informed, and quietly influential.

From time to time, he would poke his head into the cockpit during cruise. He never asked how fast we were going or what altitude we were at. Instead, he told stories—casually, without preamble—about people and events I had only seen in books. Not as lectures. Not as bragging. Just as memories that happened to involve presidents, prime ministers, and the shaping of nations.

I listened carefully and spoke very little.

His wife, Pamela, moved through that same orbit. She was his second. She had also been married before—to Randolph Churchill and later to Hollywood producer Leland Hayward. She carried herself with the kind of assurance that didn't require volume. When she spoke, people adjusted.

That was the Harriman world.

The flight operation ran smoothly. Requests were phrased politely but carried weight. Expectations were never stated; they were simply understood.

On occasion, we flew their friends and associates. One of them was Jackie Kennedy Onassis.

When she returned to the U.S. and needed transportation, the Harrimans offered their airplane. By extension, they offered Jim and me. We flew her more than once, and she treated us not as staff, but as people—asking about our lives, listening to the answers, making the space feel unexpectedly normal.

On one trip to New York, her limo was delayed. After shutdown at LaGuardia's Marine Air Terminal, I walked her across the ramp and waited with her at the curb.

Standing there, I was aware of who she was—but she never made it awkward. We talked quietly. Easily. She asked me about my life; in return, she talked about her life and family. When her ride arrived, she thanked me as if I'd done her a personal favor. The moment closed so neatly that it took me a second to realize how unusual it had been. What struck me later was how easily she made a stranger feel seen.

Not long after that, we were flying another special person at the request of the Harrimans—a man named Winston Churchill.

I of course asked for his autograph. I knew immediately how absurd that sentence sounded. But I had to ask.

It wasn't that Winston Churchill—history had already claimed him—but his grandson, Winston Churchill Jr., Pamela Harriman's child from her marriage to Randolph Churchill. He smiled and signed our flight plan paperwork. I joked about leaving the "Junior" off. He laughed like he'd heard it before.

Winston didn't arrive alone. He was dropped at National by an American instructor pilot named Kim Frizzell, who had just finished preparing him for his commercial pilot checkride. Kim struck me as relaxed and competent—the kind of pilot who didn't need to explain himself. In a business full of noise and ego, that stood out. We shook hands briefly on the ramp, exchanged a few words, and that was it.

Our role was simple. Once Winston was officially handed over, Jim and I were to take him from Washington to Kennedy Airport, where a Concorde was waiting to carry him home.

At JFK, we parked behind the Concorde. No announcements. No explanations. Just a marshal's hand signal and a place cleared where one shouldn't have been. British Airways representatives met us at the airplane and escorted him onboard, bypassing the usual lines entirely.

Rules didn't get stretched. They simply stepped aside. The privileges of a name… of wealth. A society we touched but were never a part of.

Later that week, we were landing at Dulles shortly after midnight with only Mrs. Harriman onboard. Jim was the pilot flying, and for a moment it felt routine—the approach steady, the runway lights rising, the deceleration initiated.

Almost immediately after touchdown, the landing lights revealed something directly ahead.

It wasn't debris. It wasn't a shadow.

It was a deer—full-sized, upright, standing squarely on the runway centerline, staring directly into the airplane's bright lights.

We were still doing roughly a hundred miles an hour. At that speed, distance collapses brutally fast. There is no time to wait and see.

Unlike debris, a deer chooses. It can jump. It can turn. Or it can freeze and become a projectile. With the Westwind sitting so low to the ground, a four-foot-tall animal wasn't something you "hit." It was something that could be driven straight through the nose of the airplane and into the cockpit where Jim and I were sitting.

Photo #28. Our Westwind, N84PH.

Jim reacted instantly, swerving the airplane to the right while fighting inertia, brakes, and physics all at once. For a heartbeat, the deer stayed frozen in the lights—locked in place, mesmerized.

Then the airplane slammed into it.

The impact was violent and unmistakable. A heavy, sickening thud followed by a sharp shudder as the deer struck the left main landing gear. The sound and the motion arrived together. My attention went straight to the gear and the wing above it—not the animal. If the gear collapsed or the wing had been breached, we would not have time to debate next steps.

Jim wrestled the airplane gently back toward the centerline, keeping it upright and controllable, and brought us to a stop on the runway. We were no longer moving—but we were far from safe.

I keyed the microphone. "Tower, N84PH has struck a deer on the runway. We're stopped and preparing to evacuate."

Jim immediately shut down the left engine. If we had a fuel leak or a compromised gear, staying put inside the airplane could be worse than getting out.

I went back to check on Mrs. Harriman. She was alert and clearly concerned but composed. I told her we had struck a deer and were assessing the airplane. She took it in without comment. A woman who had lived through the German bombing blitz in London had a very different scale for sudden danger.

I exited the airplane onto the runway to determine whether evacuation was necessary—fuel leaking, gear near collapsing, anything that would force us out immediately.

Within moments, fire and rescue vehicles arrived, their search lights flooding the scene and turning night into hard white glare. Working alongside them, my flashlight cutting through shadows, we examined the airplane from nose to wingtip.

The damage was severe but localized. The landing gear doors on the left side were gone—ripped clean away. Blood and hair were smeared along the strut and underside of the wing.

Standing there under the combined lights, it was impossible not to picture the alternative geometry: a foot higher and the deer might have penetrated the wing; a fraction more centered and it could have punched through the nose and into our laps instead of careening off the gear.

I ran my light carefully along the wing and integral fuel tank area, searching for anything wet, anything dark, anything that didn't belong. Fuel on the ground would have changed everything. We found none.

Evacuation was no longer the safest option.

I installed the gear pins to mechanically lock the landing gear in place. With the gear secured, we checked what else could have been damaged—brakes, hydraulics, gear structure—before preparing to move.

With the gear pinned and the fire crews satisfied there was no fuel leaking, we taxied slowly off the runway under escort.

At the FBO ramp, Jim shut the remaining engine down and the airplane finally went quiet. Only then did I step back into the cabin and escort Mrs. Harriman off to her waiting limousine. She thanked us calmly, as if we had just completed an ordinary flight. Then the car door closed, and she was gone.

When the ramp finally emptied and it was just Jim, the airplane, and the night, the intensity began to drain away. Standing beside the Westwind under the ramp lights, it became possible to replay the last few minutes in our heads—slowly, frame by frame—in a way that hadn't been allowed before.

If Jim hadn't swerved when he did, the deer would have come straight through the nose instead of striking the landing gear—and we would have been sitting ducks.

ANOTHER BULLET DODGED

The deer had been thrown clear of the runway and did not survive. At roughly 250 pounds, it never stood a chance against a seventeen-thousand-pound airplane.

The next day, with the landing gear down and pinned, we flew the plane (under an FAA ferry permit) all the way to Wilmington, Delaware for repairs.

Forty-five thousand dollars later ($145,350 in 2026 dollars), the Westwind was good as new.

Learning Point:

- True influence often speaks softly because it doesn't need to raise its voice.

CHAPTER 9

LAST WILL AND TESTAMENT

PART 2

AGE 26-27 · 1984-1985

The Westwind mostly functioned as the family's aero SUV, moving the Harrimans wherever they needed to be for the ordinary reasons important people travel. At other times, it carried the Harrimans' investment team—accountants, CFOs, and occasionally a CEO—to inspect holdings around the world. Those trips were straightforward. Our job was transportation. Their job was to review the books and observe operations in person to be sure the numbers matched reality.

Occasionally, the work took us to enviable places. Every six months we flew accountants to St. Lucia, where the Harrimans owned a sailing yacht rental business. While they spent days reviewing books and meeting with managers, Jim and I were handed one of the company's forty-foot live-aboard sailboats and told to enjoy ourselves. The boat was free; we paid only for a captain and food. At the time, it felt like just another perk of the job.

In 1984, we took the accountants and the CEO to a Harriman-owned resort in La Paz, on the east coast of the Baja Peninsula. After landing, Jim and I rented a car and decided to drive to Cabo San Lucas. When we told the rental clerk where we were headed, he hesitated—just long enough to suggest we might want to reconsider.

On the map, the distance looked insignificant. In reality, the road turned rough quickly, and what we expected to be a short daylight drive stretched into nearly five hours—much of it after dark.

This was years before Cabo had an airport, long before most Americans had heard of it. When we finally arrived—hot, dirty, and exhausted—we discovered the town had only three hotels. Naturally, we checked into what we were told was "the best hotel in Cabo." The clerk asked, "Señor, do you want towels with your room?"

I asked for towels and air-conditioning.

We received towels.

Cabo was known then for deep-sea fishing, not tourism. Catching a marlin felt like a worthwhile use of the layover, so we booked a fishing trip for the next morning.

Before sunrise, tired and blurry-eyed, we waited at the water's edge for our captain. Language was a problem immediately. Few people spoke English, and neither Jim nor I spoke Spanish. El Capitán arrived and waved us toward a wooden fishing boat that looked more like a relic than a working vessel.

A cloud of black, sooty diesel smoke poured out behind us as the boat shook and vibrated. Around us, a dozen similar relics idled in the harbor, each spewing exhaust until the air became nearly unbreathable. One by one, the boats fanned out toward their chosen fishing grounds. Eventually, so did we.

After about an hour of motoring through moderate swells—and inhaling fumes—the captain idled the engine, looked at Jim, and said, "Let's fish! Señor, do you have the bait?"

We stared at him, dumbfounded. I tried to explain that we had chartered the boat to go fishing and assumed bait was included. He didn't understand my words, but he understood my reaction.

The captain didn't argue. He didn't apologize. He simply turned the boat around and headed back toward land.

Thirty minutes later, we were tied alongside a floating bait store that looked barely afloat. If the fishing boats were rough, this one was worse—unpainted wood, a missing door, and resting so low in the water that she looked moments away from joining Davy Jones' locker.

The mate ordered mackerel. The captain looked at me and said, "Pay for it." I passed pesos across the gunwale without moving from my spot.

With bait finally aboard, we motored back toward the fishing grounds. Nearly two hours had been lost before we dropped a single line, and our expectations were low. Neither of us was much of a fisherman, but we knew early and late mattered. We had missed early—and had no desire to be on that boat after sunset.

For a while, nothing happened.

Then my line went tight.

The reel screamed as line poured out. The mate shouted instructions, motioning for me to let the fish run. I could feel the vibration in the line, the tension in the rod, and hear the high-pitched whine of the reel as the fish surged away.

It fought fiercely—sometimes darting toward the boat, sometimes pulling away, taking yards of line with it. Periodically it leapt clear of the water, twisting its muscular body side to side to dislodge the hook. To me, this was sport—exhausting, physical, and temporary. I didn't yet understand it was something else entirely.

After forty-five minutes, exhaustion set in for both of us. I managed to reel the marlin within five feet of the boat. The mate motioned for me to hand him the rod. The fish drifted on its side, barely upright. Its body shimmered in the sunlight. Its dark eye fixed on me.

Jim raised his camera. I leaned in for the photo.

In the next instant, the mate leaned over the rail and gaffed the fish.

Blood spread through the water.

I had assumed the fish would be photographed and released.

I was wrong.

We hauled the marlin onboard for the photo I no longer wanted. The crew called it a two-hundred-pounder—"a nice one." I didn't feel proud. The fish had died on my line, and whatever satisfaction I had expected never arrived.

Photo #29. David and his catch in Cabo San Lucas.

At the dock, the fish was lifted by crane and taken away to be butchered. The process was efficient and practiced, as if this ending had always been assumed. When it was finished, the meat filled four large coolers. One went to the captain, one to Jim, one to me. The fourth went to a local restaurant whose owner offered to prepare the fish and host a public dinner.

That evening became a party—tequila, strangers, laughter, and plates of marlin ceviche moving hand to hand. For a few hours, the mood carried us along. However, the image of the fish alongside the boat never fully left.

The next day, we drove back to La Paz to retrieve the accountants and CEO for the flight home. When they arrived at the airplane the next morning, they surprised us with a request. Instead of a standard climb and direct route to New York, they wanted to tour the entire Baja Peninsula at low altitude. I joked, "What a wonderful way to burn jet fuel."

Visibility stretched for miles, and the mood in the cabin softened as sport coats came off and people smiled. Jim and I did what pilots rarely do—filled the tanks to the brim. After departing La Paz, we descended until the ocean felt close enough to touch.

In 1984, huge stretches of Baja had no road access and remained untouched. For hours we followed the coastline—south past Cabo San Lucas, then north again along the Pacific side. Jim and I traded flying duties and scanned for birds, not as a pastime but because at that altitude there was no margin for inattention.

Baja felt immense and empty from a hundred feet above the water, a place still indifferent to our presence.

When we reached Magdalena Bay near Guerrero Negro, the experience crossed into something else entirely. Gray whales filled the water below us—breaching, mating, mothers guiding calves through the shallows. From that height, we were not simply looking down at them. Our airplane's shadow moved across the water beside them, gliding and turning as they gracefully moved along, briefly seeming to swim among the whales. For a few moments, it felt as though we had been allowed to become part of their world—not intruders above it, but silent participants in something ancient and purposeful.

Eventually, we climbed away and completed the loop along the Sea of Cortez. We burned a lot of fuel and added hours to the engines, but we saw Baja as it existed then, before development changed it. That made the cost feel insignificant.

Back home in Washington, D.C., the single cooler of marlin went into my freezer. Over time, I tried baking, grilling, and broiling the meat, but it didn't matter. Any heat made it tough and inedible. Ceviche was the only preparation that worked, and even that grew tiresome. I wished we had known better that day.

We hadn't.

During my years flying for the Harrimans, I came to see Pamela as a young, energetic sixty-year-old and Averell as a sharp, vibrant nonagenarian. They lived the life of the rich and famous, and we were their air chauffeurs. Georgetown was home base, but the seasons rotated among a horse ranch in Virginia, a ski house in Sun Valley, and a beachfront estate in Barbados.

The airplane and its pilots followed the same rhythm. Most winters, we spent four weeks in Barbados. On one Caribbean transit, Mr. Harriman leaned into the cockpit and said, "Boys, do you realize when I was a young boy the automobile had not yet been invented, and today I'm flying at thirty-five thousand feet at five hundred fifty miles an hour in my own jet?"

The sweep of change in one lifetime was astonishing.

In Barbados we stayed in a guesthouse next to their mansion—complete with a cook, a housekeeper, a car, and a daily per diem. Living that close erased the professional distance we were used to maintaining. Everything was handled for us, and without realizing it, we became part of the household.

Averell remained remarkably athletic. Even at ninety-three, he swam a mile a day in the open ocean. During our stay in 1985, a wave threw him against a rock, breaking his hip. What followed came quickly and without mercy.

As his condition worsened, Mrs. Harriman called us to the house. She asked us to fly to New York immediately, collect a revised will from the family lawyers, and return to Barbados without delay. We prepared the Westwind and departed that night. In New York, two lawyers met us, handed over a sealed envelope, and instructed us to give it directly to Mrs. Harriman—not to Averell.

The next morning, we returned to the mansion. Mr. Harriman lay motionless in a hospital bed, eyes open but vacant. Mrs. Harriman opened the envelope, glanced at the pages, and said, "Averell, the boys are back with your will; we need your signature." She placed a pen in his hand and guided it across the paper. Whatever resulted passed for his John Hancock.

She handed the document to me and said, "Witness it." There was no discussion. No hesitation. If I refused, my job would likely end. If I signed, I would be complicit.

I signed.

Ten months later, I left their employment for Northwest Orient Airlines.

Mr. Harriman died a few months after that.

I expected to be called.

I never was.

The will stood.

I moved on, aware the outcome could have been very different.

I still don't know whether what I signed was proper, improper, or simply how power operates when few people are watching.

ANOTHER BULLET DODGED

Learning Points:

- *Average people worry about having enough money; wealthy people worry about who and how people are taking their money.*

CHAPTER 10

THE PRICE OF ADMISSION

"Dull the edge of your pride, and sharpen the edge of your humility."
—Dr. Eugene Slattery

AGE 26-27 · 1984-1985

Unable to contain my excitement, I was dancing in the street at my suburban D.C. mailbox, waving a card over my head. American Airlines (AA) was instructing me to call the number provided and set a time to fly to New York for a pilot job interview. At last, I had a shot at the big leagues!

Flying for an airline had always been my ultimate goal. That interview card confirmed I had cleared the industry's price of admission—an Airline Transport Pilot rating and the 1,500-hour minimum—requirements I had surpassed long before, with nearly 3,000 hours in my logbooks by the time that letter arrived.

American Airlines had not hired a single pilot in five years—and now they were about to hire thousands. For someone standing at a mailbox with his ATP in his pocket, the timing couldn't have been better.

Two weeks later I stood at the American ticket counter at Washington National Airport, dressed in my blue suit, and bound for LaGuardia (LGA). In my hand was the paper that mattered—the one that turned me from an applicant into a candidate. I was vibrating with nerves. I truly believed I was holding the golden ticket to my future.

This was a moment I had mentally prepared for my entire life. Ever since that cold, damp day in Cleveland in 1963 on an Eastern Air Lines DC-7, this was to be my destiny.

In 1984, American wasn't the largest airline in the world—or even the country—but a massive MD-80 order signaled rapid expansion. For a young pilot watching from the outside, it felt like the right airline at exactly the right moment.

American had a two-stage interview process; day one was HR and a physical; day two was the simulator.

Day one went smoothly—almost too smoothly. The questions felt familiar, the exam uneventful. When I flew home to D.C. that evening, I replayed the day in my head and couldn't find a misstep. I was confident. I knew I'd be invited back for the simulator.

Then came the waiting.

Days passed. Then weeks. Nothing. No phone call. No letter. I was packed and ready to move wherever they sent me, already imagining the American wings pinned to my chest. I couldn't focus on work, friends, or anything else. My life felt paused, waiting on one envelope.

Once again, I stood at the mailbox, ready to dance.

I tore open the envelope and scanned for the words that mattered.

American Airlines regrets to inform you…

I didn't read the rest. My legs gave out and I sat down hard on the curb. The card fluttered to the pavement beside me. I had gone from airborne to grounded in a single sentence.

I had never felt silence that loud.

I called the number listed on the letter, hoping for a mistake.

The woman on the phone was polite, professional, and efficient. She asked for my file number and put me on hold.

When she came back, she said, "According to your records, you failed the drug screening."

I didn't respond.

"Sir?" she asked.

"That's not possible," I finally said. "There has to be a mistake."

I hung up in a state of shock.

I had never failed anything in my life that mattered this much.

I sat there for a moment, replaying every question, every possible scenario, searching for something—anything—that could explain what I had just heard.

I called American back and reached the same woman.

"If I fly to New York on my own dime," I asked, "would American retest me? I know this must be a false positive."

She paused, then told me I had already been removed from the pilot pool. There was nothing she could do. Once an airline stamped your file rejected, it was almost impossible to reverse.

I hung up the phone, heartbroken.

It felt like my quest to become an airline pilot was over. I had failed in the pursuit that had been all-encompassing for so many years.

Depressed barely described my emotional state.

I called my older brother Alan, a physician, because I needed help making sense of all of this. I had never taken a drug test before and didn't understand how a testing mistake—if that's what this was—could end everything.

He listened quietly and then asked, "Did you eat any brownies at my wedding?"

"Of course," I said. "Chocolate is my kryptonite."

There was a pause.

"Those were pot brownies."

Alan's words just hung in the air.

I was nearly in tears before the call—now a lump formed in my throat, and I couldn't speak. I hung up the phone and sat motionless, staring at the wall. Like a torment, I could see each bite of the confection that had canned my future.

An innocent moment—a brownie at a wedding—had detonated years of effort.

I sat there for a long time, staring at nothing. American Airlines was only one of many carriers, and intellectually I knew there would be other chances. But in that moment, reason didn't matter. The dream felt dead, and I felt responsible for killing it.

He said he'd personally handed them out and warned people what they were. That may have been true—but someone passed one to me, and I never asked. That was the mistake.

That single lapse crushed my chances at American and could have cost me my pilot's license. I was angry at my brother—but the harder truth was that I should have known better. I knew pot would be at his wedding. Brownies should have raised a red flag.

I didn't verify. I paid dearly for that assumption.

I went back to flying for the Harrimans and sending out applications—all of the airlines except American. Twenty-two airlines. Every six months. Paper forms. Updated logbooks. Envelopes. Stamps. And then nothing. No calls. No letters. No rejections. Not even an acknowledgment. Rejection would have been easier. Being ignored made me wonder whether anyone had even opened my application.

That changed in June of 1985, when a card arrived from Northwest Orient Airlines inviting me to Minnesota for a job interview. The process would take three days.

Day one: fly to Minneapolis for interviews with HR and Northwest line pilots.

Day two: a full physical at the Mayo Clinic in Rochester.

Day three: back to Minneapolis to fly a 747 simulator.

My interview date was July 13th.

With 3,200 flight hours and five years of corporate jet experience, I knew I was professionally ready. I was excited—of course—but this time I kept my hopes in check. I'd learned the hard way what unchecked optimism could be costly.

And I made absolutely sure… not to eat any brownies.

Day 1

With my blue suit freshly cleaned, I arrived at the DCA ticket counter carrying a letter that explained how to retrieve my flight ticket to Minnesota. By noon, I deplaned in Minneapolis and walked toward Northwest's headquarters, a squat, blue, corrugated-metal building dating back to the 1950s.

It had no windows.

None.

That should have been my first warning.

Inside, a guard examined my interview letter and handed me a visitor badge granting access to all Northwest buildings for the next few days. Before moving on, I asked him the obvious question.

"Why no windows?"

He shrugged. "None of our buildings have them. The big man doesn't want employees wasting time looking outside while on his clock."

That should have been my second warning.

But I wanted an airline job badly enough to ignore what felt like an architectural personality test.

I joined twenty-three other candidates in a windowless waiting room. Dark suits. Tight smiles. Everyone scanning everyone else. Eventually, conversation started. That's when I learned about the gouge.

A group of military aviators explained it casually, like it was common knowledge. Squadron mates returned from airline interviews, wrote down every question they'd been asked, and shared them. Over time, those notes evolved into a kind of underground survival manual for airline interviews.

I had never heard of "the gouge." These guys weren't just prepared—they were networked. Squadron mates passed interview questions back and forth until answers were nearly rehearsed. Information was currency, and merit wasn't the only thing that mattered in airline hiring.

As a lone wolf civilian, I was at a disadvantage.

Despite the obvious competition, a few guys showed real character. They shared the gouge freely. Some admitted they'd already been turned down by multiple airlines. One of them leaned over and said, "Don't worry about American. There's no rhyme or reason to who gets picked. You're here today—that's what matters."

A total stranger had just done what months of silence couldn't: he reframed the loss.

When my name was called, I was escorted into a small office—windowless, of course—that looked more like a storage closet than an interview room. A cluttered desk sat in the center. Papers were stacked along the walls.

The HR representative greeted me warmly and proceeded to ask many of the same questions I'd just read in the gouge. When we finished, she asked if I had any questions.

I couldn't help myself. I had to ask.

"Why, after three years of sending in applications, did Northwest finally invite me in?"

She didn't hesitate. She gestured toward the stacks of paper surrounding us.

"We're not computerized," she said flatly. "This is the first year we're hiring enough pilots to reach the W's."

I almost fell out of my chair.

"So, if I'd been an Alvarez…"

She smiled—just barely—stood up, shook my hand, and sent me back to the waiting room.

An hour later, three Northwest line pilots brought me into yet another windowless room. They reviewed my logbook and asked straightforward questions. Nothing tricky. Just measuring whether I was someone they'd want to sit next to in a cockpit for days at a time.

Later, eighteen of us were escorted to the departure gate for a twelve-minute Boeing 727 flight to Rochester. Five of the original twenty-three were sent home without explanation.

Airline hiring never made sense from the outside.

All I knew was that I was still standing.

After the flight, vans were waiting to take us to a hotel near the Mayo Clinic, where we were given instructions for the next morning's physical.

Day one was over. Day two loomed.

Day 2

The next morning began early at the Mayo Clinic. If Northwest Day 1 felt like an exercise in control, Day 2 was about extraction.

We were herded through the Mayo's endless corridors like parts on a moving assembly line—vision, hearing, blood, digestion, reflexes, balance. No explanations, just directions. Sit here. Stand there. Read this. Listen to that. Give us this sample. Now another.

By midmorning, any illusion of dignity was long gone. By afternoon, so was privacy.

Every system was inspected. Every weakness cataloged. By the time they finished poking, prodding, and sampling my body in ways I didn't know were even possible, I began to understand that Northwest wasn't just hiring pilots—they were underwriting human machines.

If the physical exams were thorough, the psychological evaluations were relentless.

Several guys struggled with the Minnesota Multiphasic Personality Inventory—the MMPI. Hundreds of repetitive questions, many only slightly different from the last.

Some of the candidates were visibly unraveling.

I believe, too much gouge.

They were trying to game the test instead of just answering it. Overthinking every question, chasing consistency rather than honesty.

I stayed simple. Answered truthfully. Trusted that whoever I was that had gotten me this far would be good enough.

Then came the final test—the one nearly everyone around me feared.

A thirty-minute session with a psychiatrist.

The gouge had pages devoted to this part. What not to say. What never to admit. What phrases supposedly got pilots disqualified forever. Nobody wanted to talk to a headshrinker.

Here, the gouge did real damage.

Guys tied themselves into knots trying to perform sanity instead of simply being sane.

For me, it was anticlimactic.

I had spent decades speaking with a psychiatrist—my father. Compared to dialog at family dinners, this was light work. The interview felt less like an interrogation and more like a conversation.

I walked out wondering what everyone had been so afraid of.

Just after 5:00 p.m., Day 2 finally ended.

I left the Mayo physically drained, psychologically wrung out, and oddly calm. My blood pressure—which I had worried about for forty-eight straight hours—never peaked, never became an issue.

I believed I had passed everything.

But I'd believed that once before. This time, I kept my confidence in check.

Tomorrow was the simulator check—the remaining hurdle—the biggest flying day of my career.

Exhausted and convinced the hard part was behind me, I did exactly what an over-confident twenty-seven-year-old shouldn't have done.

I celebrated.

With five of my new pilot friends, I went out. We chased girls. We drank—a lot. We stayed out far too late.

Today, I can't explain it. I can only confess it.

I felt invincible. I felt done. I felt like I'd earned a night off.

If you're keeping score, this one goes firmly in the not-proud column.

As the saying goes: Too soon old. Too late smart.

Day 3 — Simulator Check

The next morning, all eighteen of us flew back to Minneapolis. No one talked much. Whatever bravado had surfaced the night before was gone. The weight of what lay ahead settled in quietly, pressing down on all of us sitting in the cabin.

From the airport, we were driven to yet another windowless Northwest building—the only one where the lack of windows made sense.

Inside sat the Boeing 747 simulator.

This was it—aviator judgment time.

We met the simulator evaluation pilot, a calm, seasoned professional who immediately put us at ease. He explained that we would fly in groups of four. He would sit in the right seat as our copilot, and each of us would take turns in the left seat—the captain's seat—for about fifteen minutes.

He knew exactly what he was doing.

He made it clear that none of us were expected to know the 747. That wasn't the point. He wasn't evaluating systems knowledge or memorized callouts. He was watching how we flew—how we thought, how we communicated, how we handled pressure.

In short, he was deciding whether he'd trust us in a cockpit someday with his family in cabin.

When it was my turn, I slid into the left seat, adjusted my harness, and wrapped my left hand around the yoke.

I remember thinking, this could go very badly.

And then something strange happened.

Short on sleep and long on regret, I flew that simulator like I was playing a Stradivarius.

I don't know where it came from. I don't know how it happened. I just fell into the groove.

The weather was set at a half-mile visibility, a 200-foot ceiling, and a fifteen-knot left crosswind—my good side. When I intercepted the ILS at 3,000 feet the needles locked in and stayed there. *(See Inside the Story: What an ILS Approach Does.)*

Localizer centered. Glide slope centered. All the way down.

It was as if the instruments were broken. They never moved. I didn't chase them. I didn't overcorrect. I simply flew.

The runway lights appeared exactly where they were supposed to. Touchdown was smooth. Centerline never drifted.

I did not deserve that performance.

I hadn't prepared for it. I hadn't respected the stakes the night before. I had no business flying that well under those circumstances.

And yet, there it was.

Even the three other interviewees standing behind in the simulator commented on it afterward—something pilots almost never do. I was also the youngest person in the group, which made their acknowledgment mean even more.

When it was over, I climbed out of the simulator with my heart still pounding, unsure whether to feel proud, embarrassed, or simply relieved.

We all left Minnesota not knowing who would receive job offers—and who would be left studying gouge for the next interview somewhere else.

Two weeks later, I got the call.

Northwest Orient Airlines offered me a job with a new-hire class date of October 4th, 1985.

ANOTHER BULLET DODGED

What I learned was this: luck can mask poor judgment, but it can't replace preparation—and sooner or later, it runs out.

Forty years later, I know that had I landed that job with American, my life would have unfolded very differently. I would never have married Jillian Feldmann from Minnesota, and we would not have had the three wonderful children we share.

So, when I think back on the brownie episode, I find it hard to call it a tragedy. I missed out on what surely would have been an amazing career at American Airlines—but life had other plans.

The road twists. The ride is unpredictable.

Learning Points:

- *Twenty-two years of working toward a dream may seem like forever, yet 35 years of living the dream seems like a flicker in time.*
- *Perseverance to achieve one's goals, despite rejections, is a noble cause.*

Inside the Story *(Optional Reading)*

What an ILS Approach Does

An Instrument Landing System—usually called an ILS—is a radio guidance system that helps pilots land when weather makes the runway difficult or impossible to see.

Two radio signals guide the airplane to the runway. One signal, called the localizer, keeps the aircraft lined up left and right with the runway centerline. The other signal, the glide slope, guides the airplane down the proper descent path toward the touchdown zone.

In the cockpit these signals appear as two moving indicators—often called "needles." When the localizer needle is centered, the airplane is lined up with the runway. When the glide slope needle is centered, the airplane is descending at the correct angle.

In practice, the needles rarely stay perfectly centered. Crosswinds, turbulence, and small control corrections usually make them drift slightly from side to side. Pilots constantly make small adjustments to keep them centered as the airplane descends toward the runway.

When everything works perfectly—as it did on my simulator approach—the needles barely move at all. The airplane simply rides the electronic path down through the clouds to the runway.

CHAPTER 11

ETERNAL VIGILANCE

PART 1

"If one took no chances, one would not fly at all. Safety lies in the judgment of the chances one takes. That judgment, in turn, must rest upon one's outlook on life."
—Unknown

AGE 27 · 1985

Northwest Orient Airlines hired me on October 4th, 1985.

Six weeks later, after a blur of airline indoctrination (Indoc), Boeing 727 systems school, 727 Flight Engineer (FE) simulator training, and supervised revenue flying called Initial Operating Experience (IOE), I was finally signed off as a qualified Boeing 727 FE. *(See Inside the Story: Why a Boeing 727 needed a Flight Engineer (FE).)*

Very exciting for me! I could now actually claim to have made it to the next level of my career… an airline pilot!

Photo #30. New hire David in Northwest Uniform.

Two days after IOE ended, on Sunday, December 8th, 1985, I departed Minneapolis International Airport (MSP) for Rochester, Minnesota (RST). This wasn't just another flight assignment. It was the first leg of the first day of my new career at Northwest Airlines.

The flight from MSP to RST was notorious among pilots—a twelve-minute leg spanning less than sixty miles. For experienced Second Officers it was brisk; for a new hire it demanded constant anticipation. Tasks arrived faster than they could be mentally queued, and the climb checklist and landing data had to be completed almost on top of one another.

As we arrived in the Rochester area, hearing approach control clear us for a visual approach to runway 31, four miles behind a Learjet, I felt a rush of relief. The most compressed part of my workload was easing, even as the pilot flying grew busier with the approach. *(See Inside the Story: What a Learjet Is.)*

When I felt the slight rumble of the first flaps moved into the airstream, I knew I had made it through the hardest part of the leg.

At 3,000 feet the flying pilot turned our jet to line up with the runway centerline, and we prepared for the landing. The non-flying pilot switched to the tower controller who radioed, "Northwest 462, cleared to land, runway 31, following a Lear four miles ahead." We accomplished the landing checklist and then waited for the Lear to touch down and clear the runway so we could land.

For landing, the Second Officer swivels his seat 90 degrees to face forward and slides it up behind the center pedestal, wedged between the two pilots.

I leaned forward once more, eyes moving across the instrument panel, confirming that all three engines were behaving. For the first time since takeoff, my hands were still.

Then it happened.

I was looking through the windshield at the runway when the Learjet ahead suddenly veered, rolled inverted, and tumbled down the pavement. For a fraction of a second, my mind struggled to reconcile what my eyes were seeing.

Then the tower controller broke the silence:

"Northwest 462, go around!

Maintain runway heading, 3,000 feet.

The Lear ahead has just crashed!"

The captain immediately called for a go-around and go-around power. I reached forward and adjusted all three engine power settings as we climbed away from the runway, shifting without hesitation from witness to Second Officer, fully engaged in the go-around duties and the after-takeoff checklist.

With the Learjet now a crumpled, smoldering wreck on the runway, the airport's operations, fire rescue, and the tower controllers were all engaged in managing the emergency and coordinating incoming flights. *(See Inside the Story: Why Witnessing a Crash Felt So Unthinkable.)*

The captain leveled the airplane at 3,000 feet with a flurry of coordinated action in the cockpit as we settled into a modified holding pattern near Rochester.

As the reality of the crash set in, the cockpit grew noticeably still. No one spoke, not from shock, but from discipline. There would be time later to process what we had seen. For now, the airplane demanded attention.

Whatever had happened to the Learjet ahead of us was no longer an abstraction—it was a reminder of why this profession leaves no room for distraction, even in moments that shake you.

On my first day in the big leagues, only eleven minutes into my first unsupervised flight, we had been forced to transition from landing to managing an abnormal. A go-around led directly into a holding pattern, with a diversion increasingly likely. Each step required coordination, discipline, and time—none of which could be compressed.

In the holding pattern, my first responsibility was to understand how much time and flexibility we truly had. I calculated our fuel reserves and reported to the captain that we had several viable options: returning to MSP, remaining in the Rochester area, or reducing weight to land on a shorter runway. *(See Inside the Story: Why Runway Length Matters for Landing.)*

The numbers told us we didn't need to rush. Time was available, and with it, choices.

After about 15 minutes of circling Rochester with no information forthcoming from Air Traffic Control (ATC), we decided to request a divert clearance back to MSP. At that same moment the controllers in the tower let us know the RST airport was again open. Emergency vehicles were fully occupied on runway 31, dealing with the crash, but the shorter runway, 02, was now available.

The captain accepted that option and turned the airplane to a newly assigned heading, positioning us for an approach to runway 02. He advised ATC that we would need to climb to 5,000 feet to dump fuel—intentionally releasing fuel overboard to reduce the airplane's weight before landing. He then tasked me to calculate the aircraft's maximum allowable landing weight for the shorter runway and determine how long it would take to reach it.

My calculations showed we were roughly 3,000 pounds too heavy for the shorter runway. At our burn and dump rates, we needed about three minutes of fuel dumping to become legal.

After leveling the airplane at 5,000 feet, the captain turned to me and said, "Dump to 5,500 pounds remaining." That target provided enough fuel to fly another approach at Rochester, execute a go-around if necessary, divert back to Minneapolis, and still retain sufficient fuel for additional contingencies.

Fuel dumping on the 727 was a defined, six-step checklist procedure, and it was mine to execute. I had practiced it repeatedly in the simulator, and the steps were familiar. What was unfamiliar was doing it for real—over Minnesota, barely sixty miles from where we had departed, on my first trip.

Training had prepared me to perform the procedure correctly. But now I would be responsible for the outcome.

While waiting for my dump to complete, I coyly leaned over to the captain and asked,

"Do you guys dump fuel often at Northwest?"

He chuckled and told me, "I've been flying the 727 as captain for 10 years, This is my first time!"

Once the dumping was complete and the checklist finished, we configured for the approach and began our descent from 5,000 feet.

Inside the cockpit, the work itself was routine, but the atmosphere was not. No one spoke about the crash or the likely loss of life, yet the image of it stayed with all of us as we focused quietly on the approach.

The landing itself was uneventful, exactly as it should have been.

We taxied past what was left of the Lear. No one said anything at first. Then someone in the cockpit broke the silence and said, "There but for the grace of God go I."

ANOTHER BULLET DODGED

For me, there was no sense of arrival in the big leagues—no moment when the work suddenly felt different or safer. Whatever excitement I might have felt about flying for an airline vanished in the shadow of what had unfolded in front of us.

I did not yet know why the Learjet had crashed. But I understood again that aviation is indifferent to experience, rank, reputation, or how routine a day may appear. Vigilance is not something a pilot eventually outgrows or graduates from. It is a daily choice—a responsibility renewed every time an airplane leaves the ground.

Our flight arrived late at the gate in Rochester, and the passengers were a bit shaken by what they had seen through the side windows, but otherwise unharmed.

Three people in the Learjet ahead of us were not as fortunate. At 1:39 p.m., their airplane flipped upside down and crashed, killing all onboard.

Learning Points:

- *Anything man creates may possibly bite back; vigilance is the only antivenom.*
- *Humans are predisposed to make errors! Most of our errors don't result in death. However, some errors do carry a certain percentage likelihood of a fatal outcome.*

Inside the Story *(Optional Reading)*

Why a Boeing 727 needed a Flight Engineer (FE)

The 727 was designed in the early '60s, and it had no computerization. Instead, the FE operated all the aircraft systems, managed the fuel, calculated weights for takeoff and landing, and ran the checklists for the entire flight. It was a very important and often busy position in the cockpit. At Northwest, this position was also called the Second Officer—the third pilot on a three-man flight deck.

What a Learjet Is

A Learjet is a small corporate jet designed for point-to-point executive travel. Introduced in the 1960s by Bill Lear, it quickly became one of the most recognizable private jets in the world. By the 1970s and 1980s the name "Learjet" was so widely known that many people used it as a generic term for any small business jet.

Learjets typically carry six to eight passengers and are much smaller than airline transports like the Boeing 727. Despite their size, they are fast, capable aircraft that often operate into the same airports as airliners, where air traffic control sequences them into the same arrival streams for landing.

Why Witnessing a Crash Felt So Unthinkable

Even in 1985, when airline accidents still occurred with uncomfortable regularity, it was rare for a professional pilot to witness one firsthand. Commercial aviation was becoming safer, but that progress came through rigorous accident investigation, revised procedures, and constant professional scrutiny.

That was why what we had just seen felt so disorienting: we had watched, in real time, the kind of outcome our entire profession was organized to prevent.

Why Runway Length Matters for Landing

Runway numbers are not just identifying names for the pavement; they correspond to the runway's magnetic direction. Runway 31 at Rochester, Minnesota, points roughly 310 degrees on a compass.

In 1985 that runway was 7,500 feet long—adequate for most airline operations but not generous for a Boeing 727. The aircraft's highly swept wings required relatively high approach speeds, which meant more energy had to be dissipated after touchdown.

Another important factor is landing weight. Large aircraft are certified with both a maximum takeoff weight and a lower maximum landing weight. If conditions require landing on a shorter runway than originally planned, crews may need to reduce the aircraft's weight—usually by burning or dumping fuel—before attempting the landing.

These calculations are routine in airline operations and ensure the airplane has enough runway to safely decelerate after touchdown.

CHAPTER 11

ETERNAL VIGILANCE

PART 2

AGE 51 · 2009

Fast forward to 2009, twenty-four years later, in a profession that had grown safer—but never immune to the cost of lost vigilance. I had been a Captain on the Boeing 757/767 for eight years and was once again based in Minneapolis.

On February 24th, we launched from MSP at 5:30 p.m. for an overnight crossing to Schiphol Airport in Amsterdam—a route I had flown often, arcing north over Canada, Greenland, and Iceland before arriving in Europe the next day.

The weather on arrival was typical for the Netherlands in winter—overcast and gray. It had been nine hours since departure, and while we had missed a night's sleep in a bed, each of us had managed two hours of rest in a first-class seat. Red-eye crossings are always tiring, but we were alert and operating comfortably.

The arrival was smooth, with no gusty winds or adverse weather, and my copilot Tom flew the approach and accomplished a beautiful landing on runway 18R.

It was 10:24 a.m. in Amsterdam, and our Atlantic night crossing—a day-night ocean journey—had been uneventful. We cleared the runway at the customary exit taxiway, V2, with about a quarter of the pavement still ahead of us. We had just made the turn south onto taxiway V when Ground Control instructed us to hold position.

At first, we registered the instruction as odd, but reasonable. We set the parking brake and waited for the follow-on clearance that normally comes within a minute or so.

We sat in silence.

Five minutes then became ten, with still no word from ATC. We sat motionless, waiting for any acknowledgment that we hadn't been forgotten. After a nine-hour flight and a night without real sleep, the continued silence began to feel heavier than the delay itself.

By the fifteen-minute mark, the silence had crossed from unusual to unacceptable. None of us had ever experienced anything like this on the ground at a busy international airport. We exchanged confused glances, the stillness outside our windows matching the absence of any explanation.

After conferring quietly in the cockpit, I finally keyed the microphone and asked ground control,

"What are we waiting for, and can we taxi to the gate?"

The reply came back sharp and unmistakably Dutch:

"It is not possible. Hold your position!"

That response offered no explanation for the delay, no sense of when we might move, and no usable information.

In our current location, there was nothing to explain our predicament. Runway 18R sits nearly three miles from Schiphol's terminal complex, far enough away to have its own control tower. The taxi-in can normally take twenty minutes.

Instead of terminals and ramps, all we could see out the front windows was open Dutch countryside.

That isolation would matter.

As the minutes ticked by, the silence grew heavier. After being rebuffed by ATC for asking why we were being held, it was clear that nothing was going to change anytime soon. With our Pratt & Whitney engines burning roughly 700 gallons an hour at idle, we shut them down and committed to waiting.

With more than three-quarters of our passengers bound for onward connections, I knew a delay like this would amplify their anxiety. I made regular announcements, explaining that the airport itself appeared to be shut down and that connecting flights were likely delayed as well. It was an educated guess, offered to reassure, one more way of managing the uncertainty we shared.

For a full hour we sat motionless, wrapped in a silence that was more than the absence of sound. It was the pressure of not knowing. Having already been denied an explanation, we didn't key the microphone again, though each of us wanted answers. Instead, the three of us began quietly working through possible explanations for what could shut down an airport like Schiphol.

An eerie puzzle began to take shape during the long quiet. After nearly an hour, rumors from the cabin started making their way forward. The irony wasn't lost on me. We sat at the front of the Boeing 767 in complete communication blackout.

ATC wasn't talking to us. There was nothing meaningful to see out the front windows. The company back in Minnesota had no information about the ground stop. And since personal phone use in the cockpit was prohibited while we were operating the airplane, we had no connection to the outside world—though our passengers were free to use their phones and piece together whatever information they could find.

Nothing was confirmed, but we heard that operations at Schiphol might be shut down because a Turkish 737 had crashed short of the runway.

Hearing that news, the three of us exchanged looks. A Turkish flight had followed us in to Runway 18R.

In the absence of any confirmed information, our minds went to wake turbulence. *(See Inside the Story: Wake Turbulence Between Aircraft.)* Large aircraft like ours leave invisible disturbances in the air behind them, much like the wake left by a large ship. If the crash involved the airplane that had been behind us—and if it was a Boeing 737 or something similarly light, barely a third our weight—our wake, if it reached them, could have been significant.

It wasn't something we wanted to believe: that they might have encountered our wake. But based on what we knew at that moment, we could think of no other explanation.

As that possibility settled in, the cockpit grew quiet in a way I recognized. Twenty-four years earlier, silence had followed a crash I had watched unfold. This time, it followed a crash we could not see. The difference was subtle but profound: back then, I wondered how it had happened. Now, I wondered whether we might somehow be part of it.

With nothing to confirm or dismiss it, the weight of that possibility pressed down hard.

An hour and a half after landing, Ground Control finally came back on the frequency. "If your engines are shut down, start them up and be ready to taxi in five minutes." We ran the checklists, brought both engines back online, updated the passengers, and waited for the taxi clearance.

When we finally began moving again, we asked ATC what had happened. The answer came simply: the airplane that had followed us to runway 18R had crashed just short of the runway.

That confirmation made the questions we had been reluctant to voice impossible to ignore. We understood wake turbulence, and we knew how close the following aircraft had been. With no other information, we could not shake the possibility that our wake had played a role.

I taxied the airplane to the gate in complete silence. Whatever words might have come to mind felt inadequate. Until we knew more, we were left alone with the uncertainty.

Later that day we learned that the loss of life, while tragic, was not as great as we had feared. Most of the occupants survived, though five passengers and crew members were killed.

A year later, the final accident report confirmed that the crew had not encountered our wake turbulence. Instead, the investigation concluded that the pilots became distracted and allowed the airplane to stall at low altitude.

Knowing that our aircraft had not contributed to the accident offered some relief, even as the loss itself remained tragic.

ANOTHER BULLET DODGED

On February 25th, 2009, Turkish Airlines Flight 1951 crashed short of runway 18R at Amsterdam, just moments after we had cleared the runway.

Most aviators will never witness a fatal accident in their careers. That reality makes it even more striking that I encountered two—each rare, each sobering, and each a reminder of how thin the margin can be when vigilance fades.

What struck me later was how preventable the accident appeared to be.

Modern jetliners are remarkably forgiving machines, but they still rely on disciplined crews to manage distraction and maintain basic airmanship. *(See Inside the Story: Why Aviation Gets Safer One Accident at a Time.)*

Learning Point:

- *Human life is fragile. Aviation simply makes that truth harder to ignore.*

Inside the Story *(Optional Reading)*

Wake Turbulence Between Aircraft

Any airplane that generates lift also leaves swirling air currents behind its wings called wake turbulence. These rotating vortices trail from the wing tips and slowly sink as they move away from the aircraft.

The heavier the airplane and the slower it flies, the stronger the wake can be. Large transport aircraft can produce vortices powerful enough to roll a smaller airplane if it flies directly into them.

To prevent this, air traffic controllers separate aircraft on approach and departure so the disturbed air has time to dissipate before the next airplane arrives. Even with proper spacing, wake turbulence remains something pilots constantly consider when following another aircraft on final approach.

Why Aviation Gets Safer One Accident at a Time

Aviation did not become safe by accident. It became safe because every failure—whether rooted in human error, flawed systems, or broken machines—was examined, absorbed, and rewritten into the way we fly. Procedures changed. Training evolved. Airplanes themselves were redesigned to be more forgiving of human limits. Each improvement narrowed the margin for catastrophe, but none of them removed it.

For today's passengers, that progress is largely invisible. Many have never known a time when fatal airline accidents were a recurring presence in the news cycle. Commercial aviation now operates at a level of safety so high that serious accidents feel like historical events rather than contemporary risks. That reality is extraordinary, given the scale and complexity of the system and the sheer number of flights conducted every day.

It was not always this way. The safety record that exists now was built over decades, shaped by hard lessons and real loss. Technology, procedures, and training all played critical roles—but they mattered only because generations of aviators understood a simple truth: vigilance cannot be automated, delegated, or assumed. It must be carried, consciously and continuously, by the people in the cockpit.

CHAPTER 12

THE 747 YEARS

"Rules are guidance for the intelligent, and gospel for the idiots."
—Mike Armstrong

AGE 30-34 · 1988-1992

My new-hire job at Northwest was working out better than I had any right to expect. I started on the 727 in Minneapolis, where I lived, and the airline was expanding fast enough that a young pilot could feel the ladder moving under his feet. Six months in, I was promoted to second officer/flight engineer on the DC-10. Eighteen months after that—1988—I upgraded again, this time into the Boeing 747 second officer position.

Photo #31. Takeoff of a Northwest Orient Airlines 747.

At the time, I thought that was the story—the natural reward for being in the right place at the right time. What I didn't yet understand was that the airplane I'd just climbed into carried obligations that had nothing to do with seniority, routes, or pay.

When I first upgraded to the 747, I was encouraged—strongly encouraged—to enroll in something called the Civil Reserve Air Fleet. CRAF. *(See Inside the Story: The Civil Reserve Air Fleet.)* The explanation was brief and casual, delivered with the confidence of something so routine it barely deserved discussion.

"Just do it," the instructor pilot said. "The government has never used it. Most of the 747 guys are signed up."

So, I signed.

At the time, I did not fully understand what CRAF was. It was not the name for the day-to-day military charters we flew. Those were regular peacetime Department of Defense contracts—

valuable business awarded to airlines willing to pledge participation in the Civil Reserve Air Fleet.

In exchange, the airlines contractually designated aircraft and qualified crews for possible call-up to CRAF when a major crisis created more airlift demand than the military could handle on its own. Until that happened, the airplanes remained in normal civilian service, flying scheduled routes and routine military charters.

CRAF was the reserve force behind the reserve force: peacetime business in exchange for wartime readiness. When the government needed a sudden surge of civilian lift, it could activate the program and place those aircraft under military tasking.

I didn't think much about it when I put my name on the list. I was young, newly on the 747, and focused on learning the airplane. Like most of us, I treated CRAF as theoretical—something that existed on paper, unlikely to intrude into real life.

In late 1990, that theory became reality.

CRAF was activated. Northwest's 747s—both passenger airplanes and pure freighters—were folded into a massive, quasi-military operation. More than half of the 747-pilot group was suddenly flying missions in support of what was becoming a very real buildup for war in the Persian Gulf.

I was one of them.

If we were moving troops, we flew passenger airplanes. If we were moving equipment, we flew freighters loaded with vehicles, supplies, and anything else that needed to cross an ocean quickly. The routing was consistent: a U.S. departure, a recrew in Germany, and then onward into Saudi Arabia. This went on for months as the United States built an enormous stockpile of people and materiel in preparation for war with Iraq.

It was airline flying in structure, but military in purpose. Same cockpit. Same procedures. Entirely different stakes.

About four months into the CRAF flying, while checking in for a trip, I made an offhand comment to my chief pilot.

"Did you know Saudi Arabia doesn't allow Jews into the country?" I asked.

Then, half joking, I added, "I think it's ironic that I, a Jew, am flying soldiers and equipment into Saudi Arabia to help save them from an Iraqi invasion, yet I'm not allowed to be there."

The chief pilot didn't laugh.

Instead, he investigated it.

Whatever he found raised enough concern with upper management that the airline decided—not just for me, but for any other Jewish pilots flying CRAF missions—that, for safety reasons, we would no longer fly past Germany.

From that point on, when I was scheduled for CRAF duty, Germany was as far as I went.

That was fine with me. The food was excellent, the sightseeing exceptional—and yes, the irony of a Jew enjoying Germany was not lost on me.

When the war finally began in January of 1991, it was swift and decisive. And just as suddenly as we had been flying east with quiet, withdrawn young soldiers, we were flying west with an entirely different energy in the airplane. I flew a lot of troops home. For many of them, it felt like more than the end of a deployment—it felt like the first clear victory since Vietnam.

The tension that had filled those cabins months earlier was gone, replaced by noise, laughter, and something harder to define—a release. For an entire generation shaped by a war that ended in loss, the demons that had followed American soldiers home for decades finally loosened their grip. You could hear it in their voices and feel it moving up and down the aisle.

Back on the line, life on the 747 settled into its own demanding rhythm, and I settled geographically as well. After bouncing between bases early on, I finally landed where I wanted to be—Minneapolis. That one change mattered. There was no commuting across states just to start a trip, no crash pads with strangers. I went to work from my own home and came back to it.

The 747, unlike any other airplane I flew, offered long blocks of flying followed by long blocks at home, which, with a young family, created an advantageous rhythm that felt almost normal.

A twelve-day trip often started with a deadhead. I'd leave Minneapolis in the morning and ride as a passenger to Chicago, then stay with that same 747 and go on duty for the long pull to Tokyo—ten time zones, and the International Date Line. I'd lose a day on the calendar, and if it went as scheduled, I'd lose a night of real sleep too.

Narita was the pivot point. *(See Inside the Story: Northwest's Pacific Network.)* Crews arrived, reset, and then flew onward to destinations scattered across Asia. Senior crews went to the places people bragged about. Junior crews went where the schedule sent them.

In the late eighties, I was still junior.

Which meant Guam.

Pilots had a name for the flight: the Guam-o-Rama.

It left you hollowed out. Not tired—disassembled. The kind of fatigue where time stops behaving normally and your body no longer believes the clock.

Only after an ocean crossing had already left you exhausted did the schedule reveal its worst aspect: a double red-eye. Narita to Guam in the middle of the night, then a turn and right back to Narita before the sun was properly up. It felt like a trip designed by someone who had never tried to sleep as a human being.

We'd leave Narita late—often around ten at night—and arrive in Guam around three in the morning. Each leg was about three and a half hours, and between them sat a three-hour pause where we didn't go to a hotel or even leave the airplane. We stayed on board, sitting in passenger seats with the lights dimmed, while the groomers worked around us, waiting for the six-a.m. departure back to Japan. All told, it was eleven hours—about the length of an ocean crossing—spent almost entirely in the body clock's worst hours.

By the time we got back to Narita, it was midmorning—around nine o'clock, the day after we'd left. There was nothing left in the tank. We walked off the airplane and went straight to the hotel, moving on momentum alone.

Other crews were already in the lobby—pilots and flight attendants who had slept normal hours and looked it. They'd pause when they saw us come in. No one needed an explanation. That hollow look was unmistakable. Everyone had worn it at least once.

Somebody always made a smart-ass comment as we shuffled past the front desk.

"Guam-o-Rama, huh?"

And one of us, barely lifting his head, would answer, "Only three more days of this to go."

Which meant Narita by day, Guam by night.

The hotel in Narita was owned by Northwest, built for one purpose: to warehouse crew rest. Around two hundred pilots and flight attendants stayed there each night, and we all called it what it felt like—Camp Narita. It wasn't fancy, but it was built around sleep. Blackout window covers worked, and during the day the halls were quiet—not by rule, but by instinct. Everyone knew who was trying to sleep, and why.

With a little seniority finally under my belt, the trips changed. The Guam-o-Ramas faded away and were replaced by variety—layovers shaped not just by airline need, but by bidding strategy.

Those twelve-day international trips weren't accidental, and they weren't something I endured reluctantly. I bid for them because of what came afterward. Twelve long days away could be followed by eighteen days at home—real days, uninterrupted days, without packing bags or watching the clock, spent with my young family.

It wasn't that being gone was easy.

It wasn't.

But the trade mattered. Long stretches of absence were the price for long stretches of presence, and at that stage of my life, having time at home that felt whole mattered more than breaking trips into smaller, more frequent pieces.

Business travel isn't family travel. It isn't romantic, and it isn't restorative, and it doesn't pause for birthdays or holidays. If you spend too much time thinking about what you're missing, the job will eat you alive. I learned early that the only way to survive it—maybe the only way to do it well—was to accept the cost without dwelling on it, to stay present where I was, and to trust that being reliable for my family over time mattered more than being available in every moment.

Asia remained my anchor. Japan, especially, got under my skin in the best way. But now and then, I'd bid east instead of west, and Europe would open up.

In early1990, the timing was uncanny. I was in London for the forty-fifth anniversary of the end of World War II in Europe, watching veterans in full regalia fill the streets—men who had crossed oceans for reasons and risks that bore no resemblance to my own. Later that summer, Paris was alive with the Tour de France, and in August I landed a three-day layover in Singapore during the celebration of its twenty-fifth year of nationhood.

The 747 made all of it possible. Castles in Ireland and Germany. Ancient stone in Osaka. Architecture in Seoul, Paris, and London. It was an extraordinary way to move through the world—one earned slowly, trip by trip.

By the end of that summer, it felt as if a pretty great year was taking shape.

It felt stable. Predictable.

It would not stay that way.

The CRAF call-up late that year changed the rhythm of my flying for months to come.

The Atlantic

We were headed from Boston to London's Gatwick Airport. Three pilots, twelve flight attendants, and 396 passengers. We pushed back in the evening and climbed northeast along the coast of Maine, crossed New Brunswick and Newfoundland, and then pointed the nose of the airplane out over the Labrador Sea toward the North Atlantic.

Six hours and forty minutes was the plan.

About an hour and a half into the crossing, something changed—not abruptly, not violently, just enough to register.

A needle that had lived comfortably in the green began to drift. Not fast. Not dramatically. Just in the wrong direction.

The number two engine was getting hot. Too hot.

There's a particular energy in a cockpit during a system failure—no hero rushing in to save the day, just methodical thinking and action. Within moments it was clear this wasn't something we were going to monitor our way through.

The engine needed to be shut down.

Which meant our night was no longer going to include a walk through Piccadilly Circus. It was going to look a lot more like a walk through the Boston Common.

Flying over land with Air Traffic Control, you can turn around quickly. Over the North Atlantic, inside the organized track system, you can't.

Flying a four-engine airplane with one engine shut down is not, by itself, a serious emergency. The airplane is designed for it. The checklist is straightforward, logical, and deliberate—about a dozen steps, each one there for a reason. Follow them in order and the airplane behaves exactly as advertised.

What complicates things is what airspace you are in when it happens.

The oceanic tracks—known as the North Atlantic Tracks (NATs)—functioned like highways stacked on top of each other.

(See Inside the Story: North Atlantic Track System.) Each track carried airplanes all moving in the same direction but spread vertically across four to six assigned altitudes. On each altitude, airplanes were spaced six to ten minutes apart. To our left and right, parallel tracks ran about sixty miles away, built the same way—layered, orderly, and full of aircraft. It was a three-dimensional lattice of traffic stretching across the ocean, and we were threaded neatly into it.

We couldn't simply turn the airplane around. Deviating in direction, altitude, or speed without clearance could turn a manageable problem into a catastrophic one.

And yet, with one engine shut down, we could no longer maintain the altitude and speed we had been assigned.

That was the conundrum.

To make matters more difficult, this was 1991. Our airplane had been designed in the late sixties. There were no satellite communications. No data link. No constant digital connection between the cockpit and the ground.

All we had were high-frequency radios (HF)—technology that dated back to World War II. *(See Inside the Story: High-Frequency Radio Over the Ocean.)*

HF radio transmissions worked when conditions allowed and disappeared when they didn't. The copilot kept at the radios, repeating our call through bursts of static, while the captain and I continued the *Engine Shutdown Checklist*, knowing the answer would come eventually—or not.

My role was to read the shutdown checklist, ensure the captain took the correct action, and feed him the numbers—new maximum altitude, revised cruise speed, maximum landing weight, and fuel dump requirements. After four years on the job, I knew exactly what numbers the captain would need and when he would need them.

The stress level in the cockpit was low—not because the situation was trivial, but because everyone was doing precisely what they were trained to do.

Once the engine was shut down, physics took over. Heavy airplane. Lots of fuel. Three engines instead of four. We had to slow. We had to descend.

Which meant we had to leave the track system while still waiting to receive a revised clearance.

At seven miles a minute, time compressed for all of us at once. Each pilot had a different job, and none of them could wait. While the captain flew the airplane, the copilot stayed on the radios, and I worked the numbers and procedures, all of it unfolding in parallel. Nothing could be rushed, and nothing could be delayed. Every action had to land in the right order, at the right moment, with no extra motion to spare.

First the captain made a ninety-degree turn to the right, away from our assigned track. Once we were six miles off the centerline, he began a controlled descent to the altitude our three-engine airplane could maintain. Then, just before reaching thirty miles off the track, he rolled into another right ninety-degree turn—this one placing us opposite our original course, neatly positioned halfway between our former track and the next one over.

The entire maneuver took about four minutes. But it was a busy four minutes.

We were now clear of the traffic flow, descending safely, and still waiting for a clearance back to Boston.

It took another twenty minutes of calling and waiting before it finally came through: approved routing back to where we had started the day.

Having that clearance simplified things, but it didn't end the work. We still had over an hour of flying left, much of it over open water, on three engines.

And once an engine is shut down, every sound in the cockpit seems to get louder. A faint vibration. A change in pitch. The normal hum of machinery doing exactly what it has always done. Someone would look up and say, "Did you hear that?"

Maybe it was superstition. Maybe it was experience. Either way, we stayed sharp, eyes scanning, ears tuned, waiting to see if the airplane had anything else to tell us.

It didn't.

We landed back in Boston without further incident and taxied to the gate. During the debrief, we all agreed on one thing: the timing mattered. An engine failure is a far more serious event at takeoff, when options are limited and decisions compress into seconds. In cruise, with altitude, airspeed, and time on your side, it becomes a problem to manage—not a crisis.

Still, it was:

ANOTHER BULLET DODGED

I knew that for many of our passengers, the captain's announcement from the cockpit—explaining that we were hours from land and had shut down an engine—must have sounded frightening. Maybe even life-threatening.

It wasn't.

But I understood why it felt that way.

In the cockpit, it was another day at work. A serious one, certainly, but one we handled exactly as we'd been trained to handle it—calmly, methodically, without drama.

For passengers, an engine shutdown feels very different. Yet in reality, the worst part of their day came after we parked. Their London plans evaporated into hotel vouchers and rebooking lines.

Twilight

Not long after that flight, I moved on from the 747. I upgraded to copilot on the DC-10 and slid back into the rhythm of a flying pilot's seat. That move wasn't a step into something newer or more advanced. The DC-10 was another product of the same era—a capable, long-range widebody born of 1970s thinking. The timing felt right for my career, even though the airplane itself represented continuity, not great change.

For decades, the 747 had been unmatched. For nearly forty years, it moved people, cargo, and national interest across oceans with a reliability no other airplane could touch. Airlines built global networks around it. Countries quietly depended on it.

The real shift didn't come until much later, with airplanes like the Boeing 777—designed from the ground up to do much of what the 747 did, but with fewer engines, smaller crews, and economics better suited to a changing industry. That was the moment the balance began to tilt.

I was fortunate.

I was present for the long middle of the 747's reign—not just its opening act.

Timing matters.

Learning Points:

- *Large, complex operations succeed not through drama or heroics, but through routine execution, redundancy, and disciplined coordination.*
- *Luck and good fortune play a large part in life.*

Inside the Story *(Optional Reading)*

The Civil Reserve Air Fleet (CRAF)

The Civil Reserve Air Fleet—usually called CRAF—is a partnership between the U.S. government and American airlines designed to provide additional airlift during national emergencies.

Military transport aircraft can move large amounts of cargo and personnel, but the U.S. military does not maintain enough airplanes to rapidly deploy massive numbers of troops across the world. CRAF fills that gap. Airlines agree to make specific aircraft available to the government when the program is activated.

In return, airlines that participated in CRAF received priority access to U.S. military charter contracts during normal operations, creating a financial incentive for airlines to commit large aircraft to the program. The arrangement ensures that the United States can rapidly expand its airlift capability without maintaining a huge standing fleet of transport aircraft during peacetime.

CRAF was first activated during the Gulf War in 1990, when hundreds of civilian airliners were used to move troops and equipment to the Middle East.

Northwest's Pacific Network

For many years Northwest Airlines operated one of the most extensive transpacific route systems in the world. A key reason was its hub at Tokyo's Narita Airport, which functioned as a gateway between North America and cities throughout Asia.

Flights from the United States arrived in Tokyo, where passengers and cargo connected to destinations across Japan, Korea, Southeast Asia, and beyond. The system allowed

Northwest to operate a web of routes that would have been difficult to sustain with nonstop flights alone.

Large aircraft such as the Boeing 747 were central to this network. Their range and capacity made them ideal for the long ocean crossings that linked the United States with Asia.

North Atlantic Track System

The North Atlantic Track System—usually called the NAT tracks—is a daily set of organized flight routes that guide aircraft across the North Atlantic between North America and Europe.

Because radar coverage does not extend across most of the ocean, aircraft cannot be monitored continuously the way they are over land. Instead, air traffic control organizes traffic into several parallel routes that change slightly each day based on winds and weather.

Aircraft on each track fly at assigned altitudes and maintain time-based spacing from the aircraft ahead. Crews report their position at designated waypoints using long-range radio communication.

The system creates an orderly flow of aircraft across thousands of miles of ocean where real-time radar separation is not possible.

High-Frequency Radio Over the Ocean

Before satellite communication became common in airliners, long-distance radio contact with the ground relied on high-frequency (HF) radio. HF signals can travel thousands of miles by bouncing off layers of the Earth's upper atmosphere, allowing aircraft to communicate with stations far beyond the range of normal line-of-sight radios.

The system worked—but not reliably. Atmospheric conditions, solar activity, and time of day could all affect how well the signal propagated. Pilots often had to repeat calls several times through bursts of static before being heard clearly on the ground.

For crews operating over oceans or remote regions in the 1980s and early 1990s, HF radios were often the only link to air traffic control and airline dispatch.

CHAPTER 13

BEYOND THE CHECKLIST

"My father didn't tell me how to live; he lived, and let me watch him do it."
—Clarence Budington Kelland

AGE 31-53 · 1989-2011

You can't compress twenty-plus years of parenting into one chapter without lying, so I won't try. Instead, I'll tell a few stories—moments that still live in my bones. One of them earned a permanent place in our family mythology. Another Bullet Dodged, this time not at thirty-seven thousand feet, but above thirteen thousand—on a Colorado mountain—with my whole clan.

Few things in life hit the gut the way family danger does. When my children are the ones at risk, fear doesn't arrive politely or rationally—it arrives like a gut punch.

It was 2004. Ayla was fourteen, Fran thirteen, Aaron eleven. Jillian and I were forty-six. We lived in Boulder, and we were an outdoor family. Colorado has a culture of hiking peaks—13ers and 14ers—and we liked the challenge of climbing together. Not to "bag" summits for ego points, but because the mountains gave us something rare: hours of shared effort, uninterrupted conversation, and the kind of earned views that make teenagers briefly forget their eye-roll reflex.

Mount Audubon was one of our training hikes. An approachable 13er—13,220 feet—with a trailhead around 10,500 feet and a summit high enough to put you well above the tree line. We tried to do everything right. We checked the forecast before we left our home. Nothing suggested instability. No red flags. And because we'd been taught the mountaineer's rule that matters most in summer—be off the summit by late morning—we left the house at 5:30 a.m. with the plan to summit before eleven.

There's an old hiker's mantra in Colorado: avoid lightning, especially above the tree line. Lightning doesn't need to hit you directly to kill you.

The first part of the trail was shaded and chilly, running through spruce and fir. Then the trees thinned, and the landscape opened into tundra—beautiful, exposed, and completely indifferent to human plans. The kids climbed strong. They were excited, capable, and in their element. We reached the summit at 10:35 a.m., right on schedule.

Audubon's top is wide and flat—one of those summits that feels like a rooftop. The views are enormous. The Indian Peaks cut a jagged horizon. Brainard Lake glints in the distance. On a clear day you feel like you can see half of Colorado.

For a few minutes, we did what families do on summits: we smiled, took pictures, drank water, and felt proud.

Then the light changed. The sky darkened with a speed that made no sense, the mountains closing in as if someone had pulled a lid over the world. What had felt like a postcard moment earlier was suddenly a warning.

Thunder cracked so close it felt like it had weight. Lightning began striking around us—sharp white slashes that made the air seem thin and brittle. We were standing on an exposed rocky peak, five upright human lightning rods on a high point in open terrain.

The only safe direction was down.

We scrambled off the summit into the boulder field below. Far down the trail—more than two miles away—the path dropped back into the shelter of trees. I could see the tree line like a finish line I wasn't sure we'd reach. In the boulders, speed is limited by physics and consequences. One twisted ankle would turn an emergency into a tragedy. And yet staying exposed was worse.

The lightning intensified. Wind shoved at us, urging us faster than was safe. Above us the clouds boiled into churning, black cumulonimbus. The whole sky looked like a cauldron coming to a rolling, angry simmer.

And then I saw mammatus hanging under part of the storm—bulging pouches of cloud like bruises on the underside of the sky. I knew what they meant; I didn't have time to think about what they might mean to us. I had only one job: get my family down the mountain.

The fear in everyone was real. I could see it in the way the kids moved—careful but urgent, trying to obey instructions while their bodies wanted to sprint. I was scared too. In moments like that, the leader's face becomes the family's barometer.

If I showed panic, I'd spread it.

So, I wore my serious face and kept my fear tucked just below the surface where it belonged.

Then we got a strange piece of luck.

Both my daughters had long hair, and that hair turned into a warning system. Every couple of minutes, the air would charge with static electricity so intensely that their hair would begin to lift—subtle at first, then unmistakable.

When I saw it, I yelled, "Down! Down! Down!"

We'd practiced what that meant. Immediately find a depression among the rocks, get as low as possible, and lie flat. Don't be the highest thing. Don't stand. Don't hesitate.

The first time I shouted it, they dropped without argument. Jillian dropped. Ayla dropped. Fran dropped. Aaron dropped. I dropped.

Seconds later, lightning struck in rapid succession all around us.

There's a sound lightning makes when it hits close enough that you feel it—not thunder rolling in the distance, but a hard, ear-shattering crack you feel in your teeth.

The rocks beneath our hands shuddered as if the mountain itself flinched. Nature doesn't negotiate.

We stayed down until the strike cycle eased. When the hair settled, I yelled, "Go! Go! Go!"

We got up and moved again—fast, careful, deliberate—threading through the boulders until the next wave of static.

Hair rises.

"Down!"

Flat on the rocks.

Lightning, rapid fire.

Then: "Go!"

That strange choreography repeated itself three or four times. Each cycle lasted about a minute, and each minute felt longer than the last.

The kids kept their heads down during the strikes. They heard the violence, but they couldn't see how close it was.

I could.

I watched bolts hit nearby—too nearby—and remember thinking with a clarity that still tightens my stomach: this is how it happens. This is how families become stories other people tell.

Eventually—after what felt like a lifetime but was probably thirty minutes—we reached the tree line. The forest wasn't safe, but it was safer. We kept moving downhill through the pines until the storm's violence stayed behind us.

When we finally reached the trailhead, we scrambled into the van like it was a bunker. Doors shut. Breathing loud in the quiet. My hands shaking when no one was watching.

We had experienced more than we'd bargained for.

ANOTHER BULLET DODGED

The kids held it together because Jillian and I held it together. That's one of the oldest rules of parenting: children take their emotional cues from the adults who are supposed to know what to do. I didn't feel brave. I felt responsible. There's a difference.

We never stopped hiking after that. The clan was shaken but not deterred. If anything, that morning gave the kids a lasting respect for nature and an understanding that preparation isn't something you do because you're anxious—it's something you do because you're not arrogant.

It's one of the few pieces of wisdom I can say with confidence: you don't get to control the world your children walk through. You only get to teach them how to move through it.

Jillian

Every family has an origin story. Ours began at an airline—not because it was romantic, but because it made proximity unavoidable. In 1986, Jillian Feldmann and I were both new hires at Northwest Airlines, based in Minneapolis. She was a flight attendant. I was a pilot. We flew together often enough that professionalism eventually gave way to familiarity.

Jillian and I met when we were assigned to a month of domestic Boeing 727 flying that included three five-day trips. We briefed together, debriefed together, ate together, and—more often than management probably preferred—socialized together.

Familiarity was inevitable.

By the end of it, we knew each other well enough to drop the professional veneer. A few months later, we started dating.

Our first date set the tone. I invited her to a concert, only to discover when I picked her up that I'd been confidently—and completely—wrong. I was a month off. The concert was long over. We adjusted without drama, walked around a Minnesota lake instead, then had dinner. It turned out to be a better test than any plan executed perfectly.

Jillian was excellent at her job in all the ways that mattered most. She worked hard, cared deeply about passengers, and took responsibility seriously. But she had one significant Achilles heel for someone who made a living in the air: she got airsick—badly. Short flights were the worst, and it wasn't just airplanes. Trains, boats, even cars could do it to her. Motion sickness was simply part of her wiring.

That reality quietly placed an expiration date on her flying career.

Pilots dating flight attendants was—and still is—a stereotype, not unlike doctors dating nurses. Jillian and I fit the mold without much imagination. When we married in 1988, two years after meeting, we did so with an unspoken understanding that would later become explicit: if we were going to start a family, her days as a flight attendant would end.

As it turned out, the nausea didn't disappear. It just changed sources.

Airsickness gave way to morning sickness.

Good plans aren't rigid. They're honest.

Jillian didn't cling to a career that made her miserable, and I didn't cling to an idealized version of dual-airline life that wouldn't survive children. We adapted—not dramatically, not heroically—but pragmatically.

That adaptability became the backbone of our family.

It's easy, early in life, to imagine marriage as a finish line. It isn't. It's a starting gate. The job isn't to preserve the life you had when you met. The job is to build something new together without resenting the changes required to do it.

Jillian was the steady center of that effort. She didn't romanticize motherhood, and she didn't treat it like a sacrifice narrative either. She simply showed up—day after day—with patience, competence, and a kind of quiet endurance that doesn't announce itself but carries enormous weight.

In the years that followed, my job would take me across oceans and time zones. Hers would anchor our home.

Different roles, equal importance.

I flew airplanes.

She flew the family—and she did it with a steadiness that made everything else possible.

And nothing that came later—no mountain storm, no childbirth crisis, no teenage rebellion—would have been survivable without that division of labor, and the mutual respect that sustained it.

Ayla

Ayla arrived in late 1989, while we were living in Eagan, Minnesota. At the time, I was flying the Boeing 747 as a second officer, working twelve-day Asia trips once a month. With only four years of seniority, being home for a birth was far from guaranteed. I could easily have been halfway around the world when labor began. Somehow, improbably, the timing worked. I was in town when our first child decided to arrive.

Jillian's pregnancy had been, by most measures, easy. She carried naturally, without drama or excess. Minimal morning sickness. No strange cravings. A relatively short labor. Watching her, I assumed—naively—that childbirth was something the human body mostly handled on its own.

That illusion didn't survive the delivery room.

As a first-time father, I learned very quickly where I stood in the hierarchy of a delivery room.

Fathers are not participants.

We are ballast.

Useful only if we stay out of the way.

I did my best in the delivery room—which, for a father, isn't much.

When Ayla's head emerged, something was immediately wrong. She was purple. Not the healthy flushed color I had expected, but a deep, alarming shade that needed no interpretation. The umbilical cord—the lifeline—was wrapped around her neck.

Not once.

Three times.

Knotted.

With each contraction, the cord tightened.

The cord that was supposed to deliver life was now actively stealing it.

I didn't need an explanation. The room shifted instantly.

The obstetrician didn't waste time reassuring me.

He issued orders.

"Stop her from pushing. Get me a surgical kit. Be ready with oxygen."

Only Ayla's head was out. The rest of her body was still inside Jillian. The doctor slid two fingers between the cord and Ayla's tiny neck—just enough space to protect her—and then guided surgical scissors down between his fingers and the cord.

I stood frozen, holding a cold cloth on Jillian's forehead, trying to be useful in the only way available to me.

"Try to relax," I told her, hearing how inadequate the words sounded even as I said them. "The head is out. The cord's around the neck. He's cutting the baby free. You're almost there."

I kept calling the baby it. We didn't know the gender yet. That ignorance felt strangely protective in the moment—like one less thing to be afraid of losing.

The obstetrician worked with a calm urgency that felt instantly familiar—no wasted motion, no panic, just training, experience, and decisive action.

When the cord was finally cut away, he looked at Jillian and said, "Push. You're almost there."

One shoulder. Then the other.

And then Ayla was out.

As the nurse rushed her away, I watched the purple fade slightly from her face. Not enough to relax—but enough to breathe again.

Jillian was exhausted.

I was shaken.

Seeing your child start life already in distress has a way of stripping away any illusions you had about control.

In hindsight, I understand that what had just happened was, for the doctor, another day at work—serious, yes, but familiar and manageable. That realization gave me a strange comfort. When the stakes are highest, competence matters more than emotion.

Ayla recovered fully. Today, she's a nurse herself and the mother of two healthy children. Watching her now, it's hard to reconcile the confident woman she's become with the fragile moment of her arrival. I'm deeply proud of the person she grew into—and of the life she's built.

I sometimes think about how that birth would have ended two hundred years earlier, in a log cabin on the frontier. Ayla almost certainly wouldn't have survived. Neither might Jillian.

That thought did something permanent to my understanding of fatherhood.

Being a father wasn't about control or protection in the absolute sense. It was about stewardship. Doing everything you reasonably can and then trusting the people and systems around you to do the rest.

You don't get many moments in life when you understand, with perfect clarity, how much is truly out of your hands.

Ayla gave me that lesson on her first day.

Fran

Fran arrived sixteen months after Ayla, in 1991, while we were living in a drafty old farmhouse in Woodbury, Minnesota. The house had charm if you were generous, but mostly it had character in the way cold things do. In winter, frost formed on the inside of the single-pane windows, matching the ice on the outside as if the glass had simply given up trying to mediate between indoors and out.

Jillian's pregnancy this time was unremarkable—in the best possible way. No drama. No emergencies. No frantic voices in the delivery room. Fran entered the world quietly, as if saving her energy for later.

She was an easy newborn at first. Our family of four settled into a rhythm that felt, finally, like something we might be good at. Then, around six months in, Fran stopped sleeping through the night.

No illness. No clear reason. Just a baby who woke—again and again—unsettled and inconsolable.

Jillian was exhausted. Two young children demand everything during the day, and nighttime interruptions compound fatigue in ways that are hard to explain to anyone who hasn't lived it. So, without much discussion, on the days I wasn't flying, the night shift became mine.

Night after night, I sat in the parlor rocking chair with Fran cradled against my chest. The house was dark and silent, save for the soft creaks of old floorboards and the rhythmic sound of the chair moving back and forth. I spoke quietly—sometimes nonsense, sometimes reassurance, sometimes nothing at all. Mostly, I let my voice and heartbeat do the work.

Those hours were strangely sacred.

Fran's body seemed to be in some private revolt, and I felt for her. Whatever discomfort she was fighting, she couldn't articulate it or escape it. But for me, those nights were a gift disguised as fatigue. Alone in the darkness with my daughter, there was no competition for attention. No schedule. No performance.

Just presence.

Night after night, for months, that routine repeated itself. And without realizing it at the time, a bond formed that felt deeper and quieter than anything I'd expected fatherhood to offer so early.

Fathers don't often get that kind of uninterrupted intimacy with a six-month-old.

Fran gave it to me by necessity.

Eventually, the phase passed. She slept. The rocking chair returned to its corner. Life moved on.

But something stayed.

Years passed. Childhood gave way to adulthood, and the sleepless nights became stories instead of routines. Fran grew into a compassionate, steady person—one of those people whose strength isn't loud but is always there when it's needed. Like her sister, she became a nurse, choosing a profession built around caring for people on their worst days. Hearing stories from her work now, I sometimes catch glimpses of that infant who needed calm and learned how powerful it could be.

The chair is gone. The memory isn't.

Aaron

Aaron joined our family in early 1993, while we were living in Hawaii. By then I had upgraded to copilot on the DC-10 and was flying mostly three-day trips out of Honolulu to Asia. Once again, improbably, I was home for the birth. Three kids. Three births. Three appearances. I was batting a thousand.

The hospital was only fifteen minutes from our house, which turned out to be fortunate. Once Jillian's body decided it was time, it wasted no energy on ceremony. We were off to the races.

We didn't know the baby's sex ahead of time, and this time the surprise came with a Y chromosome. A boy. After a household dominated by women, the dynamic was about to shift.

And it did—almost immediately.

Before Aaron arrived, I would have confidently argued that personality was mostly socialization. Maybe sixty percent environment, forty percent genetics. That theory lasted about as long as it took Aaron to become mobile.

Within a few years, it was obvious I'd underestimated biology. This kid came preloaded. Testosterone-fueled. Curious. Energetic. Inventive. A sweet, happy child—but a boy in ways that required no instruction.

The girls could sit quietly for hours, coloring or playing games. To them, a pencil was a tool. To Aaron, it was a sword. He'd drift into their peaceful orbit, introduce chaos, then wander off in search of fresh mischief. We called him The Tasmanian Devil—and we hadn't taught him any of it. He came that way.

Despite our best efforts to parent all three children the same, the differences were undeniable. And oddly comforting. Aaron's mind worked in patterns I recognized instantly. Through him, I caught glimpses of the boy I had once been.

I loved all my children equally. But I won't pretend there wasn't something uniquely intuitive about raising a son. After all, I had once been one.

For years, raising Aaron had taught me about temperament—about how much of who we are is already there and how little parenting can rewrite the core. What came later would teach me something different. It wouldn't be about guiding a child. It would be about how men show up for each other when the situation is unpleasant, unavoidable, and best handled without commentary.

That connection came into sharp focus years later, when Aaron was a senior in high school.

As a family, we had an unspoken rule: when Dad comes home jet-lagged and sleep-deprived, no major issues get dumped on him for at least one night—preferably three days.

I had just returned from a twelve-day Asia trip. I appreciated everyone's restraint that evening, but something felt off. The energy in the room was strange.

After some gentle prodding, the truth emerged.

While I was gone, the lower level of our new house had flooded with sewage.

It was still flooded.

The bathrooms downstairs sat below the city sewer line, which meant they relied on a sewage ejector pump—a sump pit with an electric motor driving an impeller that lifts everything ten feet upward and out of the house. I had a pretty good idea where the failure lived.

I grabbed Aaron, a set of tools, rubber boots, and headed downstairs.

Sure enough, the pump was dead.

Ten bolts held the impeller assembly in place. Aaron handed me tools while I labored. We were both standing in eight inches of six-day-old sewage. My hands were submerged in it as I worked blind, feeling for bolt heads and threading them out one by one.

It was revolting. Surely memorable. And oddly clarifying. There are moments when instruction matters less than simply standing shoulder to shoulder and doing what needs to be done.

When the assembly finally came free, I lifted it out of the pit and turned it over to inspect the impeller.

And then I started laughing.

A deep, uncontrollable belly laugh.

Aaron stared at me like sewer gas had finally broken my brain. We were ankle-deep in human waste, and I was laughing.

The jammed impeller wasn't caused by what I had been expecting—but I recognized it immediately.

Wrapped tightly around the impeller shaft
was a used condom.

Without saying a word, still laughing, I untangled it, held it up between us, and said,

"I'm really glad you're using these—but they don't go down the toilet."

The color drained from his face.

"Please," he said. "Please don't tell anyone."

I swore an oath of silence—for ten years. We are now well past the statute of limitations. *You're welcome for the visual.*

We reinstalled the pump, pushed what sewage we could back toward the pit, and left the rest for morning.

That night, I gained a new respect for my son—and I think he saw me not just as his father, but as another guy who understood the terrain.

Aaron dodged a bullet that evening.

Watching him grow confirmed something I had learned slowly and without much certainty: parenting shapes expression, not essence. Some traits are there from the start. The real work is knowing when to guide—and when to simply stand there and do the job alongside them.

Aaron grew into a good man—thoughtful, capable, and interesting in his own right. I'm proud of him, just as I am of his sisters.

He's a new father, and I'm looking forward to hearing his own stories of parenting. And yes, from time to time he and I still chuckle about what doesn't go down the toilet.

David

At twenty-seven, parenthood felt abstract—something best postponed or quietly avoided. From a distance, it looked like a responsibility that would alter a life in ways that were hard to imagine and easy to defer.

Then it happens.

And abstraction disappears.

Raising children doesn't just add something to your life—it rearranges it. It demands a kind of selflessness that can't be simulated or practiced in advance. You either rise to it, or you don't, and you often don't know which one you'll be until the moment arrives.

I made plenty of mistakes as a parent. Some from ignorance. Some from fatigue. Some from misjudgment. I learned on the fly—sometimes literally. But I can say, honestly, that most of my decisions came from love rather than anger, and that counts for something.

One advantage I had—one I didn't fully appreciate at the time—was my job. I was gone from home twelve to sixteen days a month, which sounds like a deficit. And sometimes it was. But it also gave me space to reset. When I came home, I was present in a way that daily accumulation rarely allows.

And when I was home, I was really home.

Fourteen to eighteen consecutive days each month. Morning's rituals. Breakfasts. After-school hours. Practices. Homework time. Bedtime.

Most fathers I knew had evenings and weekends.

I had full stretches of ordinary life with my kids.

Those early years are formative in ways that can't be recovered later. For the first five or six years, parents are the primary architects of a child's world. After that, influence diffuses—school, peers, culture, media, technology all compete for attention and authority. By the time kids reach adolescence, parenting becomes less about instruction and more about calibration.

You nudge instead of push.

You listen more than you lecture.

You trust—but verify.

Teenagers will test limits. They will experiment. They will lie, selectively and creatively. I certainly did. So seeing that behavior in my kids not as moral failure but as developmental exploration kept me from turning normal growth into constant conflict.

Fighting with a teenager is like pounding your head against a wall. The wall never feels the pain—but your head certainly does.

So, I tried not to do it.

That didn't mean abdication. It meant consequences without drama. Love with boundaries. Expectations clearly stated and consistently enforced. I assumed my kids were good at their core—and treated them that way—they generally rose to the occasion.

The hardest phase for me was watching my teenage daughters retreat inward. Between about fifteen and seventeen, conversation narrowed to eye rolls and single-word answers. Every question was met with "fine."

It took me longer than I care to admit decoding that response. Eventually, I realized "fine" was an acronym:

F.I.N.E.—fucked up, insecure, neurotic, and emotional.

Once I understood that, everything made more sense.

Understanding doesn't eliminate frustration, but it does prevent resentment. And resentment is poison in a parent-child relationship.

As the years passed, I began to see parenting less as a project and more as a stewardship. You don't mold children into what you want them to be. You help them discover who they already are—and try not to damage them too badly in the process.

If I did one thing right, it was this: I let my kids fail when the consequences were survivable. Failure teaches lessons success never will. And failing young hurts far less than failing later, when the stakes are higher and the safety nets thinner.

Do I think I did a perfect job? Not even close.

But I believe I did a good job at it.

Parenthood forced me beyond myself. It expanded my emotional range, sharpened my empathy, and humbled my certainty.

Loving my children didn't make life easier—but it made it larger.

And that expansion didn't stop with my own family.

In 2005, during my kids' teenage years, I spent ten days in Honduras volunteering at a boys' orphanage. The experience reshaped my understanding of children, privilege, resilience, and love. While I was there, I wrote something—not as a lesson, but as a reflection. I'll share it now.

<u>Children de El Hogar</u>
DBW 2005

They have nothing,
Yet they have everything.
We have everything,
Yet have nothing.

They have little to smile about,
Yet smile freely.
We have all to smile about,
Yet smile sparingly.

They see beauty in people,
And rarely judge others.
We see beauty in things,
And rarely aren't judgmental.

They frequently know real pain,
Yet easily forgive others.
We confuse inconvenience as pain,
Yet expect others to easily forgive us.

Their love is unconditional,
And their needs have no strings attached.
Our love is all too often conditional,
And tailored to fit our needs.

Their futures are unsure,
Yet they plow into time.
Our futures are assured,
Yet time plows into us.

They live life daily,
And daily life tests their way.
Our way is tested rarely,
And yet life we rarely live.

There is a glow about them,
And they light up this world of ours.
Our world is forever changed,
And 81 special boys know how.

They have nothing,
Yet gave more than they received.
We gave everything,
Yet received far more than we gave.

I didn't set out to become wise by having children.

I set out, at best, to do right by them.

What I learned along the way wasn't about control or perfection—it was about presence, humility, and showing up again after you've fallen short.

My kids didn't just pass through my life as dependents. They were my teachers. And the lessons they gave me—earned in fear, laughter, exhaustion, and love—are among the few I trust without hesitation.

Photo #32. Ayla 5, Fran 4, and Aaron 2.5 in Colorado.

CHAPTER 14

UNKNOWNS

PART 1

"If you can fix it with money… it's not a problem…
just a financial decision."
—Modern Proverb – Author unknown

AGE 33 · 1991

By 1991, I had been a Boeing 747 Second Officer—Flight Engineer—for four years. With a little seniority finally under my belt, the trips improved. I was no longer stuck with the Guam-O-Rama or other leftovers. Manila began to appear on my schedule—Tokyo to Manila, a desirable pairing for crews who had put in their time.

On June 6, 1991, my twelve-day trip began with a twelve-hour flight from Chicago to Tokyo as Northwest Flight 3. That route—ORD to NRT to MNL, with Flight 4 bringing us home—was the most profitable city pair the airline flew.

Legally, we couldn't fly the full Chicago–Tokyo–Manila trip, sit a few hours in Narita, and then continue to Manila. The airplane and passengers could—but the crew couldn't. So, Flight 3 was re-crewed in Tokyo, allowing more than half the passengers who boarded in Chicago to continue onward on the same airplane to the Philippines.

That day, Flight 3 was full to the brim. Four hundred passengers. A belly full of cargo. Everything about it looked routine.

At least that's how it looked from the cockpit—before the night began to bend in ways none of us expected.

Just before pushback, the Lead Flight Attendant called the cockpit with a problem and a request for help. A first-class passenger refused to stow her belongings for taxi and takeoff. FAA rules are clear: loose items must be secured before the aircraft door closes.

The passenger wouldn't comply.

The captain turned around, looked at me, and said nothing. He didn't have to. In the cockpit food chain, problems flow downhill, and the Second Officer lives at the bottom of that hill.

I headed down the spiral staircase into first class.

The Lead FA briefed me quickly, then pointed to seat 4A. A well-dressed Filipina woman looked up at me, tears streaming down her face.

"I can't do it," she said.

"Can't do what?" I asked.

"Travel without my baby Jesus."

I followed her gaze.

Only then did I really take in what she had built—a small, improvised chapel anchored to seat 4A. Three baby Jesuses on wooden pedestals of varying heights, thick candles mounted on turned wooden stands, arranged carefully with intention. If the Vatican had issued travel altars, this would have qualified.

Other passengers had begun to stare, and the atmosphere in the cabin was shifting from curiosity to discomfort. Situations like this weren't rare—just rarely this strange. Any unresolved cabin issue before pushback is a no-go condition. Doors don't close, brakes don't release, and airplanes don't move until the cabin is secure.

There's no drama in that rule. It's simply how transport-category airplanes stay boring—and safe.

The Flight Attendant had already explained that after takeoff she could rebuild her shrine—but for taxi, takeoff, landing, and turbulence, everything had to be stowed. Somehow, she had crossed the Pacific to get to the United States without encountering this issue, but now she was genuinely shocked that anyone would ask her to put Jesus away.

I tried reason. Calm voice. Uniform authority. Politeness.

More tears. Panic.

The look of someone slipping out of reality.

This wasn't a negotiation anymore. Rational conversation requires two rational participants. We didn't have that.

She was frightened, immovable, and unraveling.

Given her first-class seat, she had likely paid about six thousand dollars for the ticket—a small fortune in 1991. In her world, she was a person of means and status. In mine, she was simply a problem that needed resolution before the door could close.

Time was running out.

Finally, I made my last offer.

"I'll move the suitcases out of the overhead bin above you," I said. "I'll set your shrine up there exactly how you want it. Every statue. Every candle. But the area around your seat must be cleared—or I'll have to escort you off the airplane."

I let that sit.

More sobbing. Then, finally, a subtle nod.

The Flight Attendant and I worked fast. We relocated the shrine to the overhead bin directly above her seat, arranging each baby Jesus according to her wishes.

Once finished, she calmed instantly.

I closed the bin, relieved we'd found a solution, smiled, and thanked her for being cooperative.

I scurried back upstairs into the cockpit. My pulse was still elevated, my brain replaying the scene as I climbed into my seat. I strapped in and said only, "You aren't going to believe this story."

It would have to wait. We were now late, and they needed me to run the *Before Pushback* checklist.

Forty-five minutes into the flight, the Lead FA called again.

"It smells really bad in the back."

Not unusual. Lavatories sometimes misbehave. I increased the cabin airflow to flush more air through the system—like turning on a bathroom exhaust fan. *(See Inside the Story: How Cabin Air Circulates in an Airliner.)*

I told her to call back if it didn't improve.

Smell complaints usually came from a familiar list of causes: a poorly serviced lavatory, contaminated catering bins, a blocked drain—none of it glamorous, all of it familiar. When changing the cabin airflow didn't help, you went looking. Not with dread, but with a plan.

An hour later, she called back.

"It still really stinks. Can you come look?"

Pre-9/11, with three pilots up front, stepping out for a while was routine. Leaving the cockpit wasn't viewed as unusual—it was simply part of how long-haul flying worked then.

So once again, the Second Officer was dispatched.

Unfortunately, this was the perfect task for me—because I have the nose of a bloodhound. It's not a gift. It's a curse. I often smell things other humans don't—things better left un-smelled.

I headed down the spiral staircase, passed the fully reassembled baby-Jesus shrine, and walked aft. This is a big airplane. Twenty-six aisle laps equal a mile. Tracking the source should have been tedious. It wasn't.

The farther back I went, the worse the smell became—stronger on the left side than the right.

That told me it wasn't the air system.

By the time I reached the rear galley, the odor had crossed a line—from unpleasant to something no airplane should smell like.

I'm sure I looked ridiculous sniffing like a dog all over the back of the airplane, but it worked. I had the scent and was firmly on the trail.

At the very back of the 747, behind the last left-side emergency exit, sat the garment-bag closet. In those days, many passengers traveled with hanging garment bags, and airlines provided dedicated closets for them.

I pulled the curtain back.

The stench hit like a punch.

Thirty garment bags hung inside. I slid them one by one past my nose, muttering, "No…no…no…"

Then—Eureka.

I swung the offending bag outward, so the zipper faced me and tugged it.

It came down about eighteen inches—

A human head fell forward toward me.

My brain stalled. Every instinct fired at once—revulsion, disbelief, adrenaline.

I shouted something unintelligible.

The Flight Attendants—three of them now—were crowded in behind me, leaning forward to see what I'd found, and they screamed.

For a suspended moment, the airplane, the passengers, the outside—it all vanished.

Thankfully, the head was still attached to a body.

Tiny grandpa. Maybe ninety years old. Filipino. About five feet tall, eighty pounds.

Very dead.

I stuffed the head back into the bag and zipped it closed.

I'm no expert on death, but the fluids and the smell suggested he hadn't been embalmed.

And there he was—hanging in a garment bag at thirty-five thousand feet, halfway to the Pacific, on my airplane.

Over the years, we'd seen many elderly Filipinos travel home to die in their country. Culturally, it mattered deeply. Apparently, this family missed the timing by a few days.

Once shock gave way to responsibility, adrenaline faded into logistics. I asked the Flight Attendants to settle down so we could deal with this professionally.

I wasn't sure yet what "professionally" meant—but screaming wasn't helping.

Our feelings were first a mixture of outrage and disbelief, followed later by laughter—the kind that arrives only after responsibility has been handled.

I was thirty-three, so it was easy for me to say, "That's a new one for me!" But even the senior mamas, with forty years flying this route, admitted they'd never seen anything like it.

I was sure the captain would not divert for an already-dead man. We had to solve this onboard, and now.

We had two problems: where to put Grandpa to reduce the smell, and how to discreetly summon the family.

The 747 has vast unused spaces above the cabin ceiling that passengers never see. We solved the first problem by stowing the bag behind the galley, above the ceiling—at the end of the cabin airflow before it exits the fuselage. The smell diminished quickly.

For the second, I avoided a blunt PA announcement.

Instead: "Could the Filipino family traveling with a sickly little grandpa please come to the back of the airplane? He can't...hang out back here anymore."

It was the most delicate phrasing I could manage.

Eventually, after two announcements, two young men appeared. Once I explained why bringing their grandfather onboard—dead, in a garment bag—was a problem, they were devastated. Apologetic. Ashamed. They explained they were fulfilling his final wish: to be buried in his village.

I explained—gently—that transporting human remains this way was illegal. Japanese authorities would be notified. Grandpa wouldn't continue to Manila tonight.

They were upset. They came from a small village, and I genuinely believe they didn't understand what international air-travel rules required. I felt awful. But rules exist for reasons.

Thirty-five minutes later, I returned to the cockpit.

The captain turned and said, "You've been gone a long time. I need to pee."

All I could say was, "You aren't going to believe this story."

Only then did I finally exhale.

We landed in Tokyo with police and immigration waiting. Grandpa and his family were escorted off first. I never learned what happened afterward. I hope they weren't in too much trouble—and that Grandpa rests peacefully today in his village burial grounds beside the little Catholic church.

ANOTHER BULLET DODGED

Normally, a bad smell would not qualify as another bullet dodged. But with dead people in a garment bag aboard my airplane—oozing fluids and giving off odors—this one did.

Learning Point:

- *Do everything in your power to ensure one's final flight is not from inside a garment bag.*

Inside the Story *(Optional Reading)*

How Cabin Air Circulates in an Airliner

Airliners constantly move large volumes of air through the cabin. Fresh air is drawn from the engines, cooled and conditioned, and then mixed with filtered cabin air before being circulated through the airplane.

That air enters the cabin from overhead vents and flows steadily toward the floor. From there it is pulled out of the airplane through outflow valves located near the rear of the fuselage. Those valves regulate cabin pressure while also controlling how quickly air moves through the aircraft.

Because of this constant airflow, the entire cabin air supply is replaced every few minutes. Increasing the airflow rate can help flush odors out of the cabin—much like turning on a powerful exhaust fan in a building.

CHAPTER 14

UNKNOWNS

PART 2

AGE 33 · 1991

After one night and part of a day in Tokyo, we departed Narita on June 8th for another long leg—this time south to Singapore. Seven and a half hours later we landed, enjoyed a comfortable thirty-three-hour layover, then flew back to Tokyo for another thirty-hour break. It would be day six of our twelve-day trip—June 11th—when we became the change-out crew scheduled to take Flight 3 from Tokyo down to Manila.

On paper, it was a routine continuation of the Chicago–Tokyo–Manila route. It was the kind of flight crews barely remembered once it was over.

On this day, we were flying toward something none of us yet understood.

Our day started in the Narita pilot briefing room with weather charts, winds aloft, and routine hazard updates. One of those hazards—volcanic ash—was something pilots took seriously, but only after a volcano had already erupted would it appear in the paperwork. In 1991, we were not briefed on volcanoes that were merely restless. If a mountain hadn't exploded yet, it simply wasn't something crews were warned about.

Our flight to Manila that night was uneventful. We landed just after 1:00 a.m. on June 12th and reached our hotel around 2:00 a.m. Still completely unaware of what was brewing elsewhere on the island, the first officer and I went out for a beer or two. I finally crawled into bed around four.

Less than five hours later, Mother Nature woke me up.

At 8:51 a.m., Mount Pinatubo erupted for the first time in five hundred years. The blast lasted forty minutes and hurled an ash column nearly twelve miles into the sky. The ground shook.

Windows rattled. I came awake instantly, not yet knowing what had caused it.

Pinatubo sits just fifty-five miles from Manila. Both are on Luzon, the most densely populated island in the Philippine archipelago. And yet that morning, life in the city carried on as if nothing had happened.

Two hours later, the volcano erupted again—longer, stronger, and dirtier. By midday, massive amounts of ash and sulfur dioxide were drifting toward Manila on prevailing winds. Local news stations advised residents that a bandana would be sufficient protection outdoors. Scientists suggested the worst was likely over. The mountain, they said, had already vented most of its pressure.

We believed them.

Photo #33. The second of Pinatubo's exploding eruptions.

The airport remained open. Flights were still scheduled. Our departure back to Tokyo the next morning seemed secure. From my insulated vantage point—a five-star hotel, room service, air conditioning—the eruptions registered as background noise.

When the airport "temporarily" closed later that afternoon, I didn't think danger.

I thought bonus.

An extra day in Manila.

And this is where I need to pause and be honest. I wasn't ignoring danger—I was choosing comfort instead.

So, the next morning, June 13th, the airport was closed, and there was no immediate plan forward. Instead of flying back to Tokyo, I defaulted to my usual Manila layover ritual: the Boulevard Health Club.

The experience unfolded with the kind of indulgence that only feels reasonable when you're young and temporarily unmoored from consequence. Hot tub. Cold plunge. Steam room. Sauna. Repeat until the edges of the world soften and time becomes optional. Later, limp and compliant, I was guided onward, convinced—incorrectly—that this was an entirely acceptable response to a natural disaster unfolding just beyond the walls.

Even after multiple visits, the bathing room still felt surreal. Naked men crouched on plastic stools while young Filipina attendants—fully clothed—scrubbed us down with soap, loofahs, and handheld sprayers. No impropriety. No flirtation. Just an earnest, efficient dismantling of grime and dignity. It always left me with one of those classic thoughts:

We aren't in Kansas anymore.

I was then deposited into a lounge chair, handed a San Miguel beer, a bowl of fried rice, and left to drift in and out of contentment. Later came a haircut, shave, manicure, and finally a ninety-minute Shiatsu massage. Four hours. Twenty-six dollars. I emerged feeling like a king—completely oblivious to how small and selfish that comfort would look in retrospect.

By June 14th, reality began pushing back.

The airport remained closed. The mountain continued pumping out enormous quantities of pulverized airborne rock. Ash thickened in the air around Manila. Visibility dropped. Breathing outdoors became unpleasant, then uncomfortable, then ill-advised. Life in the city began to degrade in small but unmistakable ways.

So, while families near the volcano fled with what they could carry, and thousands in Manila evacuated their homes, I was still being pampered at the club, convincing myself the situation was "handled."

This wasn't cruelty.

It was immaturity.

I mistook distance for safety, comfort for clarity, and money for insulation. I completely missed the larger picture unfolding around me.

What our crew still didn't know—and what the public wasn't being told—was that a dome of gas-charged magma was building beneath the volcano's surface. Pressure was increasing, not decreasing.

Pinatubo was loading a gun.

On June 15th, it fired.

The eruption that day was the largest in recorded history near a major city. More than a cubic mile of material was blasted into the atmosphere. The ash cloud climbed twenty-two miles high—four times higher than commercial aircraft cruise altitudes. Pyroclastic flows raced down the mountain's slopes, filling valleys hundreds of feet deep and causing the summit to collapse inward, forming a massive caldera.

Within hours, Manila was engulfed.

Ash fell thick and heavy, turning daylight into dusk. Breathing outdoors became dangerous—two parts rock to one part oxygen. Then came the knockout blow: a typhoon arrived, soaking the ash and multiplying its destructive weight. Roofs collapsed across the city. Entire buildings failed. Infrastructure crumbled.

Photo #34. Volcanic ash causing buildings to collapse.

Eight million people were living inside a natural disaster.

By that point, there was no pretending this was just an inconvenience.

It was dire.

We were confined to our hotel, watching the city disappear behind gray curtains of ash. Every breath indoors felt borrowed. Every hour underscored how thin the line was between interesting flight delay and catastrophe.

The civilian airport remained closed for six days.

When ground crews finally began clearing runways, the scene looked like a Midwestern blizzard had hit the tropics. Bulldozers pushed ash into enormous piles. Mechanics unsealed aircraft that had been cocooned in debris.

When we finally boarded our flight back to Tokyo on the eighth day, patience was universal. Everyone—crew and passengers alike—just wanted out. Arrivals were prohibited, and only four departures per hour were allowed. We were tenth in line.

After a long wait, we were towed onto the runway. Engines were started, and only after the previous aircraft was fifteen minutes ahead were we cleared to depart.

The takeoff roll was long and deliberate. Ash swirled around the airplane as we accelerated. To some degree, it was certainly being ingested by the engines. They ran hotter than normal on takeoff and the ash likely shortened the engines' service life. *(See Inside the Story: Why Volcanic Ash Is Dangerous to Jet Engines.)*

But they did the job we asked of them.

And then we were airborne.

As we climbed away from Manila, we could see Pinatubo in the distance—still pumping ash. An enormous column towered above it, flashing constantly with lightning generated by ash particles colliding in the plume. *(See Inside the Story: A Famous 747 Encounter with Volcanic Ash.)*

It was magnificent.

And terrifying.

Manila was to be a thirty-three hour layover. It became eight days. We missed our Hong Kong layover and didn't get home until June 20th, days later than planned.

But far more important, we missed being airborne during that first volcanic eruption by mere hours. Had the ash cloud been created eight hours earlier, in the dark of night, there would have been no checklist for the situation we would have flown into. (Actually, today there is a checklist for ash cloud entry.)

This wasn't skill.

It wasn't judgment.

It wasn't professionalism.

It was luck.

That realization landed hard.

ANOTHER BULLET DODGED

Aftereffects

Only later did the scale become clear. The eruptions of Mount Pinatubo killed more than 800 people and displaced over 200,000.

Ash and sulfur dioxide altered global climate patterns for nearly two years, cooling average temperatures and producing extraordinary sunsets worldwide.

Clark Air Base, on Luzon—one of the most important U.S. military installations in the Pacific—was destroyed. It was never rebuilt.

At thirty-three, I didn't understand how close I came to becoming part of that statistic.

Now I do.

Learning Points:

- *Looking beyond one's own needs and desires often will clear the fog of selfishness.*
- *Mother Nature's ultimate power should never be underestimated.*
- *Clean air is indispensable.*

Inside the Story *(Optional Reading)*

Why Volcanic Ash Is Dangerous to Jet Engines

Volcanic ash is far more dangerous to jet aircraft than ordinary dust or smoke. The particles are made of tiny fragments of rock and glass that remain suspended in the air for long periods.

When these particles enter a jet engine, they are exposed to temperatures hot enough to melt them. The molten material can then stick to turbine blades and internal components, where it cools and hardens into a glass-like coating. This can disrupt airflow, damage turbine surfaces, and in severe cases cause the engine to lose power or shut down entirely.

Even when engines continue to run normally, ash ingestion can increase operating temperatures and accelerate engine wear. For this reason, modern aviation procedures avoid flying through volcanic ash whenever possible.

A Famous 747 Encounter with Volcanic Ash

In 1982 a Boeing 747 flying from Kuala Lumpur to Perth unknowingly entered a cloud of volcanic ash from Indonesia's Mount Galunggung. At first the crew noticed an unusual glow around the engines and a strong sulfur smell in the cabin. Then the engines began to surge.

Within minutes all four engines failed.

The aircraft began descending through the night with no power, losing altitude at several thousand feet per minute while the crew attempted repeated restarts. Only after dropping out of the ash cloud did the engines slowly come back to life, one by one.

The airplane eventually landed safely in Jakarta, but the encounter demonstrated how volcanic ash can disable jet engines and nearly brought down one of the largest aircraft in the sky.

CHAPTER 15

COGNITIVE DESCENT

"Well, if I talked a lot I should be like a parrot, which is the bird that speaks most and flies least"
—Wilbur Wright

AGE 34-36 · 1992-1994

The next few miles on the approach unfolded faster than they should have. The DC-10 was descending, but the normal sequence—slowing, configuring, stabilizing—wasn't happening in the order I expected, or at all.

At one thousand feet, the landing gear should have been down. It wasn't. Our speed should have been near 160 knots. It wasn't. We were still racing along at 200 knots, gear up, flaps barely extended.

I turned to face the captain.

"Let's go around and try this again."

Jim stared straight ahead.

"I got this. We'll be fine."

"Jim."

Then, more firmly:

"We are not going around."

He never did.

I remember the thought flickering through my mind—the thought every copilot may eventually face.

Is this the moment?

I didn't act on it.

At the time, I knew only that something felt wrong. *(See Inside the Story: What Pilots Mean by a "Stable Approach.")*

In late March of 1992, eighteen Northwest pilots—including Jim Sacmore, as I'll call him, and me—had completed DC-10 ground school, simulator (sim) training, and passed our final checkrides.

On paper, we were ready—legally and professionally—to fly passengers out of our new domicile in Hawaii.

But for some of us, there was one more hurdle.

At the time, Northwest required pilots who had never flown a widebody airplane for the airline to complete three takeoffs and landings in a real airplane with no revenue passengers onboard. It was an old rule, based on the quality of the simulators of that era—proof that you could manage a large airplane outside the sterile environment of the schoolhouse.

By sheer luck, my father happened to be visiting on the day my flight was scheduled. The instructor pilot was kind enough to allow him to join us, and not only to ride along, but to stand in the cockpit doorway while I flew three full traffic patterns—three takeoffs, three landings. Smooth. Controlled. Professional.

Thirty-four years later, we still talk about that day. For me, it was a chance to show my father how I performed my profession. For him, it was a chance to see that his son had grown into a competent professional pilot, entrusted with serious responsibility.

That kind of cockpit access would be unthinkable today. Very rare back then. An amazing moment for a father and son to share.

Shortly afterward, thirty-six of us were sent to Honolulu to open Northwest's newest DC-10 domicile. We were the beginning. Over time, the base would grow to nearly two hundred pilots, covering seven premium routes—the West Coast, Japan, and Australia.

With only seven years at the airline, I felt fortunate. After years in a non-flying seat, moving into the DC-10 copilot position felt like real career progress. It came with more authority and responsibility, a meaningful pay raise, and—just as important—a widebody to fly. It was good to be back in a front seat again.

Moving my family to Hawaii for two years wasn't an easy decision, but it turned out to be a good one. We lived near the water on the windward coast of Oahu. Days off were simple—beach time and preschoolers—which suited thirty-four-year-old parents just fine. Friends and family visited often, and whatever homesickness might have crept in never had much room to take hold.

Professionally and personally, life felt settled.

Operationally, I was still junior. As the fourth most junior DC-10 copilot in Honolulu, I sat at the bottom of the list. That meant reserve status—no schedule, no say, and no choice of crewmates.

The consequences of that lack of control showed up on June 13, 1992, when crew scheduling called and assigned me a red-eye to San Francisco with Captain Jim Sacmore, departing in two hours.

Months earlier, my friend Richard Lefritz had spent several weeks paired with Jim during DC-10 sim training in Minnesota. Afterward, Rich had simply said, "If you ever get assigned to fly with him, you'll understand."

That wasn't much to go on, yet Northwest didn't hand out widebody captain's stripes lightly. Jim had passed the same training and checkrides as everyone else.

Still, when I saw his name on the pairing, I remembered Rich's comment.

What I didn't know was that it would become one of the most unsettling flights of my career.

As I drove to the airport that night, his warnings kept looping through my mind. By the time I reached the flight ops trailer, I was uneasy—not afraid but concerned.

Jim was already in the briefing room when I checked in. He was pleasant and friendly, and he talked nonstop. Within minutes he was talking about subjects that had nothing to do with the flight. The words came in a steady stream with almost no pause between them.

That much, at least, matched Rich's description.

Thankfully, Jim wasn't one of those old, bitter captains who complained about everything. He'd been with the airline twenty-four years, and on paper his upgrade timeline wasn't unusual. More importantly for tonight's flight, though, he had only two months of DC-10 and oceanic experience.

I may have been new to the DC-10 right seat, but I wasn't inexperienced. I'd spent a year as a DC-10 engineer before upgrading to the 747 and then crossed the Pacific for five consecutive years as a 747 engineer. I knew the DC-10, the routes, the procedures, and I felt prepared.

The second officer arrived shortly after—also on reserve, also assigned only hours earlier, and also new to his seat. Before departure, I mentioned to the second officer that I'd heard mixed opinions about Jim from another pilot. He nodded and filed it away. Then we got on with the business of preparing the flight.

About fifteen minutes after boarding, the lead flight attendant quietly pulled me aside and asked if I could keep Jim out of the galley. He was in the way, talking incessantly and distracting them from their work.

"I'll try," I said, "but he is the captain, you know."

Departure was scheduled just before midnight.

Honolulu departures always felt low-key compared with San Francisco. *(See Inside the Story: Why Departures from Honolulu Felt So Different from San Francisco.)*

Jim was the pilot flying; I was the pilot monitoring. That was customary when captains didn't know their copilots. Still, Rich's comment lingered in the back of my mind.

Startup, taxi, takeoff, and climb were normal.

Cruise was uneventful. Five routine hours passed, with Jim talking nearly the entire time.

He flew competently in the low-stress environment.

That changed the moment we pointed the nose downhill.

About 120 miles from San Francisco, as the workload increased, something changed.

ATC began issuing more frequent instructions—headings, altitudes, speed assignments. Routine, arrivals into San Francisco often became busy as traffic compressed.

Jim began missing things.

A heading had to be repeated.

A speed assignment was acknowledged but not set.

I found myself prompting more often than usual.

None of it was dramatic.

Not yet.

But the rhythm in the cockpit felt different. The airplane was moving ahead while Jim seemed to be working harder just to keep up.

Near the top of the approach, a realization settled in—not panic, not fear, but weight.

Whatever was happening with Jim was now my problem too.

Twelve miles from touchdown, ATC turned us toward the runway.

We should have been slowing and configuring.

We weren't.

The airplane continued toward the airport at a speed that left little margin for getting stabilized. Every mile that passed made the problem harder to fix.

I turned to Jim.

"We're not stable. Let's go around and try this again."

In 1992, that wasn't a command. It was a recommendation. The decision still belonged entirely to the captain.

"No," he said. "I've got it."

The second officer and I exchanged a glance.

At one thousand feet, we were still fast. The landing gear was still up. The flaps were only partially extended.

Nothing about the approach met company standards.

"We need to go around."

Jim said nothing.

The second officer tried again, louder this time.

"We need to go around. Now."

The urgency in our voices carried no authority.

Jim stared straight ahead.

At six hundred feet we broke out of the clouds. The runway suddenly filled the windshield.

We were still far too fast.

The gear was still up.

Now both of us were shouting.

"GO AROUND!"

"GO AROUND!"

Nothing.

I reached for the power levers—not out of defiance, but because the moment demanded action he wasn't taking.

There was no hesitation left.

Only action.

Jim reacted instantly.

He clamped a hand over the power levers, stopping me from advancing them. At the same moment, he reached past the power quadrant and dropped the landing gear.

The gear doors opened with a heavy thud. The landing gear slammed into the slipstream.

The added drag slowed us.

Not enough.

It didn't feel confrontational. It felt reflexive—as if, in Jim's mind, I was about to make the wrong move at the worst possible moment.

At two hundred feet, he called for full flaps.

I did not select them. I was still focused on taking the airplane and initiating the go-around.

"No, WE'RE NOT GOING AROUND," he said again.

Then he lowered the flaps himself.

At eighty feet—eighty—Jim pulled the power levers to idle.

The engines began spooling down.

The window for a normal go-around had disappeared.

Fast and high, we crossed the runway threshold.

The airplane floated past the touchdown spot.

The excess speed carried us further down the runway.

The remaining runway rapidly disappeared behind us.

Then, with excess speed finally dissipated and too little runway remaining, the DC-10 dropped onto the pavement.

It was a landing. Technically.

Only a third of the runway remained ahead.

I immediately mashed the tops of the rudder pedals, applying maximum braking.

Jim deployed the spoilers and pulled the engine reversers to maximum reverse thrust.

The cockpit filled with noise as reverse thrust came up to full power.

The airframe convulsed under maximum deceleration, the force driving straight through muscle and bone.

The runway disappeared faster than my brain could process.

G-forces pressed us hard into our seats and harnesses.

I stopped thinking in procedures.

For the first time, I stopped wondering whether we'd stop on the runway.

I started wondering what we would hit.

"One-twenty knots."

The end of the runway rushed toward us.

"Hundred."

The anti-skid pulsed beneath my feet, brakes cycling as hard as physics would allow.

Four hundred thousand pounds of airplane still refusing to slow.

"Eighty knots."

My thinking narrowed. Not whether we would stop—but how violent the impact would be.

Then—without warning—the deceleration changed.

The anti-skid stopped pulsing, and the brakes went full on.

Just… enough.

Just… in time.

The airplane shuddered and stopped.

There was no pavement left.

None.

Every inch of runway lay behind us.

I exhaled a sound that didn't feel voluntary.

For several seconds, nobody spoke.

The cockpit felt smaller now—the noise gone, the consequences settling in.

We sat motionless at the end of the runway.

Then reality spread beyond the cockpit.

The airplane behind us was instructed to go around.

Departures sat frozen on intersecting runways.

Controllers were left untangling the disruption we had created in one of the busiest airspaces in the country.

What had begun inside one cockpit was now everyone else's problem.

By the time we shut down at the gate, the adrenaline had drained away, leaving something heavier in its place. The flight was over, the passengers were gone, and the airplane was intact—but none of that felt like resolution.

What had happened on final wasn't a close call you simply shrugged off. It stayed with me, replaying in fragments that refused to settle.

With time to think, I began to understand what Rich had been trying to tell me.

According to Rich, Jim had struggled throughout training with procedures, situational awareness, and basic aircraft handling. He compensated by talking—constantly. Rich had been stunned when Jim passed his final checkride and upgraded to widebody captain.

After the approach into San Francisco, Rich's concerns no longer seemed exaggerated.

Once the airplane was parked and the paperwork was complete, there was nothing left to do except decide what responsibility required next.

I took the issue of Jim's competence to our union's Professional Standards Committee. It was a confidential peer-to-peer process intended to address safety concerns before they became disciplinary matters. For copilots at the time, it was the only meaningful avenue available.

I believed adding my voice to the others was better than staying silent.

Eventually, after months of complaints, the company sent Jim back for additional simulator training and another checkride.

Somehow, he passed.

On paper, that was the end of it.

He returned to Hawaii still wearing four stripes and still flying the DC-10.

By early 1993, I had enough seniority to come off reserve. Jim became the only captain on my personal "no-fly" list, and for nearly two years I managed to avoid him.

But the airline industry has a habit of imploding every decade or so, and 1994 was one of those years.

Another cyclical convulsion swept through U.S. airlines, and Northwest was no exception. Pilots were furloughed, those who remained took a fifteen percent pay cut, and the Hawaii operation was scaled back as international routes disappeared.

Rich Lefritz and I found ourselves back near the bottom of the DC-10 copilot list. Once again, I was on reserve.

The protection seniority had given me disappeared just as quickly as it had arrived.

Two months before my Hawaii assignment was set to end, the copilot scheduled to fly with Jim to Fukuoka, Japan called in sick.

As the junior reservist on duty, Rich Lefritz got the first call. He promptly informed scheduling that he was sick as well.

Minutes later, my phone rang.

I didn't need to answer to know why.

The Hawaii operation had shrunk. There were few reserves left and even fewer options.

It was my turn in the barrel.

I drove to the airport uneasy and preoccupied.

I had no intention of ever flying with Jim again, but I had no idea how I was going to avoid it.

Northwest's Honolulu operation was housed in a single-wide trailer parked in the employee lot.

I walked straight into the Chief Pilot's office.

I wasn't there to explain myself or be persuaded.

I knew I was about to put the Chief Pilot—Dennis, as I'll call him—in an impossible position. He was a good man, a professional, and someone I respected. But I also knew I had built credibility during my time in Honolulu.

"I refuse to fly this trip with Jim Sacmore," I said.

Dennis looked at me steadily.

"Is there any way I could change your mind?" he asked. "Anything that would make it acceptable to you?"

"No," I said. "Not if Jim is flying the airplane. This isn't personal. I simply believe he's unsafe."

Dennis didn't argue. He leaned back in his chair for a moment.

"You know he passes his checkrides."

"I know," I said. "But you've seen the copilot reports.

Either he finds focus in the simulator, or he's being carried through it. I'm only one of many pilots who won't fly with him."

Dennis picked up the phone and called scheduling.

When he hung up, he looked directly at me.

"We don't have another DC-10 copilot in legal rest," he said. "And we don't have another captain either."

He paused.

"It's you and Jim—or 280 people don't go to Japan tonight."

"I'll do anything else you ask," I said, "but I won't fly with Jim again."

Dennis sat quietly for a moment.

Then he stood up and left the office.

Dennis found the second officer assigned to the trip. He also had concerns about flying with Jim. As a new hire still on probation, however, he was understandably more cautious about challenging a senior captain's competence to the Chief Pilot.

A few minutes later Dennis returned with Jim.

Jim took a seat beside me.

The tension was thick. I knew Jim knew I had turned him in to professional standards a few years earlier.

Dennis got right to the point.

"Jim," he said, "David says he won't fly with you because he believes you're unsafe. If David goes home sick, this flight cancels. That strands 280 people here and another 290 in Fukuoka. That's not acceptable."

Jim said nothing.

To his credit, he didn't argue. He didn't attack me. He didn't claim the copilots were conspiring against him.

Dennis then delivered a long-overdue dressing-down for behavior many Honolulu copilots had reported. It probably should have happened in private, but time was short and the reckoning was necessary.

Jim, a former Marine, absorbed it in silence.

The room stayed quiet long enough to become uncomfortable.

Then Dennis turned to Jim.

"Would you be willing to stay off the controls for this trip?"

For the first time since entering the room, Jim seemed fully present.

He looked up sharply.

His mouth opened as if to speak, then closed again.

For several seconds he stared past us.

Finally, he nodded.

Dennis turned to me.

"If Jim does not touch the controls," he said, "and you fly the airplane both ways, will you take the trip?"

I waited a long moment before answering.

"Yes," I said. "But only if Jim does not touch the controls at any point during the trip."

Jim gave a slow, resigned nod.

We left the office in silence.

Walking out of the ops trailer, I knew we were crossing a line.

Three pilots walked toward the airplane carrying an agreement that should never have been necessary.

I wasn't worried about flying the DC-10. I knew the airplane.

What worried me was everything else.

The arrangement rested entirely on trust.

Trust that Jim would keep his word.

Trust that nothing would happen requiring him to take the controls.

Trust that the second officer and I could handle whatever the flight presented.

There was also the simpler concern.

Jim could change his mind.

He didn't.

I flew the airplane both ways.

Jim worked the radios and navigation systems.

The DC-10 did exactly what it was designed to do. Systems behaved. Procedures flowed.

Nothing happened.

Jim kept his hands off the controls throughout the trip, and we completed it without incident.

But the tension never left the cockpit.

ANOTHER BULLET DODGED

In hindsight, the solution Dennis devised worked—but only because everyone involved honored an agreement that should never have been crafted.

It was an improvisation born of pressure, not a model for safety.

We got away with it.

That doesn't make it right.

It was, however, one of the last dominos to fall for Jim.

Not long afterward, management gave Jim a choice: retire early or be terminated.

He retired.

For years, I thought about Jim whenever the subject of mandatory retirement came up.

The rule at the time required airline pilots to retire at age sixty. The logic was straightforward: eventually age would remove pilots whose abilities had begun to decline.

Jim was fifty-seven when I first flew with him. Clearly that exposes the weakness in that logic. Nothing about him suggested sudden failure.

He wasn't incapacitated.

He wasn't obviously unfit for duty.

What I witnessed instead was something far more difficult to identify—a gradual loss of the ability to process information, prioritize tasks, and stay ahead of a rapidly changing situation.

A pilot who seemed able to function normally until workload rose beyond his mental ability to manage it.

The clock hadn't caught him in time.

Over the decades that followed, I watched another change unfold. The next generation of pilots approaching retirement began looking very different from the generation that preceded it. Fewer smoked. More exercised regularly. Drinking moderated. Pilots generally remained healthier and active far longer than many had when the Age-60 Rule was created in 1959. *(See Inside the Story: The Airline Pilot Age-60 Rule.)*

When the retirement age eventually moved to sixty-five, the change made sense for many pilots. I flew with some approaching sixty-five who remained sharp, decisive, and fully capable in demanding environments.

But I also flew with others who seemed to be losing pace years before retirement.

The problem was never the number.

The problem was assuming that one number could accurately describe everyone.

Age may correlate with risk, but age itself is not a reliable test of cognitive fitness.

That remains one of aviation's unresolved challenges.

We still lack a reliable way to identify subtle cognitive decline before it becomes visible to the people sharing a cockpit.

The arrangement Dennis devised in 1994 would be far less likely today. Cockpit culture has changed dramatically since the early 1990s.

Back then when I urged Jim to go around in San Francisco, I was making a recommendation.

The decision remained entirely his.

Today, that same situation would unfold very differently.

Modern crew resource management places far greater emphasis on shared authority, and intervention when safety margins are eroding.

Captains remain responsible for the flight, but they no longer operate in the isolated decision-making environment that existed when I flew with Jim.

A go-around is no longer a matter of pride or negotiation.

Today, when an approach becomes unstable, the expectation is simple:

Go around.

There would be no gray area.

It now would be a command: Go around.

Even if spoken by the copilot.

When the call is made, it must be flown.

My own experience illustrates why those changes became necessary.

Learning Points:

- *Cognitive decline often appears gradually.*
- *Authority without accountability is a risk multiplier.*
- *Silence in the face of clear danger is still a decision.*

Inside the Story *(Optional Reading)*

Why Departures from Honolulu Felt So Different from San Francisco

Honolulu departures usually felt easygoing. Most long-haul flights used the same runway and a familiar overwater departure, and even when traffic was busy, the operation often felt orderly and unhurried.

San Francisco was different. The airport was constrained by runway layout, crowded surrounding airspace, and a steady mix of arrivals and departures. Oceanic traffic returning from the Pacific often converged there in the morning, while nearby Oakland and San Jose added to the complexity. What felt relaxed in Honolulu could feel compressed and demanding in San Francisco.

That contrast mattered.

What Pilots Mean by a "Stable Approach"

Airline crews begin preparing for landing long before the runway is in sight. As the airplane descends, speed is gradually reduced and the aircraft is configured step-by-step: flaps extended in stages, landing gear lowered, and engine power adjusted to maintain a controlled descent.

The goal is to reach a specific point on the approach where everything is already settled. By about 1,000 feet above the ground, the airplane should be fully configured for landing, aligned with the runway, descending at the proper rate, and flying the correct target speed. From that point forward, only small adjustments should be required.

Pilots call this condition a stable approach.

If the airplane is still too fast, too high, poorly aligned with the runway, or requiring large corrections at that altitude, today, the safest option is simple: abandon the approach and try again.

Most airlines treat this as a hard rule, because many landing accidents begin with crews attempting to salvage an approach that was never properly stabilized.

The Airline Pilot Age-60 Rule

For decades, airline pilots in the United States were required to retire at age sixty. The rule dated back to 1959, when the Federal Aviation Administration concluded that the physical and cognitive demands of airline flying made age-related decline a safety concern.

At the time there was no reliable way to measure subtle cognitive deterioration in high-workload environments like airline cockpits. The mandatory retirement age became a blunt but simple safeguard: pilots could fly until sixty, but not beyond.

The policy remained unchanged for nearly fifty years. In 2007 the United States raised the retirement age to sixty-five, aligning with international standards adopted by many other aviation authorities.

The debate surrounding the rule never fully disappeared, because pilots age differently. Some remain sharp well past sixty-five, while others begin to struggle earlier.

COVER ART

PHOTO 1 · CHAPTER 1
A U.S. Air Force AWACS aircraft in Saudi Arabia.

PHOTO 2 · CHAPTER 2
An Eastern Air Lines DC-7 on the tarmac.

PHOTO 3 · CHAPTER 4

The replica 1956 MG TD kit car Jim McGrath and David built—Jim in the left seat, David in the right.

PHOTO 4 · CHAPTER 4

John and Kathy Gaubatz with David, Ayla, Fran, and Aaron in Hawaii.

PHOTO 5 · CHAPTER 5
Buddy Goodman, Andy Magar, and David reunited in 2023.

PHOTO 6 · CHAPTER 5 PART 2
Buddy Goodman and David in the Utah mountains, 2023.

PHOTO 7 · CHAPTER 6
David with the engine he had just removed from a 1966 Corvette.

PHOTO 8 · CHAPTER 6
David, a flight instructor, beside a Cessna 172 in 1979.

PHOTO 9 · CHAPTER 7 PART 2
Ortner Airport in 2023—cleaned up and operating again.

PHOTO 10 · CHAPTER 7 PART 2
Our home for more than a year: a trailer beside the hangar at the abandoned airfield.

PHOTO 11 · CHAPTER 7 PART 2
N751Z, one of the planes the Whitesells acquired at Ortner Airport.

PHOTO 12 · CHAPTER 7 PART 3
David, in a polyester suit and ready for town, hanging from Dulcinea's nose wheel well shortly after the repainting.

PHOTO 13 · CHAPTER 7 PART 3
Dulcinea's No. 3 and No. 4 engine cowlings in their new paint scheme.

PHOTO 14 · CHAPTER 7 PART 3
Dulcinea's cockpit, repainted cream by David and Bruce.

PHOTO 15 · CHAPTER 7 PART 3
Dulcinea, nearly repainted, awaiting new engines and propellers.

PHOTO 16 · CHAPTER 7 PART 5
The company truck arrives in Wakeman with freshly overhauled propellers from Miami.

PHOTO 17 · CHAPTER 7 PART 5
Installing the first of four overhauled propellers on Dulcinea's No. 2 engine.

PHOTO 18 · CHAPTER 7 PART 5
With Dulcinea on jacks, the landing gear retracts for the first time in more than eight years.

PHOTO 19 · CHAPTER 7 PART 6
The great escape from Wakeman: Dulcinea begins her takeoff roll at Ortner Airport.

PHOTO 20 · CHAPTER 7 PART 6
Dulcinea climbing away from Ortner Airport—barely airborne.

PHOTO 21 · CHAPTER 7 PART 6
Bill Whitesell returns to Ortner Airport for a low farewell pass.

PHOTO 22 · CHAPTER 7 PART 9
Dulcinea in New Smyrna Beach, Florida, in 2022, awaiting conversion into a restaurant.

PHOTO 23 · CHAPTER 7 PART 9
Vic Hardy flying a Boeing 737 for America West in the 1990s.

PHOTO 24 · CHAPTER 7 PART 9
Bruce in front of a DC-7 after a 1981 flight, two years before his death.

PHOTO 25 · CHAPTER 7 PART 9
Bill Whitesell at the controls of his old girl, Dulcinea, in 1982.

PHOTO 26 · CHAPTER 7 PART 9
David on Dulcinea's No. 3 engine in 1979.

PHOTO 27 · CHAPTER 9 PART 1
David in the Westwind cockpit before a Barbados trip with the Harrimans.

PHOTO 28 · CHAPTER 9 PART 1
The Harrimans' Westwind, N84PH.

PHOTO 29 · CHAPTER 9 PART 2
David with a marlin in Cabo San Lucas.

PHOTO 30 · CHAPTER 11
New-hire David in his first Northwest Orient uniform, 1985.

PHOTO 31 · CHAPTER 12
A Northwest Orient Boeing 747 lifting off.

PHOTO 32 · CHAPTER 13
Ayla, age five; Fran, four; and Aaron, two and a half, in Colorado.

PHOTO 33 · CHAPTER 14 PART 2
The second of Mount Pinatubo's explosive eruptions.

PHOTO 34 · CHAPTER 14 PART 2
Volcanic ash collapsing buildings.

PHOTO 35 · CHAPTER 20
David in the captain's seat with copilot Mike Miller during a Colorado Avalanche charter, 1996.

PHOTO 36 · CHAPTER 20
Newspaper photograph of David's Northwest Boeing 727 in San Antonio, signed by the newly crowned NBA champion Spurs.

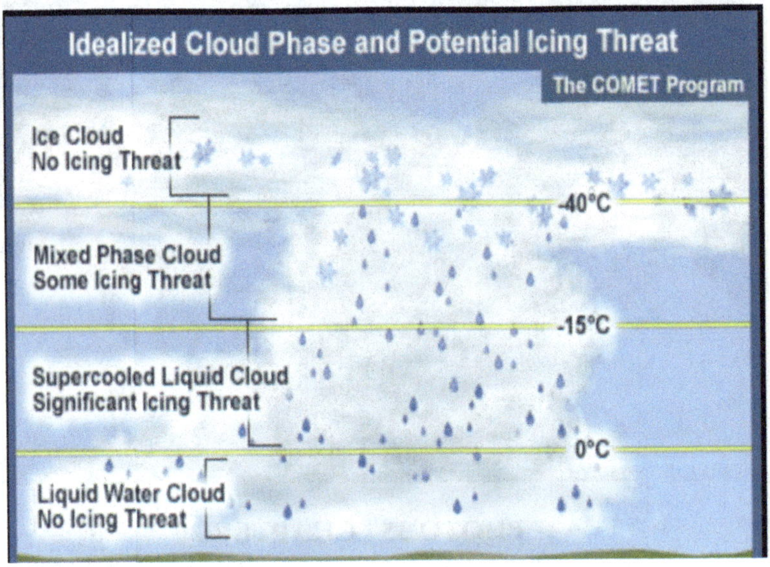

PHOTO 37 · CHAPTER 22
Cloud-phase and temperature profile for aircraft icing.

PHOTO 38 · CHAPTER 24
The CD and case for “Kitty Hawk.”

PHOTO 39 · CHAPTER 25
Cockpit view on approach to Saipan International Airport.

PHOTO 40 · CHAPTER 25
Banzai Cliff, Saipan.

PHOTO 41 · CHAPTER 26
Kim's Flight Design CT at 3,000 feet over Minnesota at the start of our flight to Colorado.

PHOTO 42 · CHAPTER 27
David inside the nacelle of a Boeing 757 engine.

PHOTO 43 · CHAPTER 28
Solar panels atop Concourse C at Denver International Airport.

PHOTO 44 · CHAPTER 29 PART 1
The 41-foot Beneteau we sailed down Mexico's Pacific coast, moored at the San Carlos marina with Mount Tetakawi behind.

PHOTO 45 · CHAPTER 29 PART 1
David, wearing four layers and still cold, shortly before sunrise in Mexican waters.

PHOTO 46 · CHAPTER 29 PART 5
A beach café overlooking Zihuatanejo Bay.

PHOTO 47 · CHAPTER 29 PART 6
The Mexican Navy/Coast Guard alongside our boat during an unexpected at-sea interdiction.

PHOTO 48 · CHAPTER 30
Bryn stripping linen wallcovering during our 2016 renovation.

PHOTO 49 · CHAPTER 30
David in front of a Boeing 777 engine, months before Delta retired both the airplane and the pilot.

Captain's hats from my two airlines: Northwest and Delta.

When Northwest hired me in 1985, we were told we would someday fly the 1,800-mph "Orient Express" SST pictured at the bottom of the photograph above.

CHAPTER 16

I KNOW WHAT I DIDN'T SEE

"When you have eliminated the impossible, whatever remains, however improbable, must be the truth."
—Sherlock Holmes

AGE 34 · 1992

The cockpit had settled into that low-grade vigilance unique to night ocean flying. Systems operating normally. Engines steady. Navigation stable.

Minds drifting just close enough to sleep to be dangerous.

We were eastbound across the Pacific Ocean, midway between Japan and Hawaii, with nothing outside the windshield but stars, dark sky, and black water.

Routine had settled in, carrying the subtle risk that comes with nothing demanding your attention.

Then something moved rapidly across the windshield from left to right.

White. Brilliant. Fast.

Close enough that all three of us reacted at the same instant—not a thought, not a word—just a violent snap to attention as our bodies came upright in our seats.

The sensation landed before language did.

Adrenaline surged, compressing time and sharpening focus.

"That was close." One of us blurted out.

"Too close."

Someone reached up and killed the cockpit lights. The flight deck went black.

With the autopilot flying and nothing demanding our hands, all three of us leaned forward, faces close to the glass, scanning the darkness ahead for the aircraft that had no business being there.

A navigation error.

A crossing jet.

Anything that fit the rules and explained why we were still alive after such a near-miss.

There was nothing.

Instead, a solid white light hung perhaps eight to ten miles ahead of us, slightly right of our nose and a few thousand feet above.

No strobe.

No position lights.

No visible structure.

Just a defined sphere, holding station relative to us—fixed to our airspeed and course—as if it belonged there.

That alone broke expectation. The absence of recognition registered without discussion.

Then it moved.

Not accelerated—simply relocated.

The transition took less than a breath, yet long enough to register with unsettling clarity.

It crossed our path from right to left and stopped again.

Same distance. Now slightly below us. Perfectly matched to our speed and direction.

No one spoke.

We were trying to force what we were seeing back into training, into physics, into any framework that preserved order.

It moved again.

Traversing about sixteen miles in the blink of an eye.

Back to our right. Above us this time. And once more it froze in place, motionless relative to us, as if tethered.

Three moves.

Each deliberate.

Each precise.

Each incompatible with everything we knew about flight.

A single, bright white sphere, not emanating from any visible structure—yet unmistakably present. *(See Inside the Story: What It Couldn't Have Been.)*

For a brief, unspoken moment, I think we all entertained the same possibility: the movements seemed too precise to be random. The light crossed our path, repositioned itself, then did it again—as if following a pattern we could not recognize. Like hearing dots and dashes without knowing Morse code, we were left wondering whether the sequence carried meaning or whether we were attempting to imposing order on something we simply did not understand.

The idea surfaced and was immediately dismissed. Speculation had no place in the cockpit, and we had neither a method to test the thought nor a way to respond even if it were true.

What remained was the tension.

The original urgency of collision avoidance had drained away, replaced by something heavier. The recognition that explanation was our responsibility—and that none of us had one.

The common ocean chat frequency—Guard—crackled alive.

Measured voices. Careful phrasing, as if everyone understood that precision still mattered.

"Anyone else seeing a light out here?"

No laughter. No dismissal. Just confirmation—carefully worded, deliberately incomplete—offered as if assigning it too much definition might make the unthinkable real.

Then the spherical light shot straight up out of our visual frame.

Not a climb. Not a rocket engine burn. It simply departed—vertically, instantly—accelerating out of sight in a way that left no room for reinterpretation.

The frequency erupted back to life. The professional veneer finally cracked—measured voices giving way to disbelief.

Then it went quiet again—as if nothing useful could be said.

The rest of the flight was uneventful.

At cruise altitude, over open ocean, with clear skies and no traffic conflicts, there was nothing left to manage.

No reports were filed.

No notes were made.

Nothing abnormal was written down.

There was no system failure, no traffic conflict, no category into which the event could be responsibly placed.

But the absence of consequence did not erase the encounter.

We had been startled out of routine night flying by what felt like a near miss—and then shown something that behaved with intent inside our airspace, on our geometry, at our speed.

I can state with certainty what I did not see: no aircraft, no atmospheric reflection, no astronomical object behaving within known patterns. Beyond that, I offer no explanation. *(See Inside the Story: UFO vs. UAP.)*

ANOTHER BULLET DODGED

This encounter stayed with me. I did not speak about it for decades. It altered how I understood our place—not as the center of anything, but as participants in a much larger system, governed by rules we do not yet understand.

I will say this quietly and without qualification. What we observed that night behaved beyond any human capability known to me then—or now.

Whatever its purpose, it did not end us.

Learning Points:

- *Not all anomalies yield explanations.*
- *Silence can be an appropriate response when evidence is incomplete.*
- *When one experiences the unexplainable, one should try to think outside of one's self-imposed constraints for answers.*
- *We don't need to always understand the world around us, but we need to stay open-minded.*
- *Trillions of exoplanets in the Universe indicate a vast number of possibilities!*

Inside the Story *(Optional Reading)*

What It Couldn't Have Been

Professional pilots are trained to identify objects and phenomena in the sky quickly. Years of experience allow them to recognize the visual signatures of aircraft, satellites, meteors, atmospheric reflections, and weather phenomena. When something unusual is observed, the first step is not speculation—it is systematically eliminating known explanations.

In this case, several common possibilities can be ruled out immediately.

The airplane was cruising at 33,000 feet, far above the operating ceiling of helicopters. Conventional jet aircraft also follow predictable flight paths and cannot maneuver with the abrupt acceleration, stopping, and direction changes that were observed.

Rockets or spacecraft in boost phase also behave differently. They travel along continuous ballistic trajectories and do not stop, reverse direction, or maneuver laterally once underway.

Natural atmospheric or astronomical explanations were also unlikely. Meteors or space debris entering Earth's atmosphere travel in a straight path dictated by gravity and velocity. They do not abruptly halt or change direction before leaving the atmosphere again. Reflected light was also improbable—the sky was clear, and there were no clouds present that could have produced reflections or optical illusions.

Aurora activity was another possibility considered and dismissed. Our latitude was far too southerly for charged solar particles to create auroral light displays at that location.

After four decades of flying, a professional aviator develops strong confidence in recognizing what is normal in the sky. On that night, the object we observed did not match any known aircraft, weather phenomenon, or astronomical event.

What it actually was remains unexplained.

UFO vs. UAP

Technically, what we witnessed would be classified as a UFO—an unidentified flying object. In recent years the U.S. government and scientific community have shifted to the term UAP, meaning Unidentified Anomalous Phenomenon. The change reflects an effort to remove the cultural baggage attached to the term "UFO," which for decades became synonymous with extraterrestrial speculation.

By definition, a UFO or UAP simply means that the observer cannot identify what was seen. It does not imply alien technology or anything supernatural. It only indicates that the observed object or phenomenon could not be explained with the information available at the time.

Researchers who study these events often describe several observable characteristics that separate routine aircraft or atmospheric events from truly anomalous observations.

These include:

- instantaneous acceleration
- apparent immunity to gravity or inertia

- travel between different media (air, water, space)
- hypersonic speeds without visible propulsion
- the ability to hover motionless
- maneuvering beyond known aerodynamic limits

Most sightings exhibit none of these characteristics and are later explained as conventional aircraft, weather balloons, satellites, astronomical objects, or atmospheric optics.

The event described in this chapter was unusual because the object appeared to demonstrate five of these six characteristics as we observed it from the cockpit. You can draw your own conclusion.

CHAPTER 17

SMALL WORLD

"If any man thinketh that he knoweth anything, he knoweth not yet as he ought to know."
—Paul

AGE 25-60 · 1983-2018

It was January 1983. The holidays were over, and Barbados had settled back into its winter rhythm—busy enough to feel alive, quiet enough to disappear into.

The Harrimans were at their beach house, and I had time on my hands. One evening, I wandered into a small local bar I liked—nothing notable, just a place where the stools were worn, and the talk came easily.

The bartender was new to me. He spoke with a Midwestern accent, which stood out on the island. The place was nearly empty, and over the course of his shift, we did what people do when there's nothing else to manage—we talked.

At some point, I mentioned that my brother was also a bartender.

"Where?" he asked.

"Chicago."

"Where in Chicago?"

"The north side."

"Where?"

"Armitage and Halsted."

"What bar?"

I paused. Then, a little snarkily, I said, "A small neighborhood place called Nick's."

His expression didn't change. "Is that the one with the bullet hole in the painting?"

"Yes," I said. "You know it?"

He leaned closer over the bar, looked straight at me.

"Is your brother's name Lee?"

I nearly fell off the stool.

Lee had worked at Nick's for years—first bouncing, then bartending.

But I wasn't in Chicago.

I was sitting in a quiet bar on a Caribbean island, more than two thousand miles away, talking to someone who knew details I hadn't offered.

There were explanations.

Nick's was a known place—but most definitely a local place.

Lee was outgoing.

People remembered him.

All that made sense. And none of it made sense.

That was the first time I noticed the feeling—not amazement exactly, but a sudden awareness that the world was smaller and stranger than I'd assumed.

In 2017, while preparing a flight at Charles de Gaulle Airport in Paris, I was standing at the gate podium reviewing weather and paperwork when I noticed a woman seated nearby. I recognized her—but out of context, it took time.

Then it came to me. Lisa Honeycutt.

Lisa owned a restaurant in San Carlos, Sonora, Mexico—a small fishing village at the edge of the desert. I'd been there often enough to know her well. But I had only ever seen her in an apron, working hard—not sitting in an international terminal thousands of miles away.

I walked over and said hello. She hesitated—she had only ever seen me in shorts and sandals, not a pilot's uniform—then recognized me.

We laughed, surprised.

She came from a town of just over five thousand people, half a world away.

She was returning from a trip with friends and, remarkably, was on my flight from Paris to Salt Lake City. From there, she continued to Mexico.

We talked briefly. Then I returned to my work.

Paris fed traffic in every direction. At least ten airlines flew daily to the United States, and Delta alone launched fifteen departures a day. Lisa could have been on any of them—but she was on mine. A small-world collision inside the fourth-busiest airport on Earth.

On another layover in a random U.S. city, I met a hotel cleaning woman in the hallway outside my room. I told her she could skip the room that day and asked only for an extra towel. We exchanged a few polite words.

Somehow, we touched on the topic of hometowns. She mentioned Cleveland.

My childhood city too.

We narrowed it down—neighborhoods, then schools.

When I listed mine—"Boulevard Elementary, Roosevelt Jr. High, and Heights High"—she went still.

Then she said, "My mother taught at Boulevard Elementary. Mrs. Allison."

I had to steady myself.

Mrs. Allison had been my kindergarten teacher.

I told her how kind her mother had been.

How safe that classroom felt.

How much those early lessons—listening, sharing space, treating people decently—had stayed with me long after I left it.

She nodded quietly. Then said, "That sounds like my mom."

She told me her mother had passed away a few years earlier.

We stood there for a moment, each holding a memory the other hadn't known they shared.

None of these moments were dramatic. There was no danger, no urgency, no decision required. And yet, each one left the same residue—a sense that expectation alone was an incomplete tool.

Training teaches you to anticipate outcomes based on probability, proximity, and preparation. Most of the time, that works. But occasionally, the world introduces a variable that doesn't announce itself as important—only incompatible.

I didn't draw conclusions from these encounters.

I simply noticed them, set them aside, and continued—aware now that some patterns do not reveal their purpose when they appear.

Over the years I stopped asking, *"What are the odds?"*

None of these encounters changed my life, but they changed my confidence in coincidence.

The world is enormous—oceans, continents, billions of people—and yet our paths cross and recross in ways no spreadsheet can predict.

I've come to believe the world is simultaneously much larger and much smaller than we imagine.

Learning Points:

- *The world is crowded—and still somehow personal.*
- *Probability is a useful tool—right up until it isn't.*
- *The fastest way to shrink the planet is to start talking about where you're from.*
- *Some moments don't require meaning. They just require noticing.*

CHAPTER 18

THE MARIANA ISLANDS—GUAM

PART 1 — MOTHER NATURE

"It's only after you've stepped outside your comfort zone that you begin to change, grow, and transform."
—Roy T. Bennett

AGE 35 · 1993

By 1993, Guam wasn't new to me anymore—it was familiar work. I'd been flying there for years. Like Puerto Rico, Guam is a U.S. territory. On the ground, the similarity mostly ends with the fact that both are islands. Different cadence. Different priorities. Different clock. Different people. *(See Inside the Story: The History of Guam.)*

By this time the old Guam-o-Rama on the 747 was behind me. Promotion to DC-10 copilot meant better trips—and fewer nights wrecked by the schedule.

The week of August 7th, 1993, I was a DC-10 copilot on the Honolulu–Guam trip: mostly a daylight leg out of HNL, arriving in Guam in the late afternoon with a 24-hour layover before the return. A long layover by airline standards. Good duty—when the weather cooperated.

That weekend, it wasn't going to cooperate.

Two typhoons were out there. Both barreling toward the islands of the central Pacific. The first was close enough to make Guam ugly all day. Its eye wasn't forecast to cross the island—it was expected to pass west—but the bands that radiate off a typhoon can reach for hundreds of miles. Even without a direct hit, it would throw thunderstorms across our route like a field of land mines. The second was still days back, but its projected track had everyone watching it like a slow-moving threat you couldn't ignore.

Thunderstorms are not just turbulence. They are not only "a rough ride." They are a physics problem with teeth that pilots are trained to deal with.

Company policy was simple: stay at least twenty miles from the cells, and if you can top them, clear them by at least five thousand feet—though in the tropics, the big ones can reach into the high forties and fifties, where "topping" isn't a plan. The only winning move is to go around them. *(See Inside the Story: Weather Deviations Over the Ocean.)*

We expected deviations and carried extra fuel for them. Scheduled time was a little over eight hours, but we planned longer because over the ocean, you don't play games with margin and thunderstorms.

Before walking to the jet, we found the flight attendants and briefed them. The captain kept it mostly light on the surface—he knew they had eight hours of cabin reality coming.

"The last couple hours could get sporty," he said. "First part should be smooth. Get the service done early."

The lead flight attendant didn't bother hiding her opinion.

"Great," she muttered, "more half-digested food for them to throw up later."

We pushed on time. Honolulu gave us a perfect send-off—warm, calm, blue—and for the first few hours the flight felt like it was trying to prove the forecast wrong. Smooth air above sixteen thousand and beyond. The kind of visibility and ride that makes you believe the atmosphere is simple.

Just past the International Date Line—August 8th now on the clock—the lines began to form ahead of us, the way they always do when a large system is feeding the air in front of it. Thunderstorms stacked and spread, and the radar filled with colors depicting storms we had no intention of touching.

We called Tokyo Radio on HF and requested wide deviation authority—up to two hundred miles east and west—with a block altitude two thousand feet above and below our cleared level. HF never feels urgent, even when it is. Static, repetition, delay. While we waited for permission, the weather didn't.

The turbulence settled into a sustained, jarring motion—the kind that doesn't spike and fade but simply stays. It wasn't violent so much as relentless. Reading instruments took concentration. Simple tasks took effort. You found yourself rechecking the same gauge not because it had changed, but because the motion made it hard to trust that it hadn't.

By the time permission came, geometry forced our hand. A gentle thirty-to-forty-degree deviation only works if you get it started early. We didn't. We turned nearly ninety degrees, flying southeast—perpendicular to our course—ultimately pushing more than two hundred miles off track to keep the worst of the weather off our wings and not our nose.

Even staying clear of the strongest weather, the ride stayed ugly in the way tropical weather does: not patterned, just constant motion that wears people down. "Clear" on the radar didn't mean comfortable in the cabin. Calls started coming forward—sick passengers, anxious questions, and the same answer each time.

"It ends when we land."

After roughly ninety minutes of zigging and zagging, a thinner section finally appeared on the radar. We turned back toward Guam—still in bumps, but clear of the thickest bands of thunderstorms. It wasn't smooth, but it was survivable, and over time the edge began to come off the ride.

Airport weather was low and wet: one mile visibility, a six-hundred-foot ceiling, moderate rain, and wind running hard across the island. Not beach weather. But within both the pilots' and the airplane's limits. The ILS *(Instrument Landing System)* would do what it was designed to do—lead us to the runway when visibility alone could not.

The captain made a solid PA—an apology for the ride, an explanation for the delay. Calm. Professional. No drama. People don't want a story when they've been holding a bag in front of their face for an hour.

With a strong crosswind, the approach was sporting. The landing was a handful but controlled—the kind you get when the runway is wet and the atmosphere has claws. As we rolled out, the captain gave me the kind of ribbing that releases tension without celebrating it.

"Nice," he said, "but anybody can grease it on when it's wet. Show me what you got when it's dry."

Passengers deplaned slowly—some pale, some angry, most just relieved to be standing on something that didn't move. With no jetway, they filed out into the humid air and down the airstairs.

I went to the back to help a few elderly folks with heavy bags down the aft stairs. The cabin looked like a small war had been fought in the aisle. Everyone was depleted, including the crew.

The terminal was small and tired, built for a different era, now doing a job it had outgrown. Customs took longer than normal. We stood in a long line under signs that read HAFA ADAI—the Guamanian welcome greeting. It sounds like "Half a day."

We'd been on the ground maybe forty-five minutes when it started.

At first, it was subtle—something you feel before you name it. A vibration through the floor, felt in the balls of my feet. Then the visuals confirmed it: fixtures shifting when nothing should shift. Finally, the sound arrived—a low, steady note, like the building had started humming.

I'd felt earthquakes before. Recognition doesn't calm your body. It just removes hesitation.

I stepped out of line, left my bags, and moved for the exit.

Across the room, heads lifted together—faces turning the same direction, confused, searching for a cue. For a moment, everyone looked like prairie dogs sensing danger without knowing where it lived.

The shaking escalated.

I picked up my pace and yelled back to anyone who would listen.

"To the door—move! Leave your bags! Out of the building!"

Seconds later, the quake hit with full force.

Then the building began to rupture.

Ceiling tiles dropped in sheets. Glass flexed, then cracked. The noise climbed past where speech mattered. People screamed. Most didn't move.

I held the door open, motioning hard with both arms. A few came. Not enough.

Outside, the ramp erased the last comforting assumption.

The concrete was rolling—long waves, like ocean swells. Solid concrete, feet thick, moving like water. I'd read about it. Reading isn't seeing. Seeing is being forced to accept it.

Our DC-10 bounced on its gear as if alive, the fuselage jumping and yawing like an animal shaking off a swarm. The airstairs danced and slid away from the airplane, separating farther with each wave.

Getting everyone back aboard was no longer an option. The stairs would not stay put.

I let go of the terminal door. There was no more directing. The only viable plan was distance.

Running wasn't possible. Walking felt like crossing a deck in heavy seas. People moved like they were drunk, clawing for balance as the ground threw them sideways.

Inside, the building tore at itself—cracking, popping, twisting—until even that sound blurred into the larger roar.

Then it stopped.

The rocking and rolling felt like it had lasted at least a minute.

The silence afterward was deafening.

A big, burly Guamanian ramper said, "Man, dat was a big one!"

A few of us stood out on the tarmac and looked back.

The terminal building was still standing.

We went back in carefully, expecting carnage. What we found was chaos and fear—but not the pile of bodies your mind produces when a building shakes that hard. Ceiling tiles everywhere, broken glass at the perimeter, people scraped and shaken but mostly intact.

ANOTHER BULLET DODGED

The captain shifted immediately into control.

Triage.

Accountability.

Regroup.

Flight attendants were instructed to retrieve some first-aid kits. Customs tried to re-form lines with unsteady hands.

The second officer and I walked around the airplane—scrapes along the skin from the airstairs, oxygen masks hanging from the ceiling, minor damage consistent with what we had watched unfold. But the airplane did what she was designed to do. She moved with the ground, absorbed the motion through her landing gear, and did not break.

The airport was another question.

After watching the taxiways ripple, no one was ready to declare the field open. Not yet. The concrete had to be inspected, the systems checked, and someone had to decide it was safe to start moving airplanes again.

Eventually, we cleared Customs and stepped into the familiar humid air of Guam, rain still falling lightly, the larger questions left behind us—for the moment.

And there—like any other day on the roster—the Hilton van was waiting.

We climbed in soaked and exhausted, still carrying the quake in our bodies.

"Condition of the hotel?" someone asked.

The driver—big Guamanian, easy smile, booming voice used gently—shrugged like the question hadn't quite arrived yet.

"I'd bin here wait'in for da crew tince schedule time," he said. "No idea 'bout da hotel. When de quake hit, I jus' stay in da van."

The captain's voice tightened.

"Have you radioed the hotel? Do you know if it is still standing?"

The driver blinked.

"Din't tink to assk."

The crew was unusually quiet in the van, listening intently to the driver as he called the hotel on the two-way radio that dangled precariously under the dashboard ashtray, held on by one loose screw.

"Dis is van numba 2 to hotel."

A pause.

Static.

"Hotel, dis van numba 2 do yah hear me?"

Silence. You could have heard a pin drop in the van

Then he turned on the music and put the van in drive.

No one said anything. The tension in the van rose.

At last, the local broadcast finally broke through.

An 8.0 earthquake. Sixty-two seconds long.

Epicenter: Guam.

No tsunami. Low casualties so far.

Then one more line.

A five-story parking garage collapse on Pale San Vitores Road. Near Ypao Beach Park.

That meant little to an aircrew from Hawaii.

The driver spoke without turning his head.

"Man," he said, "dat is rite nex to da Hilton."

Inside the Story *(Optional Reading)*

The History of Guam

Guam sits in the western Pacific Ocean and is the southernmost island in the Mariana Islands chain. Long before European explorers arrived, the island was settled by seafaring people from the Philippines and nearby island groups around 1400 BCE. These settlers became known as the Chamorro people, whose culture still forms the foundation of Guam's identity today.

The first recorded European contact occurred in 1521, when the Portuguese explorer Ferdinand Magellan, sailing for Spain, encountered the island during his circumnavigation of the globe. Spain later colonized Guam in 1668, turning the island into an important provisioning stop for Spanish galleons traveling between Mexico and the Philippines.

Guam remained under Spanish rule for more than two centuries until the Spanish–American War of 1898, when U.S. naval forces captured the island without resistance. Spain formally ceded Guam to the United States the following year in the Treaty of Paris, making it an American territory.

During World War II, Guam was attacked and occupied by Japanese forces at the same time as the assault on Pearl Harbor—December 7, 1941, December 8th Guam time. After nearly three years of occupation, American forces recaptured the island in July 1944 during a fierce battle that helped secure the Mariana Islands as a strategic base for U.S. operations in the Pacific.

Today Guam remains a U.S. territory and an important military outpost. Major U.S. Air Force and Marine installations operate on the island, projecting American military presence deep into the Pacific. Despite its strategic role, Guam is also a major tourist destination, particularly for travelers from Japan who visit for its beaches, coral reefs, and shorter travel time compared to Hawaii.

Weather Deviations Over the Ocean

Air behaves as a fluid, much like water in an ocean. It forms currents, waves, and rotating structures that can move enormous amounts of energy through the atmosphere. When this motion becomes strong enough, it produces turbulence that can make an aircraft ride uncomfortable—or in extreme cases, dangerous.

Pilots often rely on clouds as visual clues to understand what the air is doing. Towering thunderstorms reveal strong vertical air movement, while certain cloud shapes indicate wind shear or turbulence. But many disturbances in the atmosphere are invisible, especially over the open ocean where there are fewer visual references.

Modern airliners have weather radar, which detects precipitation inside clouds. The radar displays areas of rainfall intensity as colored returns—typically green for light rain, yellow for moderate, and red for heavy rainfall associated with powerful thunderstorm cells. The radar allows crews to identify hazardous weather hundreds of miles ahead of the aircraft. Even so, avoidance requires planning. A jet traveling at typical cruise speeds covers roughly seven miles per minute, meaning a storm 300 miles away may be only forty-five minutes ahead.

Over oceans, crews must begin requesting deviations well before reaching the weather because air traffic controllers generally do not have radar coverage. Instead, aircraft positions are tracked using radio reports and estimated times over navigation fixes. Any change in course must be coordinated through long-range radios—traditionally by High Frequency (HF) communications.

HF radio can be slow and unreliable, especially near thunderstorms where atmospheric electrical activity creates heavy static. It may take several attempts—and sometimes many minutes—to establish contact with the appropriate radio station, relay a request through multiple agencies, and receive clearance to deviate around a storm.

Because of these limitations, pilots crossing large oceanic regions carry extra fuel and often begin planning weather deviations long before reaching the storms themselves. In tropical regions, where thunderstorm towers can reach 45,000 to 50,000 feet or higher, climbing above the weather is rarely possible. The safest strategy is almost always simple: go around it.

Chapter 18

THE MARIANA ISLANDS—GUAM

Part 2 — Aftermath

Age 35 · 1993

The word came out of us all together.

"What?"

"Yah," the driver said, still calm. "Rite nex to da hotel. Waz dere fine when I lef."

Fine. When he left.

No one spoke after that. The van rolled on through wet streets and broken traffic lights, the rain tapping steadily on the roof. Each of us did the same quiet math and came up with different answers. If five stories of reinforced concrete had failed next door, no one knew what that meant for the buildings beside it.

We crested a low rise and started down toward Pale San Vitores Road. The driver leaned forward slightly and pointed.

"Dar it is."

The Hilton tower was still there.

The Hilton complex at Tumon Bay wasn't a single building—it was three: the tall tower, a lower garden building, and an odd octagonal wing where crews often stayed. Seeing the tower standing answered one question, but not all of them.

The van rolled closer.

The garden building came into view.

The footprint looked intact.

No one said anything for a few seconds.

Then, as we pulled up the long drive, we passed directly alongside what used to be the parking garage.

Five levels lay flattened into one, like plates stacked on a shelf.

Emergency vehicles ringed the site, their lights flashing across the wreckage.

A car's front end protruded from the pile at an angle that made it impossible to misread what had happened.

It was too early for questions and too late for guesses.

Inside the hotel, order had not survived the earthquake.

Employees moved quickly but without coordination. Voices overlapped. People were redirected, then redirected again. Phones were dead. Power was out. The front desk clerk appeared and disappeared as staff were pulled away to deal with other guests.

We had been awake all night. We were exhausted and just wanted our rooms.

We waited patiently.

When someone finally addressed us, the message was short and absolute.

"The tower is off limits. The garden rooms are full of 'real guests'. The octagon wing has shifted and is unsafe. We don't have rooms for airline crews."

The captain asked where yesterday's crew was.

"In their rooms."

"In the octagon?"

"Yes."

"Do they know it's unsafe?"

She snapped, already looking past us. "The phones are dead. How would we tell them?"

Up to that point, chaos had felt temporary—something to endure until systems reasserted themselves. That answer made it clear we were no longer inside the system. We were no longer anyone's problem.

We asked for yesterday's crew sign-in list. Names. Room numbers.

She handed it over without comment and walked away to deal with other issues she considered more pressing—real customers.

No one debated what to do next. We turned and walked toward the octagon.

The corridor smelled humid and musty from dust shaken loose from places it wasn't meant to come from. Halfway down, the second officer stopped and pointed up. Where the hallway met the octagon wing, the ceiling had separated—not simply cracked but shifted. The building had moved and left evidence.

"This isn't cosmetic," he said quietly.

Someone asked what would happen if there was another aftershock.

The captain didn't soften it. "I don't know."

Then he gave people a choice.

"If you don't want to go in, turn back now. No shame. Find water. Find information. Do something useful from the safe side."

Five flight attendants turned around immediately. No hesitation. They didn't look embarrassed. They looked relieved.

The rest of us split into pairs and kept moving.

The hallways were unnaturally quiet.

No televisions. No voices. Doors sat slightly crooked in their frames. Thin cracks traced the walls like veins.

First door on the list.

We knocked hard.

"John! We're crewmembers from today's inbound flight. Are you in there?"

A voice answered, tight and irritated. "Phones are dead. My door won't open."

"Unlock it and stand back."

Two kicks. The door released. John stood there blinking, trying to catch up to a reality he hadn't been briefed on.

"My crew's scattered in the octagon," he said. "I can't reach anyone."

"We've got the list," I told him. "Grab your things. Meet in the lobby. You're not flying tonight—the airport's shut down."

Room by room, floor by floor, the pattern repeated.

Unlock. Kick. Release.

Each crewmember reacted the same way: relief first, then the delayed understanding of how easily they could have stayed trapped without information, without power, and, more pressing, without a way out.

No one answered at four rooms. We left notes at the base of the doors and hoped whoever was missing had been outside when the ground moved.

By the time we regrouped, nineteen of the twenty-three Northwest people were accounted for.

There was nowhere to go.

The lobby was crowded and oppressive, lit unevenly by emergency lighting that never quite filled the space. We drifted to the Pool Tree Bar because it was open-air and felt less like a trap.

Rain settled into a steady, miserable drizzle, but a huge Banyan tree covered the entire bar area.

When we finally stopped moving, the fatigue arrived.

Then Stan Swenson appeared—the outbound crew's captain. He'd been on the beach when the quake hit.

"When I got back, hotel staff was in a panic," he said. "Phones were dead. No one could tell me anything. I went to the airport to find the station manager. He's agreed to come later tonight to brief us about the runway and aircraft status."

No one interrupted him.

Unfortunately, the Hilton had nothing more to offer.

Not answers. Not supplies. Not hotel rooms.

We were airline people, not "real guests." Once that settled in, the waiting took on a different weight. The day stopped feeling chaotic and started feeling excruciatingly long.

The hotel gave us a meeting room to stow our bags and change out of our uniforms, along with access to the Tree Bar's beer fridge. We changed in the dark, then gathered beneath the banyan to drink the beer before it got warm.

I had a few minutes before the planned 8:30 crew meeting and walked down toward the beach.

Beaches had always been my reset. When schedules frayed or fatigue stacked up, I gravitated toward the beach—sand, water, open space. They slowed my breathing, reordered my thoughts. No matter how chaotic a trip became, the shoreline usually put things back into proportion.

I crossed the coral outcropping and stepped onto the sand at Tumon Bay. The light was fading. For a moment, my body started to settle.

Then I looked to my right.

The collapsed parking structure sat a few hundred yards away. Emergency lights pulsed against the Hilton walls. Wreckage was front and center.

I stood there longer than I meant to.

The beach didn't feel like my sanctuary anymore.

I turned back toward the hotel and the rest of the crew.

Our meeting provided an update that we still had no update. The free beer helped a little, but most people were too exhausted to feel much of anything.

Then another aftershock rolled through. The fragile calm that had settled over the group evaporated instantly. Fear rushed back in, sharper this time, with nowhere left to go.

Midnight came with the final insult: no rooms. Not at the Hilton. Not nearby. Not anywhere.

The earthquake had pushed every contingency plan past its breaking point.

We were a tired, frayed group, and the silence that settled over us wasn't acceptance—it was resignation.

Most of us tried to sleep on pool loungers in a windowless meeting room. With no A/C, no airflow, and twenty-plus exhausted bodies, it wasn't sleep so much as slipping in and out of consciousness, jolted awake by heat and noise. The loungers left us no choice but to sleep on our backs, and that's when the noise took over—snoring, wheezing, coughing, plastic creaking, an involuntary racket in the dark. No one had the energy to be annoyed.

We had been awake for more than twenty-four hours by then, bodies wired past usefulness, minds desperate for rest that wouldn't come. Time lost its shape. Minutes stretched. Hours dissolved. The room felt smaller as the night wore on, the air heavier, the noise unavoidable.

Around three a.m., I gave up.

I carried my lounger back outside toward the Tree Bar, where at least there was a hint of breeze and overhead cover from the rain. Water drummed softly on the branches. The air moved. It wasn't comfortable—but it was better. I slept in fragments, short, shallow pieces, waking and drifting again until dawn.

Morning came reluctantly. The sky was still bruised with storms, low and gray, as if the night hadn't quite finished with us.

The station manager arrived when he said he would. That mattered.

The runways were still closed. Inspections were slow. No timeline anyone trusted.

"If the airport opens," he said, "it will be because the concrete passes inspection. Not because the clock on the next typhoon runs out."

"You'll need to stay ready for an immediate departure," he said, then paused.

The National Weather Service was now predicting that the second typhoon would make a direct hit—possibly as a category

4 or 5 storm. If we don't get you out soon, you won't be leaving for a while.

That was when the captain said, "Then we need to go to the airplane for provisions." He asked for volunteers.

Two of us went back with the station manager.

Inside the DC-10, the air was hot and still. Overhead bins opened. Galley compartments were unlatched.

Water came out first—heavy, awkward. Snack boxes followed. Crackers, nuts, packaged food meant to bridge time. First-aid kits after that.

We stopped when every non-perishable item had been pulled—everything that might matter if the airport didn't reopen on schedule.

We weren't starving. We weren't dying of thirst. Not yet.

But without this, the next days could turn into something else entirely.

That distinction mattered.

On the drive back to the Hilton, the rain and wind were escalating—harbingers of what was inbound for the island.

Later that morning, the station manager returned with news.

"The airplane's damage has been fully rectified," he said, "but the runways are still closed." He paused, then went on. "I know you all have families to get back to. I wish I had better news.

You're stranded here with us.

Soon, everyone on the island will be focused on preparing for the storm and taking care of their own families. When that happens, you'll be on your own."

No one spoke. Whatever hope we'd been holding onto drained out quietly, without ceremony.

Then he added that he'd found a small inland motel that could take all twenty-three of us. Immediately.

It wasn't near the water. It wasn't comfortable. But it was intact and open for business. For the moment, that was enough.

We moved inland together.

The motel owners welcomed us one by one at the door. They could offer little—no electricity, no air conditioning, no water, no phone, no food. But each of us had a bed, a window, and a structure around us when the storm hit.

That was when the reality hit hard. We were stranded. No way off the island, no way to call home, and no way for home to reach me.

The second typhoon arrived later that day—like an arrow hitting a bullseye.

It didn't gust. It pressed hard and long, packing one-hundred-fifty-five-mile-per-hour winds, high seas, and delivering the proverbial punch in the gut.

Sustained force that made my motel room shudder and hold, shudder and hold again. Rain drove sideways for hours, finding seams in the walls I didn't know existed. There was no sleeping through it. No distraction available. I listened and waited, knowing there was nothing left to decide.

When it finally passed, anything the earthquake had weakened was gone.

Not damaged. Gone.

The morning after the storm, one of the motel owners checked on all of us.

He looked tired, but steady.

He said, almost conversationally, that "Guam had been through worse than this." That the island always made it through. That people helped each other and kept going.

He added, without emphasis, that we would too.

Then he moved on to the next problem.

The days that followed blurred.

We had provisions from the airplane—water, snacks, non-perishables. Enough to function. Not enough to forget what we were missing. No hot meals. No cold drinks. No showers.

By day three we were all starting to smell like farm animals. It had been days with no running water, with searing humidity and heat.

The rain eventually gave us something useful.

One of the motel's downspouts had been torn loose by the storm and ended many feet above the ground. When heavier rain showers rolled through, water poured out of it in a solid stream.

Someone held up a bar of soap.

Swimsuits came out.

We took turns standing under the downspout, letting rainwater run over shoulders and backs, washing away days of sweat and salt. The water was warm, nearly the same temperature as the air, but the pressure felt miraculous.

A few quiet comments were exchanged. Nothing clever. Just acknowledgment. A little laughter, splashing, a moment where the weight lifted enough to breathe.

Clean lasted about five minutes.

The humidity returned immediately.

But for a moment, skin didn't itch, eyes didn't burn, and bodies felt marginally more human.

It was impossible to feel good in ninety-five-degree heat with ninety-five percent humidity. It was Guam.

The crew stayed mostly cohesive. The stress was palpable, but we didn't turn on each other. We shared what little space there was, passed along information when it surfaced, and checked in without making a production of it. No one complained out loud.

No one needed to.

As the days dragged on, what changed wasn't tempers—it was energy. Conversations thinned. People began peeling off alone when they could, guarding small pockets of quiet the way you guard shade.

For me, that meant walking.

With no power, no schedules, and nowhere to be, I walked the island. Hours turned to days.

I passed homes with roofs peeled back, trees stripped to trunks, storefronts open to the air. Everywhere people were already clearing debris from places they intended to return to—whether help came or not.

I didn't interfere. I didn't take photographs. I just watched.

When I spoke with people, no one complained. No one asked who was coming to help. They talked about what needed to be done that day. Where to start. Who of their neighbors needed assistance.

By the seventh day, power returned in sections. On the eighth, the airport reopened. Empty airplanes arrived to take stranded people out.

My twenty-four-hour layover became eight days.

Leaving Guam ended my ordeal, but not theirs. From the air, the damage was unmistakable.

As an unsettling reminder of how circular life can be, on this very day—May 26th, 2023—as I put these words on paper, Guam's airport is once again closed. A typhoon has damaged the airfield, stranding travelers on the same rock, waiting out the same forces. Writing about being marooned there three decades earlier, I found myself fully empathizing with those now stuck in place, watching weather and time dictate terms.

ANOTHER BULLET DODGED

Back in Hawaii, my family told me what the week had looked like from their side: few TV news reports, silence, waiting.

In those days, airline families understood a simple rule.

If something truly bad happened, the company didn't call.

Someone came to the door.

No knock meant I was still alive somewhere beyond the horizon.

Learning Points:

- *Mother Nature has dominion over all of us; control is mostly an illusion.*
- *In life, we can truly only control our own expectations.*
- *Endurance is what remains when crisis stops feeling temporary.*

POSTSCRIPT

In the years that followed the 8.0 earthquake, Guam built a large, modern, beautiful international terminal building with 17 gates, including enclosed Jetways. No more walking on the ramp and up airstairs in the heat and sporadic rain showers. Guam's shabby little original terminal building still stands as a reminder to those of us who thought it would be our tomb that day in 1993.

(Names of individuals have all been changed for anonymity)

CHAPTER 19

A KNOCK AT THE DOOR

PART 1 — NEIGHBORS

Knowledge or Ignorance:
"Between knowledge of what really exists and ignorance of what does not exist, lies the domain of opinion. It is more obscure than knowledge, but clearer than ignorance."
—Plato

AGE 36-37 · 1994-1995

By April of 1994, we had finished our two-year term in Hawaii and packed up once more. It was the eighth domicile change in eight years. The children were too young to register the disruption; home, to them, was portable. Jillian and I understood it differently. Each move required starting over again, just as the previous version of our life had begun to take hold.

So, we reversed the equation.

Instead of moving the family to chase my job, we would live where we wanted, and I would commute. Routes could change. Aircraft could change. The kids would stay put.

Jillian and I traveled for weeks, trying to decide where we could imagine raising our children. We narrowed it to four places: Boulder, Santa Fe, Boise, and Spokane. Each had four seasons, easy access to the outdoors, and a small-town feel we thought our kids could grow into.

Boulder won for one practical reason.

At the time, Denver's Stapleton Airport hosted major operations for both United and Continental Airlines. Living nearby meant I could reach almost any Northwest assignment with a single flight. Simplicity mattered.

We moved onto Riverbend Road, Superior, Colorado, in August of 1994, just in time for Ayla to start kindergarten. Fran was three and a half. Aaron barely walking. We found many kids in the neighborhood the same ages as ours and Jillian quickly became the neighborhood activities mom. I did what I always do and created a construction project of finishing the basement into a playroom.

For a while, it seemed we had landed well.

December changed that.

The first of a few dubious knocks came soon after. This one belonged to a woman from down the street. I recognized her face, not her name. Once inside our home, she didn't waste time.

She explained that the Homeowners Association had organized a Christmas-light contest. The street with the best display would win—bragging rights, mostly, but from her tone it clearly mattered.

She looked past us, toward the front of the house.

"You don't have any lights."

We explained—politely—that we were Jewish.

She paused, as if considering whether that information was relevant.

"Well," she said finally, "you should still put up Christmas lights. Everyone needs to participate if the street is going to win."

Jillian calmly tried to address this neighbor's suggestion.

"We don't celebrate Christmas."

Our neighbor's mouth tightened.

"If Riverbend doesn't win," she said, "people are going to notice."

Then she excused herself curtly from our home.

Afterward, Jillian and I had a good laugh—not because it was funny, but because it was absurd. I'd encountered that kind of ignorance before. It rarely lingered, but it always clarified where you stood.

A few days later, I left on a work trip.

When I returned the next week, the front of our house was lit like a stage.

Bright lights covered the façade. At the center, ten feet high, a blue Star of David blazed.

I hadn't known Jillian was planning it.

I didn't know the neighbor's visit had stayed with her.

I didn't need to say anything.

It was perfect.

Riverbend didn't win the contest. That wasn't the point.

The point was the question it raised: had we jumped too quickly into a community we didn't know?

Before we purchased, we had exactly two days to find a house. That turned out to be optimistic in the hot market of Boulder County.

Anything inside Boulder's open-space belt was out of reach financially. *(See Inside the Story: How Boulder Protected Its Open Space.)*

With time compressed, our options narrowed.

We settled on a two-year-old house in a new tract development called Rock Creek, in the town of Superior.

Tract developments weren't our style. But it was a corner house with lots of space, on a cul-de-sac and in the right school district. The price worked. With three small kids, it felt like a reasonable compromise.

Back then, calling Superior a town was generous. There were a handful of old mining houses, an abandoned coal mine, and what little downtown it once had had been carved up decades earlier by Highway 36. Rock Creek itself was brand new—scraped out of prairie and dust in the early '90s, two hundred houses finished, with thousands more promised on paper. It felt provisional, like a place still waiting to see who would show up.

It wasn't ideal. We didn't know anyone in Boulder or Rock Creek and moving there felt like a Hail Mary. But we had done that before—Hawaii had been the same—and it had worked.

So, we jumped again.

The second knock came from another neighbor. She asked if she could come in and speak to both of us. Once seated, she said she had just left a neighborhood meeting and felt horrible.

"What meeting?" I asked. "We weren't notified."

She hesitated. Then said it.

The meeting had been about whether neighbors should continue to allow their children to play with the Jewish kids on Riverbend.

Our kids.

The meeting had been held two doors down, at our children's pediatrician's home.

She explained who attended. What was said. Why it had been discussed.

I listened without interrupting until my chest felt tight and my hands felt cold.

I stopped her mid-sentence—not because I had heard enough, but because I couldn't hear any more. I walked her to the door, opened it, motioned for her to leave, and closed it again without a word.

Jillian and I stood in silence.

Later that afternoon when all the kids were out back playing in the yard, nothing was different. Yet everything was different.

Outside, the street looked the same.

But it never felt the same.

That spring, I admitted what I had been avoiding since December.

Rock Creek was never going to be home—not because of the houses or the schools, but because we now knew what was discussed when we weren't invited into the room.

We put the house up for sale.

Some might call that retreat.

I didn't.

We saved our powder for fights that mattered more than arguing with neighbors who had already decided who our children were allowed to be.

We moved.

ANOTHER BULLET DODGED

Later, I learned that the meeting had been a weekly Bible study attended by a group of evangelical Christians who occupied several homes near ours in Rock Creek.

They had gathered to study a book that says:

Love thy neighbor.

Learning Points:

- *Neighbors are not automatically allies.*
- *Prejudice often arrives politely.*
- *Leaving is not always retreat; sometimes it is judgment.*

Inside the Story *(Optional Reading)*

How Boulder Protected Its Open Space

During the 1960s, the city of Boulder and Boulder County adopted a land-use strategy that would permanently shape the character of the region. Concerned that rapid growth from nearby Denver might eventually consume the town, local voters approved a one-cent sales tax dedicated to purchasing undeveloped land around Boulder.

The goal was simple: create a publicly owned ring of open land that would prevent suburban sprawl from reaching the city. Over time, the program acquired tens of thousands of acres surrounding Boulder, forming what became known as the Boulder Open Space system. The preserved land created a natural buffer several miles wide around much of the city.

The policy was widely praised as a forward-thinking conservation measure. It protected mountain views, preserved wildlife habitat, and ensured that residents would retain easy access to trails and outdoor recreation. Boulder became known nationally for maintaining a strong connection between the city and the surrounding natural landscape.

However, the policy also had unintended economic consequences. Because development inside the open-space belt was limited and land outside it was tightly controlled by county zoning rules, the supply of new housing remained relatively constrained. Over time, rising demand for homes in the area drove property values sharply upward.

As Boulder grew more desirable—and more expensive—many families found themselves priced out of the city itself. Development shifted to nearby towns such as Superior, Louisville, Lafayette, and Erie, which became de facto suburbs serving people who worked in or wanted to live near Boulder.

The open-space policy succeeded in preserving Boulder's natural setting and distinct identity. But it also transformed the town from a relatively accessible college and outdoor community into one of the more exclusive housing markets in Colorado.

CHAPTER 19

A KNOCK AT THE DOOR

PART 2 — BETWEEN THE CRACKS

AGE 11-37 · 1969-1995

After the second knock, I had learned that knocks rarely announce what they carry. Authority, accusation, truth, hatred—they all arrive the same way. A sound at the door, and the certainty that whatever comes next will change something.

Two men stood on the porch. Dark jackets. Aviator sunglasses. Serious faces. They held their badges long enough for me to read them.

FBI.

I had done nothing wrong. I knew that—and still felt the involuntary tightening that comes when authority arrives unannounced.

They asked careful questions. Names. Dates. Transactions. They took notes while I spoke and waited in silence when I stopped.

They were investigating a man from whom Jillian and I had bought property years earlier. Bank fraud. Bankruptcy fraud. Crimes that live quietly on paper for years before anyone knocks.

When they left, the house felt unusually still.

It wasn't the first time I'd learned that lies can live comfortably for a long time before anyone challenges them.

I had heard that knock before.

Most notably when I was eleven.

On a summer evening in Cleveland Heights, just before sunset, my brother Lee, my father, and I sat on our front porch, rocking quietly. Two boys from up the street walked past. They slowed. Looked at us longer than necessary.

Then the words came.

"Dirty Kikes."

"Go back where you belong."

"Hitler should have killed you all."

Lee was over the railing before I was fully upright.

I glanced at my father, and with a subtle nod, I followed Lee—no plan, just motion.

The fight was short and chaotic.

No rules.

No technique.

Just fists and noise. Lee knew how to throw a punch. I did not—but I grabbed, pulled, and kept swinging until the shouting stopped.

When it ended, the boys from up the street were bruised and scraped, their clothes dirty, their bravado gone.

Hours later, the police came.

Lee and I were charged with assault and battery.

Two months later, we stood in juvenile court.

I had never been in a courtroom before. The room was small. The chairs were hard. The mood was serious. I remember worrying about that—I had a child's mind in an adult proceeding.

I didn't want to be sent to juvie. I didn't want to be labeled a bad kid.

My father leaned toward us and spoke to us quietly.

"Just tell the truth," he said.

"No matter what happens, it will be okay."

That helped. A little. I held his hand as we sat.

The judge—called a referee—asked me to explain what had happened.

My mouth felt dry. I told the story as clearly as I could, from the porch to the shouting to the fight. I didn't embellish. I didn't defend myself. I just talked.

When I finished, the judge turned to Lee.

"Anything to add?"

Lee filled in a few details. Nothing more.

Then the judge turned to the other boys for their story of events.

They didn't hesitate.

"It's what they said," one of the boys told him.

The judge paused, surprised.

"So you agree with their version?"

"Yes," the boy said. "We called them Kikes."

The silence that followed felt heavier than anything that had come before.

The judge turned to the parents.

"Do you see anything wrong with what your boys said?"

The father answered immediately. Loudly. Forcefully.

"No. They are Kikes and Christ killers."

My fist tightened in the hand that was not being held.

For a moment, the same rage rose in me—the thing from the porch—and I wanted to stand up, to say something, to hit someone. Instead, I felt my father's hand close around mine tighter. Firm. Steady. I stayed seated and silent.

The judge shifted in his chair. He looked at the man, then at the boys, then back at us. He seemed genuinely perplexed, as if none of his experience had prepared him for a courtroom where no one disputed the facts—only the hatred behind them.

Finally, he spoke.

"Charges dismissed on the Waldman boys."

Then he turned to the other family.

"I order you and your children to attend classes on 20th-century Jewish history and complete forty hours of community service."

The gavel came down.

ANOTHER BULLET DODGED

The pattern wasn't new. I had heard similar ugly fears a few years earlier in 1965, when some neighbors on our Cleveland Heights street gathered to debate whether the first Black family moving onto our street would bring crime and falling property values.

Learning Points:

- *Prejudice is learned at a young age.*
- *Hatred survives on permission, not intelligence.*
- *Anti-Semitism is a virus that can afflict the old, the young, the educated, the uneducated, people in rural and urban communities, white people, and minorities.*

CHAPTER 20

SPECIAL HANDLING

"You do not play hockey for good seasons, you play to win the Stanley Cup!"
—Guy Lafleur

AGE 37-43 · 1995-2001

Professional sports charters looked glamorous from the outside.

Sometimes they were.

More often they were simply airline flying with unusual passengers, unusual schedules, and occasionally unusual challenges.

Stanley Cup

By 1995, I had been at Northwest long enough to know how rare good news could be. When my seniority finally earned me a 727 captain position, I was ready for it—more than ready. After simulator training, I was based in Detroit and slid into the left seat with the kind of excitement that comes from knowing you have been preparing for a moment long before it arrives.

The timing could not have been better.

Northwest had just signed a charter contract to fly professional sports teams—NHL and NBA—on specially outfitted aircraft. Two of those teams mattered a great deal to me: the Denver Nuggets and the Colorado Avalanche. *(See Inside the Story: Northwest's Pro Sports Charter Aircraft.)*

I lived in the Denver–Boulder area, and when I could, I bid those charter trips.

For an airline pilot, life is usually measured in commutes. Mine had involved three trips a month from Denver to Minneapolis or Detroit just to start work. These charters changed that. Most were five-day trips that began and ended in my home city. Without even trying, I gained several extra days each month with my young family by not commuting.

The departures were often near midnight, after games finished. That's why senior pilots avoided them. I did not. After a decade of flying twelve-hour international legs at odd hours, a four-hour red-eye felt manageable.

In 1996, both the Avalanche and I were new. I was new to the left seat; the Avs were new to Colorado, having just moved from Quebec. The season built steadily, then decisively. By mid-April, they had won the division and rolled into the playoffs.

Vancouver fell first. Then Chicago. Then Detroit. Each series ended four games to two.

When my schedule showed I would be flying the team to Miami for a possible fourth and final game of the Stanley Cup Finals, I felt as though I had won something myself. I had grown up playing hockey, and this was special.

The Avalanche had been dominant all postseason. I was convinced they would finish it in four.

The drive to the FBO felt different than going to the main terminal. At the terminal, everything moved at once—cars stacking up at departures, people dragging bags, announcements overlapping into a low-grade chaos that never quite shut off. The FBO lived on the same airport but ran at a different tempo.

Corporate jets lined the ramp. A few arriving, a few leaving. Red carpets rolled out, then rolled back in. Engines spooled, stairs retracted, doors closed—but nothing was rushed. No crowds. No lines. No sense of being herded.

I parked, walked through the building, and headed onto the ramp toward my airplane.

The Boeing 727 was waiting where it always did for these trips, surrounded by Gulfstreams and Challengers that cost more than the office buildings the executives who flew in them worked in. The 727 dwarfed them all. It stood out on the ramp—larger, heavier, unmistakably an airline airplane among corporate machines.

Before the team arrived, I brought a new hockey stick onboard and leaned it against the back wall of the cockpit near the observer seat. It was a small, hopeful act—something I wouldn't normally do—but the moment got the better of me.

During that season, I got to know LJ, one of the Avalanche trainers. He made a point of introducing himself to the entire crew every trip. He understood the value of a go-between and became an informal liaison between the team and the cockpit crew.

When LJ poked his head into the cockpit to say hello, I asked him to step in.

"If the guys win tomorrow," I said, "do you think they'd be willing to sign my stick on the flight home?"

He picked it up, rolled it slowly in his hands, looked it over—then his expression changed.

His jaw set, and in a strong French-Canadian accent, he said sharply, "No, no, they will not sign your stick."

He set it down harder than necessary and stormed out of the cockpit.

I sat there, instantly realizing I'd crossed a line I normally wouldn't. I hadn't asked a player directly, and I hadn't technically violated the company charter rule—but his reaction made it clear I'd misjudged the moment.

The flight to Miami went off without a hitch.

The next night, the Avalanche swept the Florida Panthers and won the Stanley Cup. When the team returned to the airplane, the celebration in the back was exactly what you'd expect—loud, happy, uncontained. I stayed in the cockpit the entire flight home, keeping a low profile, replaying yesterday's cockpit indiscretion over and over in my head.

Days passed. Then weeks.

No call from the Chief Pilot.

No disciplinary message.

Nothing.

I couldn't tell whether that meant I was fine—or whether some action against me was still forthcoming.

After four weeks, I started to feel as though I was out of the woods.

Then it happen.

A large rectangular box showed up at my house.

Inside was Patrick Roy's goalie stick, signed by the entire 1996 Colorado Avalanche Stanley Cup team.

A note was enclosed:

"Dear Captain:

They would not sign that shitty stick of yours, but they signed this one for you.

See you next season."

Only then did I understand what LJ had done. He hadn't been insulted at all. He'd set me up—let me sweat it out—and then delivered the punchline a month later.

For the next five years I flew the Avalanche—wins and losses, long nights, quiet returns, and the occasional roar of a championship behind the cockpit door.

The work became familiar. The trust deepened. The boundaries stayed where they belonged.

Then in 2001 they won the Cup again, and once more a box arrived at my home—this time Joe Sakic's stick, signed by the entire roster.

Those sticks hang proudly in my home as reminders of my first years as a captain at Northwest, my time flying the Avalanche, and the crews I worked with on those charters.

I also remember how flying charters quietly improved my daily family life. That was the big win.

I hadn't earned those sticks by pushing. If I earned anything at all, it was by knowing when to stop talking—and leaving the moment alone.

Photo #35. David in the left seat of a Boeing 727 in 1996.

LA Clippers

Charter flying is relaxed—until it isn't.

In the 1997–98 preseason, the NBA scheduled an exhibition game in La Crosse, Wisconsin. The LA Clippers were flown in from Los Angeles on one of Northwest's specially configured Boeing 727s. The airplane arrived a few days before the game and then sat on the ramp, untouched, waiting for the return flight.

That part was routine.

What wasn't routine was what we found when our crew deadheaded in from Minneapolis on the day of departure.

The smell hit before we reached the cabin door.

Somehow, no one had ordered lavatory service after the five-hour inbound flight. The holding tanks were full—and had been sitting that way for three days in the sun.

Strike one.

The cabin air was thick and unmistakable. Opening windows and doors barely helped.

We had three hours before the team arrived.

La Crosse didn't have a lav truck.

That alone was unusual. Most airports had a solution. La Crosse didn't.

Strike two.

Flying five hours to Los Angeles with full lav tanks wasn't an option. Boarding a professional team onto an airplane that smelled like an outhouse wasn't an option either.

Dispatch and I worked the problem.

The nearest lav trucks were in Minneapolis and Madison—more than two hours away by road. Even if one could be driven legally on public roads, it would arrive about the same time as the chartered buses. The team would either wait outside or board a foul-smelling airplane.

Neither was acceptable.

So, we built a different plan.

We had two and a half hours before the team buses were due to arrive. The idea was simple: fly the airplane empty to Madison—a twenty-minute hop—dump the lavatory tanks there, then fly it back to La Crosse. If everything went as planned, the whole round trip would take about an hour and still leave us a time cushion back on the ramp.

Someone jokingly called it *Operation Brown Water*, and the clock started immediately.

La Crosse printed the paperwork, late. Closing the airplane took longer than it should have. When we called ATC for our clearance, our flight plan wasn't in the system. By the time we finally took off, flew the short distance, and landed in Madison, most of our planned sixty minutes was already gone.

Madison didn't go any better. The gate was still cluttered with ground equipment. The paperwork for the return leg wasn't ready. The lav dump itself took longer than expected. And once again, when we called for clearance, the route wasn't in the computer.

By the time we launched back toward La Crosse, nearly all of our cushion had evaporated.

We touched down fifteen minutes before the buses were scheduled to arrive, and for a moment I thought we had pulled it off.

Then, as we taxied off the runway, I saw them—two large red charter buses already parked on the ramp, next to the waiting fuel truck.

Strike three.

We parked, shut down, and moved fast. The crew split tasks without speaking.

I headed straight for operations.

I didn't make it twenty feet off the aft stairs.

The Clippers' head coach stepped directly into my path.

He didn't ask a question.

He stood inches from my face and began yelling—loud enough for players, staff, and crew to hear. His face was red. The veins in his neck stood out. Spittle flew as he shouted.

I said nothing.

Years of cockpit discipline held me in place even as every instinct wanted to push back.

"Why did you take my airplane for a joy ride?"

"Are you an idiot?"

"We've been waiting!"

I said nothing.

I stood at attention and took the reprimand.

He continued for several minutes, uninterrupted. When he finished, he turned his back on me and ordered the team to board.

Only after he turned away did the anger hit me—hard enough that I had to slow my breathing and focus my energy.

I needed to get to operations, but I stood there a moment longer, still in shock, letting the noise of boarding mask the emotional disconnect.

I was so angry my hands shook, and my voice cracked when I spoke with the operations agent printing the flight plan. I nearly couldn't sign my name to the release.

Inside the airplane, the cockpit was quiet as my crew waited for my decisions.

The original operational issue had already been resolved. What remained was deciding how to fly safely with the residue of the exchange. Removing the coach from the flight was within my authority—and it would have made things easier for me—but it wasn't the decision that best served Northwest, the team, or the operation.

But I was clearly not in the right headspace to fly safely, and the flight mattered more than my pride. I asked the copilot to fly the leg and barred the coach from the cockpit. The decision wasn't punitive. It was procedural—and necessary.

We pushed back twelve minutes late.

We arrived in Los Angeles early.

The team never knew there had been a problem with the airplane—the exact outcome we had worked for all afternoon.

Only afterward, standing alone, did the realization settle in. We had planned carefully, acted responsibly, salvaged a bad situation, and still absorbed the blame—publicly and without recourse.

San Antonio Spurs

Once again, I was part of the crew that flew a professional team home after a championship—this time the San Antonio Spurs, following their 1999 NBA title.

The arrival back in San Antonio was nothing like La Crosse.

As we taxied toward the ramp, I slid my side window open. Cheering came through—raw and unfiltered, cutting through the whine of the jet engines. Ten thousand fans stood behind barriers, packed shoulder to shoulder. Police vehicles idled nearby, lights turning slowly. I raised a hand and waved, and the noise swelled in response before fading again as I closed the window.

The cockpit settled back into its familiar isolation.

We shut down, opened the cockpit door, and stayed where we belonged.

The celebration happened in front of us. From the cockpit, it felt distant—contained—like weather you could see off in the distance but didn't need to fly through.

Days later, someone handed me a photograph clipped from the newspaper—our airplane on the ramp that night, surrounded by people. Many of the players had signed it for me.

I accepted it quietly.

The work had already been done.

Photo #36. Northwest Boeing 727 on the tarmac in San Antonio after arriving with the newly crowned NBA champion Spurs.

Learning Points:

- *Being conscientious at work does not mean others will see your actions in the same light.*
- *Titles can be assigned. Authority is revealed sometimes by what you choose not to do.*
- *Professionalism means absorbing pressure without passing it downstream.*

Inside the Story *(Optional Reading)*

Northwest's Pro Sports Charter Aircraft

During the mid-1990s, several professional sports leagues began moving away from commercial airline travel and toward dedicated charter aircraft. The demanding travel schedules of teams—often flying late at night immediately after games and needing to arrive rested for the next matchup—made private transportation increasingly attractive.

To meet that need, Northwest Airlines operated a small fleet of Boeing 727-200 aircraft for the NBA configured specifically for professional sports teams. The airplanes retained Northwest's exterior paint scheme and were flown by regular Northwest flight crews, but the interiors were dramatically different from a standard airline cabin.

A typical commercial 727 carried roughly 150 passengers in mixed seating, first and coach. The charter aircraft were refitted with only about 50 seats, creating a spacious environment more comparable to a large corporate jet than a traditional airliner.

The forward section of the cabin featured large leather seats for star players, including a four-person card table that often hosted high-stakes card games during flights. Behind that area were additional oversized seats for other players and coaches. Farther aft were first-class style seats for team staff, media personnel, and invited guests. Some aircraft even included amenities such as a massage table for team trainers, allowing players to receive treatment during the flight.

Under a seven-year agreement, Northwest maintained the airplanes, scheduled the flights, and provided the pilots and flight attendants. For the crews, these charters were unique assignments—still airline flying, but with a cabin full of professional athletes rather than typical passengers.

CHAPTER 21

WHEN THE BELL CRIED FIRE

In honor of the late Nikki Water

"Learning to fly an airplane taught me a way of thinking, an approach to problem-solving that was applicable and effective. Pilots are very methodical and meticulous."
—Chris Carter

AGE 39 · 1997

In the late '90s, as a relatively new captain at Northwest Airlines on the Boeing 727, I had very little seniority in the left seat. With only twelve years at the airline and just one year as a captain, I knew I'd be working the holidays in 1997—and for years to come.

It was a sacrifice I considered well worth it.

I'd finally made captain at the airline.

When the November '97 MSP 727 schedules published, one five-day trip jumped off the page: it would force a crew into a thirty-three-hour Cleveland layover on Thanksgiving Day.

Cleveland was my childhood hometown.

My parents still lived there.

A no-brainer. It had to be my first bid choice.

Luckily, most pilots avoided long Cleveland layovers. When the bids were awarded, I got the trip.

I would miss being with my own clan for the holiday—but that was inevitable anyway. At least I wouldn't be alone.

The trip began two days before Thanksgiving, on the 25th, with a five-leg day that ended in a short twelve-hour overnight in Kansas City (MCI). Day two had three legs scheduled: MCI to MSP, MSP to DTW (Detroit), ending with DTW to CLE.

It was going to be a good Thanksgiving—not just for me, but for my crew of six. All of us had been invited to the Waldman family feast at my parents' house. Instead of being alone and hungry on Thanksgiving in some ghost hotel, we'd eat a real meal in a real home and skip the annual scramble to find food on a holiday. *(See Inside the Story: Holiday Flying for Airline Crews.)*

The day before Thanksgiving is historically the busiest travel day of the year. Out of MCI we were booked to the brim: one hundred fifty passengers, three flight attendants, three pilots—with two extra pilots riding jump seat in the cockpit and an additional flight attendant riding jump seat in the back.

As we say in the industry: a butt in every seat.

It was an enjoyable time at Northwest—and especially on the 727. We were young, enthusiastic, junior in position, and genuinely excited to be working for a major airline. We were having a good trip together and had already gelled into a cohesive, high-functioning crew. We made work fun and no one complained about the holiday.

At that time, it was typical that all three pilots on a 727 were within about five years of each other's age, usually in their thirties. On this trip, I was the old dog at thirty-nine; the first officer and second officer were both around thirty-five.

The flight attendants were young too, and the three of them were scheduled to stay with our three-man cockpit crew for the entire five-day trip. (That's unheard of today.)

Trips like this built real camaraderie among the six of us. Sometimes they even sparked lifelong friendships—or romances. (I met Jillian, the mother of my three children, this way.)

That morning of the 26th, I lined the jet up on the centerline of runway 01L (zero-one left) at MCI bound for MSP.

The weather was cloudy with a 3,000-foot ceiling and five miles of visibility with light winds—well above minimums for takeoff or landing.

The copilot and I had been trading off who would fly each day, and this was my day to fly (PF). That meant the copilot worked the radios while I tried to fly smoothly and look competent in front of my new crew.

Because it was a short flight to MSP relative to the 727's capability, the fuel tanks were less than half full. Our takeoff weight was light. The runway was long, so we used a reduced-power takeoff that saves engine life and—just as important on these old, loud jets—spares the airport's neighbors from ear-shattering noise.

The tower controller gave us our clearance:

"Northwest 367, you are cleared for takeoff, runway 01L, wind 040 at 4 knots, fly runway heading, climb to 3,000 feet."

My copilot, Nikki Water—a very nice, very professional young lady—responded:

"Roger—Northwest 367 is cleared for takeoff, runway 01L Kansas City, runway heading to 3,000 feet."

I looked over at my two mates.

"You all set?"

With a head bob.

A thumbs up.

I released the brakes.

"Let's take her to MSP."

I pushed all three power levers forward and called to the second officer:

"Set reduced takeoff power."

He reached forward and fine-tuned the settings on all three engines.

The airplane started to roll—slow at first, then accelerating steadily. As airspeed increased, the cockpit grew louder, the familiar Boeing mix of wind and machinery noise invading our ears.

The controls felt normal.

The instruments behaved.

Everything looked exactly the way it should.

"Eighty knots," Nikki called. *(See Inside the Story: Takeoff Abort Decision Speeds.)*

About fifteen seconds later:

She shouted, "V1."

A second later:

"Rotate."

I pulled back on the yoke and our 727 broke the bonds of earth.

We were flying.

"Positive rate."

"Gear up."

Nikki reached over and raised the big, bulky gear lever. We heard the doors open and the wheels slam into the bays.

We were only about three hundred feet above the ground when the bell exploded in our ears—

BAH-DA-RING, BAH-DA-RING

—and the #2 engine fire warning light came on, bright red and directly in my line of sight.

My focus snapped to that light.

"Silence the bell," I shouted, forcing the words out over the alarm and the roar of air noise.

"The #2 engine is on fire.

She's still making good power.

Declare an emergency.

Stand by with the engine fire checklist."

The airplane was barely airborne.

My attention narrowed—not emotionally, but operationally.

The fire light demanded attention.

I registered it, and then deliberately took it out of my scan.

At this altitude, there was only one priority.

Fly the airplane.

(See Inside the Story: Reducing Distractions During Emergencies.)

Training took over. Pitch, power, airspeed.

I held the climb and kept the jet performing.

One thousand feet was the target altitude.

I heard Nikki on the radio: "Kansas City Tower, Northwest 367 out of 400 feet—we have an emergency with an engine fire, we need to return."

Tower answered, calmly and immediately:

"Roger. Fly runway heading, climb to 3,000 feet.

How many souls on board?

We will scramble the fire trucks."

Nikki responded, "Runway heading, climb to 3,000. We'll get you souls on board."

I didn't want to widen my scan even long enough to confirm the landing gear indicators.

"Can someone confirm the gear is up?"

"Gear is up. Lights out. Handle going off," Nikki said.

The second officer said, "Standing by with the engine fire checklist."

"Stand by until we get to 1,000 feet."

Then, to Nikki I explained: "At 1,000 feet I'll hand the airplane to you. You'll fly it and work ATC while I work the fire problem with the second officer."

"Roger. Passing through 650 feet."

The fire light still glared at me like it could burn through metal by sheer insistence.

The #2 engine on a 727 isn't out on a pylon where damage is external and less critical. It's buried in the tail, behind the cabin. If something back there is truly burning, there's less margin—less time—less forgiveness.

The red light glowed bright in my peripheral vision.

The climb to 1,000 feet felt endless.

It wasn't.

We were climbing around 1,800 feet per minute.

But time does strange things when your attention is pinned to one unacceptable fact.

"One thousand feet." She shouted, making sure I heard her.

I lowered the nose a few degrees to let the airspeed build to about 200 knots. As the jet accelerated, we cleaned up the wing—raising flaps from takeoff configuration to climb configuration.

I turned and made eye contact with Nikki before handing her the airplane.

She was focused and steady—fully in the moment.

"You have the airplane," I said. "She's clean. Climb to 3,000. Stay within fifteen miles of the airport.

If we can't get this fire out quickly, we'll want her on the ground fast."

"I have the airplane."

I turned to the second officer.

"Let's run the checklist."

I looked back at the forward instruments to confirm that Nikki had the airplane climbing properly.

She did.

"Engine Fire or Severe Damage Checklist."

"Go for it."

"Number 2 power lever—idle."

I placed my right hand on the #2 power lever and announced,

"Number 2?"

"Number 2 confirmed."

"Number 2 going to idle."

"Number 2 fire handle—pull."

I reached up and placed my hand on the #2 fire handle—the one still glowing red.

He confirmed I had the correct one.

"Number 2 fire handle pulled."

That single motion shut off fuel, hydraulics, and electrics to the engine. It also meant we were now committed to flying and landing on two engines.

"Nikki, #2 is shut down.

Lower the nose a smidge.

You're doing great."

"Number two engine fire extinguisher."

I pointed to the button and held there.

"Confirmed."

"Discharging."

The red glare disappeared.

The cockpit changed instantly.

"The fire is out.

Let ATC know. Souls on board is 159.

How's she flying?"

"She's flying great. I'm on downwind and I'll extend until you're ready."

"Northwest 367 level 3,000. The fire is out. 159 souls on board. Request extended downwind."

"The airspace is yours.

Call your turn whenever you are ready."

The second officer and I continued the engine shutdown checklist.

Once complete, the second officer shifted into calculations mode—landing weight, speeds, runway requirements, and whether we needed to dump fuel or not.

I'd done his job years before. I knew exactly how busy he was about to become.

Nikki held the airplane steady.

Then, loud enough for both of them to hear, I announced, "The fire is secured."

I let that sink in for a few seconds.

"Everyone, take a deep breath.

We do not have to rush.

TAKE YOUR TIME."

"Nikki, use the autopilot and set up the ILS for runway 01L. The Second O is running the numbers. I'll step out of the loop to call the flight attendants, company, and talk to the passengers."

In stereo I heard: "Roger."

I knew they had it.

First, I called the company and told them we'd declared an emergency with an engine shut down. I asked them to set up a gate and a ground crew at MCI, and to prepare for the passenger fallout.

Next, I called the lead flight attendant.

"We had an engine fire indication on takeoff.

The fire light is out now.

We're returning to Kansas City.

We'll be on the ground in about ten minutes.

We will not evacuate.

We will taxi to a gate and deplane normally.

Please repeat that back to me. And then I'll make a PA."

She read my instruction back to me—perfectly. There was a slight hesitation in her voice. Normal. Understandable.

Before she hung up, I added, quietly,

"Don't worry. We'll be OK."

I heard her exhale. A small sound.

Enough for me to know.

Then I picked up the PA mic.

"Ladies and gentlemen, this is your captain speaking. Some of you may have noticed we stopped climbing and Kansas City is still below us. Shortly after takeoff, we received an engine fire warning on one of our three engines. We shut that engine down and the warning light is now out. However, because of that event we will not be continuing to Minneapolis."

I paused.

"The airplane is flying normally on two engines. My crew is trained for this situation. We'll be landing back in Kansas City shortly and taxiing to the gate. You will deplane normally."

I added, "You will see fire trucks after landing. This is precautionary. The fire is out.

Now, please listen closely to the flight attendants' instructions.

Thank you for your patience."

"I'm back in the loop," I said.

"Cabin and company briefed.

Nikki, I can take the airplane back if you want to brief me on what you've set up and get us a turn toward the field."

"You have the airplane."

"I have the airplane."

Nikki called ATC, and Approach Control vectored us for the instrument landing on runway 01 Left at MCI.

As we turned back in, Nikki briefed me on what she and the second officer had set up while I was tied up talking to the cabin and company. They had quietly managed the airplane, the radios: ILS tuned, speeds set, plan agreed upon, workload managed.

Calm. Thorough. Unhurried. Methodical.

If I hadn't known we had an engine shut down, I would have thought it was an ordinary approach.

That is exactly what you want from fellow professional pilots.

She finished the approach brief. The second officer briefed the differences for a two-engine configuration approach. Then I briefed the go-around plan, because even with everything going right, you never fly an approach without an exit plan.

We'd decided Nikki would be pilot flying to touchdown.

Then I said, "You have the airplane back."

"I have the airplane," she responded.

A few minutes later Approach called: "Northwest 367, turn 340 degrees. Intercept the 01L localizer. You are cleared the ILS runway 01L. Contact tower on 128.20. Fire equipment is standing by.

Good luck."

We checked in with the Tower and were cleared to land.

When the talking was done, all that was left was configuring the airplane for landing, completing the landing checklist, and watching Nikki make it look easy.

Minutes later, she did.

She rolled that big Boeing onto the pavement with the lightest touchdown force possible. After touchdown, she used moderate reverse thrust and light braking.

To the people in back, it felt… normal.

"Eighty knots," I called out.

"I have the airplane."

I brought ship #289 to a full stop on the runway.

I made eye contact with Nikki.

"Nice work.

That landing just lowered the blood pressure in all twenty-six rows behind us."

I looked back at the second officer. "Great work too."

I don't remember his name today, but I remember his performance. He was calm, organized, and exactly where he needed to be throughout the emergency. He handled it flawlessly.

After any fire event, protocol demands we stop on the runway so fire rescue can inspect the aircraft before we taxi.

Three large green Oshkosh fire trucks surrounded the airplane, lights flashing, and water cannons pointed directly at us. It probably looked terrifying out the cabin windows. It was the price of prudence.

"Northwest ship #289," Fire Rescue, "We have used thermal imaging to look for hot spots under the skin in your aft tail area and find no indication of fire. We will follow you to the gate."

"Roger. Thank you," Nikki replied.

Before exiting the runway, I made a quick PA.

"Folks, as you can see out the windows, fire trucks are around the aircraft. They've inspected the engine area and told us there is no indication of fire at this time. We'll be taxiing to the gate where you'll deplane normally."

I paused, then added, "That beautiful approach and landing were flown by our copilot, Nikki Water."

I returned the PA microphone to its cradle and looked at Nikki. Her face had turned beet red. Humble as she was, she looked as though she wanted to crawl beneath the instrument panel.

But I meant what I said.

A smooth landing, in a moment like this, is more than comfort—it's a message.

We parked at the gate and the jetway came over quickly. A station supervisor boarded, made a PA to explain the bad news: this flight was cancelled.

As passengers filed off, the three of us stood in the galley and cockpit doorway saying goodbye. We accepted the wave of gratitude from one hundred fifty relieved travelers.

Fear has a way of sanding people down—especially when they realize they're going home alive, even if they're not going where they planned.

A few minutes later as our crew stepped out of the jetway into the gate area, the crowd applauded—briefly, almost reflexively.

It felt a bit misplaced.

We hadn't done anything extraordinary.

We had simply followed training and procedure. If there was reassurance in that moment, I hoped it wasn't about us—but about the system.

As the clapping faded, reality came back into focus: a line already snaking from the podium down the hall, and two overworked Northwest agents doing what they could with very little to work with.

Next, I called crew scheduling. Thankfully for us, they couldn't get a reserve crew in DTW to cover our later leg from DTW to CLE. The six of us would deadhead from MCI to DTW on the next flight in about four hours. (Deadhead—DH—means a working crew member rides in a passenger seat to reposition for an assigned flight later.)

That was good news for us.

Shortly after, one agent pulled me aside. "We have no seats out of MCI for your passengers until late tonight," she said. "And most of those won't connect until Thanksgiving morning."

I nodded. "Real bummer—especially the day before Thanksgiving."

Then I added, quieter, "But we aren't in a smokin' hole."

She nodded and went back to the podium.

It would be a brutal day for a lot of our passengers.

Many would sleep in airport chairs in MSP, DTW, or MEM. Others had no options offered—turned around, drove home, and missed their holiday entirely.

For those who waited at MCI, there might have been a small snack shop—but more likely, only vending machines. Pre-9/11 concourses did not have restaurants the way they do now. Ten hours is a long time to sit at a gate with nothing more substantial than a candy bar.

Instead, the station manager and I ordered food from a local restaurant, and we threw a pizza party at the gate for our stranded guests and tried to take the edge off the day.

My crew and I mingled, answered questions, and turned the event into something human instead of purely miserable. It still sucked for our customers. Their holidays had been disrupted. But at least they had food, a crew in front of them, and straight answers.

Three hours later, we left Kansas City.

The next day, my parents brought two cars to the hotel and picked up six wayward crew members for a Thanksgiving feast.

I will always remember that Thanksgiving trip.

We handled a serious emergency professionally and safely—exactly the way airline procedures are designed to work.

No improvisation.

No rushing.

Just training, coordination, and time bought through discipline.

ANOTHER BULLET DODGED

In thirty-five years at the airline, I worked twenty-one Thanksgivings. At least on that one, I wasn't hungry—nor as lonely as most.

Learning Points:

- *Professionalism is calm execution under pressure.*
- *Good training will always outperform hubris.*
- *Preparation determines whether luck ever gets a vote.*
- *Airline safety is a system—not a personality.*

DEDICATION

I dedicate this chapter to my copilot that day, Nikki Water.
She handled the airplane with professionalism and precision.
Sadly, a few years later, far too young, she lost her battle with brain cancer.
RIP, Nikki.
Thank you for your aviation mastery.

Inside the Story *(Optional Reading)*

Holiday Flying for Airline Crews

For airline pilots and flight attendants, working during major holidays is a routine part of the profession. Because airlines operate on fixed schedules year-round, flights continue Thanksgiving, Christmas, and other major holidays regardless of how many employees would prefer to be home.

Holiday trips can be especially difficult for crews because layovers often occur when much of the surrounding city has effectively shut down. Restaurants close early, hotel staffing is reduced, and many services that travelers normally rely on simply are not available.

Crews frequently arrive at their layover hotels late in the evening after a full day of flying. By that time, hotel kitchens and nearby restaurants may already be closed for the holiday. On some trips, the only food available might be vending machines—or whatever snacks the crew packed in their luggage before leaving home.

Airlines also face operational challenges during holiday periods. Passenger demand increases dramatically, particularly around Thanksgiving and Christmas, which means flights operate at or near full capacity. At the same time, staffing shortages can occur when crew members call in sick or weather disruptions ripple through already tight schedules.

These factors combine to make the holiday travel period one of the most demanding times of the year for airline operations. For crews on the road, even small comforts—such as being invited to a home-cooked meal during a layover—can turn an otherwise difficult holiday into a memorable one.

Takeoff Abort Decision Speeds

One of the most critical phases of any flight occurs during the takeoff roll, when an aircraft is accelerating down the runway but has not yet become airborne. During this short window, pilots must be prepared to decide instantly whether to continue the takeoff or abort it based on a myriad of possible system failures.

To manage this risk, aviation uses several standardized decision speeds.

The first important threshold is_80 knots. Below this speed, the aircraft is still moving relatively slowly, and there is always enough runway remaining to stop safely. For that reason, pilots are permitted to reject the takeoff for almost any abnormality—an unexpected warning light, a questionable instrument reading, or anything else that suggests the aircraft may not be functioning normally.

Above 80 knots, the situation changes rapidly. The airplane is accelerating quickly, runway remaining is decreasing, and the amount of braking energy required to stop the aircraft increases dramatically. From this point forward, the reasons to abort the takeoff become much more limited. Only serious problems—such as an engine failure, fire, or a condition that makes the aircraft unsafe to fly—justify rejecting the takeoff.

The final decision point is called_V1, sometimes referred to as the "decision speed." Once the aircraft passes V1, there is no longer enough runway remaining to safely stop the airplane under normal conditions. If a major problem occurs after V1, the pilots must continue the takeoff, get the aircraft airborne, and deal with the emergency in the air.

This system is designed to reduce the risk of high-speed rejected takeoffs, which historically have led to runway overruns and serious accidents. In many cases, it is safer to get the aircraft airborne—even with a problem—and return to land using the full length of the runway rather than attempting to stop with only a small amount of pavement remaining.

Reducing Distractions During Emergencies

Modern aviation training emphasizes a simple but critical hierarchy of priorities during any emergency:_first fly the airplane, then navigate, then communicate and solve the problem. This order exists because many accidents in earlier decades occurred when flight crews became distracted by a malfunction and neglected the basic task of controlling the aircraft.

Human factors research has shown that unexpected warnings—especially loud alarms or flashing lights—can capture a pilot's full attention. When that happens during high-workload phases of flight such as takeoff or landing, even a few seconds of distraction can lead to loss of control.

For that reason, pilots are trained to delay troubleshooting certain emergencies until the aircraft is safely established in flight. During takeoff the first objective is to maintain control of the airplane, achieve a safe climb, and reach an altitude that provides both time and margin to deal with the malfunction.

This principle applies even in situations that appear urgent, such as an engine fire warning. Attempting to diagnose or fight a fire while the aircraft is still only a few hundred feet above the ground can create a far greater danger than the malfunction itself. In many cases it is safer to let a problem engine continue running for a short time while the aircraft climbs to a safe altitude, rather than risk losing control of the airplane while distracted by the emergency.

On multi-crew aircraft such as the Boeing 727, responsibilities are deliberately divided during these moments. One pilot focuses exclusively on flying the airplane, another handles communication with air traffic control, and a third crew member assists with the emergency checklist and system management.

This structured division of labor—part of the broader philosophy known as Crew Resource Management (CRM)—helps crews manage emergencies methodically rather than emotionally. The objective is simple: never allow the emergency to distract the crew from the primary task—flying the airplane safely.

"Pilots should not be rushed into the fray, just as the Wright brothers achieved their remarkable flight through carefully planned methodological processes."
(Wilbur Wright)

CHAPTER 22

CLOSE TO THE EDGE

"When everything seems to be going against you, remember that the airplane takes off into the wind, not with it."
—Henry Ford

AGE 42 · 2000

For two hours, we cruised west from Boston at 34,000 feet—smooth and uneventful. The sky was clear. The airplane was stable. Outside air temperature sat at −55 degrees Celsius, leaving the aluminum skin deeply super-cooled.

To a pilot, it felt like any other winter leg into the upper Midwest—right up to the clouds.

As we descended toward Minneapolis, we turned on engine anti-ice before entering the weather.

Routine.

Automatic.

A small switch movement that didn't interrupt conversation—or thought.

Over TWINZ intersection, a published navigation point on the arrival into Minneapolis, at 11,000 feet, the world outside turned gray. Ice appeared on the windshield wiper post almost immediately—light, ordinary, and of no great concern.

Downwind of the airport, as we flew away from Minneapolis and descended to 8,000 feet, the temperature slid into a range we all recognized without saying it.

The temperature band we'd all learned to respect.

Minus fifteen degrees.

Colder than this, moisture arrives already frozen and doesn't adhere to the airframe. Above the freezing temperature, water hits the airplane and just runs off. But here—right in between 0 and minus 15 degrees—the droplets stayed liquid until impact, then froze instantly. *(See Inside the Story: How Ice Forms on Jet Aircraft.)*

They didn’t streak away.

They piled on.

We switched on wing heat.

Still not out of the ordinary.

“Approach, Northwest 674, we’re in moderate icing and need a lower altitude,” my copilot said, his voice steady.

“Maintain 8,000. Expect a turn in_five miles.”

I nodded, more to myself than to anyone else. Five miles_was reasonable. It meant a quick turn back toward the field and, with it, a descent out of the icing layer.

Five miles passed in about minute.

No turn.

In that airspace, turns and descents weren’t ours to take.

We could ask for changes, but until we were cleared, we stayed exactly where we were.

The ice continued to build.

Power crept higher.

“Approach, Northwest 674—we’re now in heavy icing.

We need lower—now.”

“Maintain 8,000. Five more miles_before your turn.”

No urgency in the controller’s voice. I’d heard that tone before—usually from someone who wasn’t feeling what we were feeling.

Five more miles zipped by again.

The pitch attitude continued to creep up just to hold altitude.

Not dramatic.

But persistent.

The kind of change that doesn’t belong in level flight. There was only one explanation.

We were carrying a lot of ice.

I adjusted the power again. The engines responded, but the airplane still felt wrong. Not enough to trigger an emergency checklist. Enough to trigger concern from years of winter flying.

We flew past the point where we normally would have turned back toward the airport.

I glanced at the distance measuring equipment, then back at the wiper post. The ice was thicker now—noticeably so.

We requested a lower altitude—again.

The controller’s voice came back strained now.

I could tell he was approaching task saturation.

But empathy didn't keep ice off the airplane, and what we needed was warmer air and an exact answer about when we would turn and descend.

The quiet in the cockpit fractured as the ice kept forming and the margin kept shrinking.

"Approach, Northwest 674—we are in extreme icing conditions. We need an immediate descent."

There was a pause—long enough to remind me we weren't alone in the sky. That others on this arrival were also squawking for altitude changes.

Ice continued to thicken on the wiper post.

Even windshield heat struggled to keep pace.

None of us spoke, but all three of us were watching the same places, waiting for the systems to catch up.

It never did.

Finally, ATC came back—not with an acknowledgment of the ice or any help, but with routine sequencing.

"You're number six for landing. Descend to 6,000. Slow to 180 knots."

Slowing made it worse.

Descending those two thousand feet didn't help either.

At 6,000 feet the temperature changed only enough to put us deeper into the icing band. Accretion didn't slow—it accelerated.

The airplane felt more sluggish now—not unstable, but burdened. Control inputs needed more intent behind them.

We flew past 20 miles downwind.

Still no turn.

Still no further descent.

Ice continued to accumulate at a rate I had never seen in twenty-four years of flying.

I looked at the first officer. He didn't look back. His eyes stayed on the approach chart clipped to his yoke, as if staring at it might somehow get us what we needed.

I waited one beat longer than I should have.

As a captain, I was trained to cooperate—but also to recognize when cooperation had reached its limit.

"This isn't working," I said. "Declare the emergency.

No more leniency."

Declaring an emergency was escalation.

It was the only way left to reclaim control.

"Approach, Northwest 674 declaring an emergency. We need 3,000 or 12,000 immediately."

Silence.

The kind that stretches too long.

"Approach, Northwest 674 declaring an emergency."

Still nothing.

That silence carried weight.

Not panic—ownership.

The moment you realize the system has stepped aside, and what happens next belongs completely to you.

Then the radio came alive.

"Northwest 674, turn left 210, maintain 6,000 feet."

I was already rolling into the turn before the controller finished speaking.

The cloud stayed solid.

Ice kept forming.

The situation didn't improve—the turn only meant the wreckage would be closer to the runway if we lost it here.

Again, I said to my crew. "We can't stay in this layer.

Declare it—make him acknowledge."

Before my copilot could key the mic, the controller came back, faster, more urgent.

"Northwest 674, turn left 120. Descend to 4,000. Cleared for the ILS one-two Left. Maintain 160 knots."

I pulled the power back and pitched down without hesitation.

The second officer reached forward and advanced the thrust levers just enough to keep the anti-ice systems operating at full capacity, while I extended the speed brakes to steepen our descent.

We all hoped 4,000 feet would be warm enough.

The airplane dropped through the cloud like a rock.

At 4,500 feet, the ice accumulation finally began to slow.

At 4,000 feet, the accumulation nearly stopped.

It took a moment for that to register fully.

No one spoke.

We stared outside at the wiper post, still shocked at what we were seeing.

The tension in the cockpit didn't leave all at once. It drained slowly—like pressure bleeding off a hydraulic line.

At least now we were pointed at the runway.

Every minute brought us closer instead of carrying us farther away.

We were still heavy.

Still carrying tons of ice.

But at least it wasn't getting worse.

By Minnesota winter standards, the weather at Minneapolis–St. Paul wasn't bad at all—a 2,000-foot ceiling, 6 miles of visibility, and a temperature just below freezing.

The final leg of the approach was long—very long—held at 160 knots by ATC due to the traffic ahead of us.

At around 2,500 feet we finally broke out of the bottom of the clouds, and for the first time in more than 25 minutes the moisture stopped pinging off the windshield.

The runway came into view straight ahead.

One airplane was ahead of us, just touching down.

Our touchdown itself was uneventful. *(See Inside the Story: Why the Boeing 727 Was Difficult to Land Smoothly.)*

Which was exactly what we needed.

We rolled to a stop on the diagonal exit taxiway.

All three of us paused, looked at each other, and knew—without saying it—that we had just shared something close to the edge.

At the gate the passengers complained about being late.

We let them.

ANOTHER BULLET DODGED

After the passengers deplaned, I walked down the jetway and onto the ramp to look her over myself.

Up close, the airplane looked unreal.

Thousands of ice nodules clung to the fuselage and wings—the size of grapefruits.

Every slightly protruding rivet head carried a white half-sphere of frozen water.

The wing leading edges and engine inlets were free of ice. Those were the only areas protected by heat; everything else was shrouded.

In my judgment, we were carrying on the order of ten thousand pounds of ice—far more than any of us were comfortable with.

Even rampers stopped to stare.

I recognize those looks.
That meant the danger had finally become visible.
A few even asked, "You flew that?"
"Not proudly," I said. "But she did her job."

Learning Points:

- *Mother Nature can ruin your day in an instant—with only water.*
- *Sometimes the most important details are invisible, while the obvious ones distract everyone else.*
- *Calm flights build habits; rare ones test judgment.*

Inside the Story *(Optional Reading)*

Standard Terminal Arrival Routes (STARs)

Aircraft arriving at busy airports are often assigned published procedures called_Standard Terminal Arrival Routes, or STARs.

A STAR is essentially a predefined path that guides aircraft from the en route phase of flight toward the airport's approach area. The route contains a series of navigation fixes where aircraft change direction, altitude, and/or speed while air traffic control sequences traffic for landing.

The_Eau Claire–TWINZ arrival_was one of the standard routes used for aircraft approaching Minneapolis–St. Paul from the east.

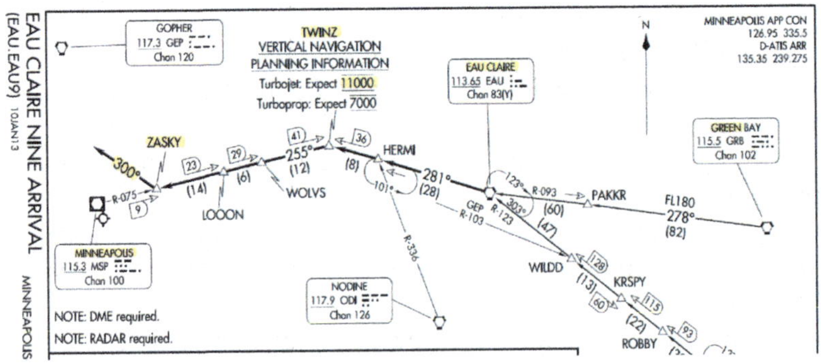

Eau Claire TWINZ arrival STAR
(See Inside the Story: Standard Terminal Arrival Routes (STARs).)

By assigning aircraft to the same arrival path, controllers can organize traffic efficiently while maintaining safe spacing between airplanes.

How Ice Forms on Jet Aircraft

Ice accumulation on an aircraft is one of the most significant winter hazards pilots face. It occurs when an aircraft flies through clouds containing supercooled liquid water droplets—water that remains liquid even though the surrounding air temperature is below freezing.

When these droplets strike the aircraft's surface, they freeze immediately. As ice builds on the wings and other structures, two serious problems develop.

First, ice adds weight to the aircraft. Even a thin coating across a large surface can increase the amount of lift required to remain airborne.

Second—and more critically—ice alters the shape of the wing. Aircraft wings are carefully designed aerodynamic surfaces. When ice distorts that shape, airflow over the wing becomes less efficient, reducing lift and increasing drag.

The most dangerous icing conditions usually occur in clouds where temperatures range between 0°C and about −15°C.

Photo #37. Cloud/temperature depiction for ice formation.

In colder air, most cloud moisture is already frozen into ice crystals that do not stick easily to aircraft surfaces. In warmer air above freezing, liquid water tends to run off before freezing.

Because temperature changes roughly 2°C for every 1,000 feet of altitude, even a relatively small climb or descent can sometimes move an aircraft out of, or into the most severe icing layer.

Modern jetliners use anti-ice systems to protect the most critical areas of the aircraft from ice buildup. Hot compressed air from the engines—called bleed air—is routed through the leading edges of the wings and engine inlets to keep those surfaces warm enough to prevent ice from forming.

However, these systems protect only selected portions of the aircraft. Large areas of the fuselage and other structures remain unheated, which means pilots must monitor icing conditions carefully and change altitude if ice accumulation becomes excessive.

Why the Boeing 727 Was Difficult to Land Smoothly

Among airline pilots, the Boeing 727-200 developed a reputation for being one of the more difficult jetliners to land smoothly. The airplane's aerodynamic design and the geometry of the main landing gear placement behind the center of lift exacerbated the challenge during landing. Because of this, the 727 required careful timing in the final moments before touchdown.

Most aircraft land smoothly when the pilot gently raises the nose just before the wheels contact the runway, reducing the rate of descent and softening the contact with the runway. On the 727 stretched version, however, since the wheels are behind the center of lift, that action—unless timed perfectly—had the effect of driving the landing gear hard onto the pavement with a firm thud.

Over time, many pilots developed small techniques to manage this behavior. One commonly used method involved applying a very slight forward pressure on the control yoke just before touchdown. Instead of increasing the pitch attitude in the final seconds, the subtle forward input allowed the landing gear to meet the runway without a downward thrust while the airplane's vertical motion was already stabilizing.

The result, when executed correctly, was the satisfying sound pilots aimed for—a light "chirp" as the tires first contacted the runway.

Like many aircraft-specific techniques, it was not something found in manuals. It was knowledge passed informally from one generation of pilots to the next.

CHAPTER 23

Dedicated to the nearly 3,000 Americans who died 9/11/2001

SEPTEMBER 11TH CHANGED EVERYTHING

"The world is too dangerous to live in—not because of the people who do evil, but because of the people who sit and let it happen."
—Albert Einstein

AGE 43 · 2001

Impact

The phone rang at home in Boulder, and my sister didn't bother with hello.

"Turn on the TV. An airplane just crashed into one of the towers."

I stood there for a second, receiver in my hand, as if the extra moment might keep the sentence from being true. Then I crossed the room and found the remote.

The screen came alive with a blue September sky and a building that shouldn't be smoking.

Jillian sat down beside me without a word. The kids were already at school. The house had that hollow quiet of an ordinary day after everyone has gone.

The camera stayed wide. The tower stood there, wounded and upright. The smoke didn't drift or curl—it poured out in a thick, purposeful stream, like something inside the building had been ruptured.

The commentators filled the air with guesses. Navigation error. Disoriented pilot. Controller mistake. Confusion. Accident.

I felt my back straighten without conscious thought, like a harness locking.

The sky over Manhattan was CAVU—perfect flying weather. High cirrus. Visibility that made flying easy. Forgiving.

A professional crew does not fly a transport-category jet into a skyscraper in that weather. Not by mistake. *(See Inside the Story: Why the World Trade Center Collapse Was Different from the Empire State Building Crash.)*

Jillian turned toward me. She didn't ask anything. She didn't need to. She could feel the thought forming in my head.

I didn't say terrorism. My mouth stayed closed. My hands stayed busy. They kept adjusting the channel—ABC, then CNN, then NBC—as if the right setting might correct the picture.

On screen, the camera framed the towers like fixed points.

Then the second airplane entered the frame.

It came in fast—too fast for that airspace—and steady. Not wandering. Not hunting. It flew like it knew exactly where it was going.

When it disappeared into steel and glass, the sound in the studio changed. The commentators stopped talking like professionals and started talking like people.

My stomach dropped hard. My brain did the opposite. It went flat and cold—the way it does when you're staring at something no training ever named.

This wasn't an accident.

This was a takeover—the kind no checklist prepares you for.

In a quiet living room, on an ordinary weekday morning, I watched the world step off a ledge and realized it wasn't ever coming back the same way. *(See Inside the Story: Airline Hijacking Procedures Before 9/11.)*

Control

By that afternoon the U.S. airspace system was shutting down in a way none of us had ever experienced. Aircraft everywhere were being told to land—now, wherever they were. Crews didn't question it. Controllers didn't negotiate. The order carried a gravity that made compliance automatic.

In the days that followed, the country looked the same but felt completely different.

People who had never thought twice about flying couldn't stop looking skywards at the lack of contrails. People who had always traveled easily now spoke about flying the way you talk about something dangerous but necessary.

People were stranded everywhere—hotels filled, rental cars vanished, highways clogged. Some slept in terminals. Some on floors. Some were taken in by strangers.

For airline crews, the time on the ground felt hostile in a way we weren't trained for. We knew how to manage risk in the air. Now the risk had moved into the terminal, into the aisle, into conversations that never used to matter.

On Friday, September 14th, Northwest planned a limited system restart.

My schedule had me working that day.

On paper, it was routine: Detroit to LaGuardia, back to Detroit, then onward. But plans had stopped meaning much.

At DTW, even getting to the gate felt foreign. The employee shortcuts were gone. Crew badges no longer opened quiet doors. Lines crawled. Bags were opened. Hands ran over bodies. Secondary checks by contract security appeared without warning—sometimes waved off, sometimes not.

Law enforcement uniforms were everywhere in the terminal. Body armor. Rifles. Pistols carried openly. I'd spent my adult life around authority, but this felt different. It didn't feel safer. It felt louder.

A new piece of hardware waited for us on the airplane, and it changed everything: a locking bar behind the cockpit door. A simple pivoting steel bar. Once lowered, the cockpit might as well have been sealed off with concrete.

The FAA guidance was blunt: the door stays closed. The door stays locked. No one comes in. No one goes out.

No breaks.

No visits.

No meals brought forward.

Pilots were being sealed inside their workplace.

My copilot—experienced, and older than I—looked at me like the new rules were a bad joke. "I pee every two hours," he said, not complaining. Just stating his reality. "How are we supposed to do this?"

"Pee before pushback," I said. "If we get stuck holding near New York, you'll be peeing into a bottle in the back of the cockpit."

We tried to laugh. It didn't land.

For a while after 9/11, that bottle really did become the solution. The 727 cockpit was big enough to make it possible. Still, there was something degrading about it—being told that dignity was now a negotiable item if you wanted to keep flying.

We were ready to leave DTW when we hit the next reality snag: we had no flight attendants.

Crew Scheduling didn't soften it. Sick calls were off the chart. Fear was winning the day.

The FAA didn't care about fear. They cared about rules. They cared about numbers. They cared that we had three flight attendants on the aircraft before boarding could commence.

So, eighty-five passengers waited in the gate area, watching an airport filled with weapons, wondering whether going home was worth the risk of not getting there.

Violation

An hour later when three flight attendants finally arrived, they looked worn thin. Professional smiles stretched just enough to pass scrutiny.

We gathered in first class for a briefing that felt heavier than any I'd given before.

"I don't have wisdom for what we've all lived through," I told them. "But if I didn't feel safe to fly, I wouldn't go. I have a family I want to get home to also. Today, I believe we're as safe as we can be."

They nodded. Not in comfort. In resolve.

We boarded. The agent closed the door. We ran the checklist. The ramp cleared us to push. We called the tug operator and gave the go-ahead call.

The tug's brakes were released.

Then the tug operator's voice snapped into my headset.

"Captain, we've got three police cars that have just surrounded your aircraft. Lights flashing and all. We can't push. Set the brakes."

I set the parking brake and looked out the window. Red and blue light washed over aluminum and glass and reflected off the wet tarmac.

The cockpit seemed to shrink, the air suddenly quiet and constrained.

A flight attendant called the cockpit.

"Passengers are getting upset back here," she said.

"They see the lights. You should make an announcement."

"I don't know anything yet," I said. "Give me a minute."

The first officer called the ramp tower.

"Someone on your flight just came up on the FBI watch list," came the reply. "Jetway's coming back. The passenger will be removed. His bags pulled. Your flight's on hold."

I made a brief PA. Controlled. Factual.

The jetway nudged the airplane. Police boarded.

From the cockpit we couldn't see the removal, but we could feel the shift. Anxiety moved through the cabin the way turbulence-induced airsickness moves through an airplane—first localized, then everywhere at once.

Then came the call that broke the day open.

"Captain," the flight attendant said, her voice tight and scared, "three bearded men just stood up, took separate locations in the aisle. They put prayer rugs down. They're praying. Out loud, in a language I don't recognize."

In another time, it would have meant little.

On September 14th, 2001, on a flight bound for New York, it was a spark dropped into fuel.

The cabin was already carrying too much fear. People hadn't come to fly—they'd come to survive the act of flying. Every sound, every movement, every deviation from normal felt amplified. Context no longer existed. Only threat.

Shouting surged in the cabin. Voices overlapped. Some screamed.

Passengers poured off the airplane into the jetway, then into the gate area, fear spilling out with them—no one tried to stop them.

Then the flight attendants flooded off too.

They faced me under harsh jetway lights; their expressions told the story.

"We're not flying to New York," one of them said.

"Not with those passengers."

I tried reason. I tried calm.

"They're Americans. Praying isn't illegal.

They are likely scared, just as are most Americans."

It didn't move them.

And the truth was, it didn't fully move me either.

I was angry—angry at the timing, angry at the choice to pray in the aisle, angry at how it landed like a challenge in a room already on edge.

Three days after the attacks, with the country raw, why provoke anything?

I didn't know what they meant by it. I still don't. But I knew what it did.

All three flight attendants walked away from me.

I started calling up the chain. Operations. Scheduling. Dispatch.

Scheduling had nothing. No replacement flight attendants.

Dispatch didn't dress it up.

"Captain, you've got two options. Cancel the flight or remove those passengers. The call is yours. We'll back you either way."

The support sounded generous. It really wasn't.

Bad or worse—that was how the choices shook out. I needed a good choice, but none was forthcoming.

I returned to the gate area and found the cabin crew unraveling. They weren't being dramatic. They were spent. They were crying. They were saying the same sentence over and over like a mantra.

"We're not going."

Meanwhile, the police finished their work with the watch-list passenger. The passenger—the one who had started this whole cascade without meaning to—was re-cleared.

"All good," the officer told me. "Passenger can reboard."

That changed nothing.

The immediate danger now wasn't physical. It was emotional, and it was feeding itself.

For an hour I tried to bring the crew back. I tried logic. I tried reassurance. I tried authority. Nothing worked.

"We won't fly with them onboard."

It wasn't said in anger. It was said as a decision wrapped in fear.

I stepped away from the gate to clear my head and walked the concourse alone. Everywhere I looked were armed officers. If fear was driving this, maybe visible protection could blunt it.

I found a lone U.S. Park Ranger and asked if he could travel with us as an armed law enforcement officer. He hesitated—then keyed his radio, spoke quietly to someone I couldn't hear, and waited. A minute later he nodded. His supervisor approved it.

We walked to the gate area together.

I introduced him to the crew, matter-of-factly, like I was simply adding a new crew member.

Two flight attendants exhaled, visibly.

One didn't.

"Not a chance," she said, voice shaking. "Three attackers against one guy with a handgun? Either they're off, or I'm going home."

We needed three flight attendants to dispatch. Her fear had become leverage strong enough to stop an airplane.

We tried again—logic, procedure, coordination. Nothing changed her mind.

Passengers hovered nearby, watching. They'd waited days to get home. Now they were watching their one chance slip away.

The decision settled into my chest like an enormous weight.

As a Jew, I knew what it felt like to be singled out because of religion. I didn't want to do that to these men.

They'd been searched. Twice. They showed no overt malice. If they were terrorists, they'd chosen the dumbest possible moment to reveal themselves.

But the airplane wasn't a courtroom. It was a pressure vessel.

Canceling the flight would strand everyone longer and hand fear the levers of power.

Removing three men would leave a different wound.

A scar I'd carry, cut deep enough to ache long after the moment passed.

I had the three men removed by airport police.

They didn't fight. They looked stunned and humiliated as they were escorted out of the gate area.

Then the flight attendants reboarded. Then the passengers reboarded.

Three hours late, the airplane finally pushed back.

It wasn't a good solution.

It was the only one left.

Aftermath

The flight to New York was quiet in the way you get when everyone is ashamed of what they just saw and still can't say they'd do anything differently.

The cockpit stayed sealed. The new locking bar sat behind us like a commandment.

Approaching Manhattan from the southwest on a clear day, the visibility was cruel. You could see for miles. The arrival route brought us adjacent to the Statue of Liberty, the river stretching ahead like a corridor. At ten thousand feet, the skyline should have had two anchor points.

It didn't.

The absence was louder than the city.

Lower Manhattan still bled smoke. Gray, heavy, relentless. The column marched north up the Avenues with the wind like a wound that refused to close.

On a normal day, flying the Hudson River invited a casual PA—"Look out your right side."

That day I said nothing.

If passengers saw it, they saw it. I wasn't going to narrate grief.

We followed the river north to the George Washington Bridge, then turned east toward LaGuardia.

Inside the cockpit, nobody spoke. Not because there was nothing to say, but because explaining it would have dulled something that needed to be felt.

Meaning

That week split aviation careers into two eras.

Before, the system ran on trust—trust that screening worked, that rules held, that a cockpit couldn't simply be taken.

After, it ran on fear, displays of force, and policies written fast enough to look like control.

The economic damage followed quickly. Passenger demand collapsed and never returned in time. Airlines bled cash trying to survive in a world where airplanes had become symbols of danger instead of freedom.

Bankruptcies followed, including my own airline's.

For pilots, bankruptcy wasn't abstract. It rewrote contracts, erased protections, and cut pay deeply and permanently. My income dropped by roughly half and never fully recovered. The career I finished was not the one I'd built toward, and the break traced directly back to that day.

I lost a college classmate on 9/11—Jason Dahl, captain of United Flight 93. He and others fought the hijackers, and the airplane crashed in Shanksville, Pennsylvania.

The cost to his family is honestly beyond anything I can write.

What I can write is this: those of us who kept flying carried a different weight into the cockpit. The job stopped being only about weather, systems, and judgment. It became about being the front door of a national trauma, flight after flight. *(See Inside the Story: How 9/11 Changed an Airline Career.)*

Months later, the three passengers removed from my flight sued Northwest and me. The company backed my decision and eventually removed me from the legal process.

I was never told the outcome.

What stayed with me wasn't the lawsuit.

It was the moment.

I had managed risk and safely delivered my passengers to their destination. Yet I was still complicit in harm.

Professionalism doesn't always protect you from moral residue.

Sometimes the job wears you down, not with danger, but with decisions that don't heal.

Shortly after that flight, I wrote this poem for my passengers. I read it on every flight for the rest of 2001.

Welcome Back
DBW 9/15/2001

I fly airplanes, that's what I do.
The big, beautiful Boeings painted red, white and blue.
It's a childhood dream, one that came true.
So welcome aboard, from your captain and crew.

Our lives have all changed, and it seems so unfair.
Yet flying is…still the best way to get you there.
So, as you stow your stuff, and settle in your chair.
I want you to know, your crew really does care!

You now are our guests, please try and relax too.
Enjoy the marvel of flight and perhaps take in the view.
For I have one promise, I will make to you.
We shall keep you safe, I know that to be true.

You mustn't worry, fret, or despair.
Our job is your well-being, both on the ground and in the air!
For no chances will we take, as the captain…I do swear!
We shall deliver you safe, to waiting loved ones… Everywhere!

Learning Points:

- *It is a shame that it often takes a disaster for Americans to remember they are one people.*
- *Systems designed for ordinary times are often overwhelmed by extraordinary events.*
- *Fear narrows options and can, if left unchecked, harden into hatred.*
- *Professionalism can involve moral compromise. Those costs are real and cumulative.*

Inside the Story *(Optional Reading)*

Why the World Trade Center Collapse Was Different from the Empire State Building Crash

In July of 1945 a U.S. Army Air Forces B-25 bomber accidentally struck the Empire State Building while flying in dense fog. The aircraft penetrated several floors of the building and started a fire, but the structure itself remained intact.

At first glance that earlier accident led some observers to believe the World Trade Center towers might survive similar impacts. The circumstances of the two events were dramatically different.

The B-25 bomber weighed roughly 30,000 pounds and was flying at relatively low speed when it struck the Empire State Building. The Boeing 767 aircraft used in the September 11th attacks weighed more than ten times as much and were traveling several times faster.

Physics explains why this difference matters. When an object's speed increases, the kinetic energy available in an impact rises with the square of its speed.

Although the structural damage from the aircraft strikes was severe, the towers themselves initially remained standing. The primary cause of the collapses was the intense fires fueled by thousands of gallons of jet fuel. These fires burned at temperatures high enough to weaken the steel support structure, eventually leading to the progressive collapse of both buildings.

Airline Hijacking Procedures Before 9/11

For decades prior to September 11th, airline hijackings followed a relatively predictable pattern. Most U.S. incidents involved individuals attempting to redirect aircraft to another destination—most commonly Cuba during the 1960s and 1970s.

Because of this pattern, aviation authorities developed procedures designed to de-escalate the situation rather than confront it. Pilots were instructed to keep hijackers calm, avoid provoking violence, and cooperate with demands whenever possible.

The primary goal was to protect passengers and crew while buying time for law enforcement to resolve the situation once the aircraft landed.

In some circumstances this guidance even allowed hijackers to be brought into the cockpit to negotiate directly with the flight crew.

Security screening at airports also reflected this mindset. Certain items that would later be banned—including small knives and box cutters—were allowed to be carried onboard aircraft.

The attacks of September 11th demonstrated that these procedures were built for a very different type of threat. After the attacks, cockpit doors were reinforced, security screening procedures were dramatically expanded, and pilots were no longer expected to cooperate with hijackers attempting to gain control of the aircraft.

How 9/11 Changed an Airline Career

The attacks of September 11th did more than alter security procedures and cockpit protocols. They reshaped the airline profession itself.

In the months that followed, passenger demand collapsed. Travelers who had once boarded airplanes without hesitation now viewed flying through a different emotional lens, and airlines suddenly found themselves trying to operate expensive fleets with far fewer paying passengers.

That drop in demand pushed much of the airline industry into financial crisis. In the years that followed, major U.S. airlines entered bankruptcy, restructured, merged, furloughed employees, cut pay, terminated pension plans, and rewrote work rules that had once defined the profession.

For pilots, those changes were not temporary disruptions. They altered the arc of entire careers. Income, advancement, retirement expectations, and quality of life were all reshaped by what happened on that September morning.

For many of us, the airline career we finished was no longer the one we had spent years building toward.

CHAPTER 24

TRIBUTE

"Hold fast to dreams. For when dreams go,
Life is a barren field frozen with snow."
—Langston Hughes

AGE 45 · 2003

In celebration of the one-hundredth anniversary of the Wright Brothers' first powered flight at Kitty Hawk, North Carolina, I wrote this song. My good friend and fellow aviator, Kim Frizzell, put it to music and recorded it with his band.

We submitted the recording to the Wright Celebration Committee in Dayton, Ohio, and our song was selected to be played on the air during the week-long centennial celebration.

It was an honor to be selected—and an honor to write this song about two heroes of mine.

Kitty Hawk
(The Song)
2003

Chorus

Did they know their dream would soar?
Change our world forevermore?
Rocket to a distant star,
Jumbo jets, wide and far.

Verse 1

As a boy, I dreamed of flight
Sixty years since Kitty Hawk
Slipped free to see the sights
All because of the brothers Wright.

Two brothers of modest means
Machinists, inventors, builders of things
One goal, one mind, to achieve their dream
To soar with the eagles and join their team.

How did they see so clear
So many summers away from home
Devoted to flight, without any fear
Designers and builders of all their gear.

The Outer Banks would witness the two
From Dayton to the dunes and back again
Tests and trials as they would stew
The race was tight—till at last it flew!

Verse 2

Frail and odd their machine did look
A leering praying mantis of wood and cloth
No rules or guidance—they wrote the book
Can anyone imagine what it really took?

Verse 3

Can we thank them for what they've done?
One hundred years since Kitty Hawk
At last, their day has come
A day of thanks for what they've done

Photo #38. The CD and case for the song Kitty Hawk

CHAPTER 25

GENTLEMAN'S FLYING

"We make a living by what we get, but we make a life by what we give!"
—Winston Churchill

AGE 42-50 · 2000-2008

Before I flew the Boeing 757, I had never been to Saipan. For years it existed only on charts and flight plans—an island we passed near on Central Pacific flying or listed as an alternate if Guam went below weather minimums. It was part of the job in a purely operational sense, abstract and distant. That changed when the Boeing 727 disappeared from the fleet and the 757 took its place. *(See Inside the Story: The Boeing 757.)* Saipan stopped being a contingency and became somewhere I actually went—somewhere I stepped onto.

Photo #39. The view from the cockpit approaching Saipan Airport.

Northwest shifted its Pacific Island service to a small fleet of 757s based out of Tokyo's Narita Airport. Once my 757 simulator training was complete, I bid the 757 Pacific routes and began commuting to Japan—deadheading across the ocean, meaning riding as a passenger while traveling to an assigned flight, then flying island legs for about two weeks before deadheading home.

What surprised me was how quickly repetition did its work. Trip after trip, Saipan stopped feeling like a destination and became a place. Before long, it was one I thought about when I left, quietly hoping the next trip back would come soon. *(See Inside the Story: The History of Saipan.)*

Flying the Pacific this way was different. Instead of living overseas, we now commuted from America to Japan. The flying was one, maybe two legs a day. No red-eyes, and we stayed within two time zones, which was kind to the body. Layovers were typically thirty hours, and except for Narita, the hotels were right on the sand.

By airline standards, it was excellent duty.

For the Narita-to-Saipan leg, I usually started the day with a long walk through the rice paddies near the hotel, followed by a midafternoon nap. Our departure from NRT was typically around eight in the evening, and the trip was just under four hours en route. One flight a day, a day off at the beach, then one leg back—what we called "gentleman's flying."

A little seniority goes a long way.

Our pickup at the Narita hotel came at six p.m., always the same routine. Out front would be a black, nondescript Japanese sedan, the driver sitting perfectly erect behind the wheel, waiting patiently. Each wore a navy-blue sport coat over a neatly pressed white shirt and black tie, with clean white driving gloves.

They looked like they were preparing to drive the Queen of England.

The drivers—usually older than all of us—loaded our bags with quiet precision, fitting them into the trunk like a perfect game of Tetris. The cars were spotless. The passenger seats were covered in clean white cloths that looked almost ceremonial. Nothing was ever out of place. No trash. No dirt. No mechanical quirks.

Once we were seated, the driver remotely closed the doors with a soft click, and we were off.

The cars themselves were unremarkable—often a Toyota Crown, roughly equivalent to a Camry—but the driving was flawless. Every bump was anticipated. Every corner taken at exactly the right speed, so no one swayed. Even stopping at traffic lights was done so smoothly it was sometimes hard to tell we were decelerating.

After nearly thirty years of flying in and out of Japan, I came to deeply admire the culture. The professionalism of those taxi drivers was just one small example of a broader national trait: pride in doing things well, quietly, without performance.

With one notable exception.

Most of our passengers to the Marianas Islands were Japanese tourists headed for the beach or the golf course. Because of that, I made all my passenger announcements in both English and Japanese.

I tried.

One day in Osaka, as I stood at the cockpit door saying goodbye, an older, well-dressed man stopped in front of me. He looked me square in the eyes and said, in a deep, flat voice, "You speak Japanese like a woman."

Then he walked off.

It felt like a knife to the side.

He wasn't wrong. All my language instructors had been women.

It was a passing remark from a man I would never see again. But it lodged itself in my head.

From that day forward, his comment followed me every time I spoke into the microphone. I knew what he meant, and I knew I couldn't change it. So, I focused on clarity, respect, and intent—and kept speaking Japanese as best as I could.

Heading to Saipan, our departures from Narita were usually fast. By that time of night, most international traffic had already pushed, leaving the ramp quiet and runways relatively clear.

Within ten minutes of takeoff, we were pointed out to sea, slipping into the quiet rhythm of oceanic flight. There was another advantage to the late departure: most of the daytime Pacific thunderstorms had already begun to wither, making for an easy ride more often than not. It was usually a relaxed night at work.

Midway across, we passed Iwo Jima—the site of one of the Pacific theater's most brutal battles of World War II. For us, its single runway was the only pavement available for hundreds of miles in any direction, our primary emergency alternate field en route to Saipan or back to Japan.

In operational terms, Iwo was safety.

Ironic for an American to say.

Thankfully, I never saw it from ground level. Others I knew had. It was never a good experience.

Once we landed in Saipan, the rhythm was familiar. Bags off, a short ride from the airport, and then the hotel—built on a stretch of private beach, idyllic in its setting.

The rooms were a little worn, but the grounds were beautiful, and the staff treated us well. By the time we arrived, it was usually just after one in the morning.

Most of the crew went straight to bed.

I didn't.

Across the street from the hotel was one of the better massage places on the island. A legitimate operation—no neon, no suggestion—just quiet rooms, low light, and practiced hands.

I would change clothes, cross the street, and ask for the three-hour shiatsu massage.

Thirty-three dollars.

Heavenly.

I slept through parts of it, drifting in and out while the last remnants of a two-week trip were worked out of my muscles.

Around five in the morning, I'd drink hot tea in the waiting area, then wander next door to a small mom-and-pop market for a bowl of rice and fried eggs.

By the time I returned to my room, the sky was beginning to lighten. Exhaustion kicked in and I slept deeply until noon.

One morning in 2004, sitting with my tea after a massage, I noticed I wasn't alone in this strange schedule. Another American sat across the room. He was enormous—easily four hundred pounds—with a thick accent from the north end of Boston.

He introduced himself as Big Tony.

When he found out pizza was my favorite food, he looked at me and said, "You wanna go make some 'za?"

Pizza. Music to my ears.

I ran next door and grabbed a couple of six-packs of beer. Tony drove us across the island in an old Toyota sedan that leaned noticeably to one side but never missed a beat. Ten minutes later, we pulled into a small strip mall off the main road. At the far end, behind salt-air-streaked windows, was his pizza place.

While the oven heated, we drank beer and traded stories—Saipan, Boston, life far from where either of us had started. He showed me how to stretch dough properly, how to spin it in the air and let it find its own shape.

"Nevah use a rollah," he told me. "That's how ya ruin it."

We each made a pie, the oven roaring hot by the time they went in. Seven minutes later, what came out looked—and smelled—perfect. Thin, firm crust underneath, a big chewy edge around the outside. Exactly the kind of pizza I loved.

Tony ate his entire pie. I did real damage to mine and carried the rest back to the hotel.

I never saw Tony again. But I still make pizza exactly the way he taught me. Years later, it still surprises me that one of the things I do best in my own kitchen came from a brief friendship on a small island halfway around the world—no plan, no intention, just openness to the moment.

By midafternoon, I usually headed out for a long walk. Walking became part of my Saipan rhythm—how I burned off restlessness and cleared the noise left over from life and distance.

The heat was oppressive, no matter the time of year. I followed a paved path along the coast, staying where Ironwood and Flame trees cast broken shade.

The path wound through several picnic areas where large local families gathered most days. Food spread across tables. Kids running barefoot. Laughter carrying easily through the humid air. Life had reclaimed the shoreline.

Near the far end of the path sat the remains of a Japanese tank, rusted and slowly melting back into the earth. Its armor had been split open by direct hits during the battle for Saipan. I stopped there often, tracing the likely lines of fire with my eyes, trying—and failing—to imagine the moment when steel stopped being protection.

By the time I turned back toward the hotel, I was usually dripping in sweat. Even a leisurely four-mile walk felt heavy in that climate. It was impossible not to wonder how anyone had fought a war here, carrying weapons and gear, day after day, in heat like this.

Because Saipan is part of the Commonwealth of the Northern Mariana Islands, a U.S. territory and played a pivotal role in the Pacific war, it is home to the American Memorial Park Museum. By coincidence or good fortune, the museum sat right next to our layover hotel.

It was there that I met Tim and Julie.

They were a husband-and-wife team, U.S. Park Service rangers who had volunteered for the Saipan assignment. We became friends quickly. They loved the island and took their stewardship seriously—not just preserving what was already known but trying to better understand and document what the land still held.

Tim and I often planned hikes together. He knew where history lay just beneath the surface, and I was more than willing to tag along. We were usually looking for remnants of the war—artifacts that could be cataloged and displayed in the museum, small pieces of a larger story still being assembled decades later.

On one of those outings, we climbed a steep hill overlooking the ocean. The hike required some bushwhacking through dense tropical growth, but nothing extreme. What made it striking was knowing that none of these plants had existed before the war.

In 1944, U.S. battleships offshore had pounded these hills relentlessly, stripping them bare so Japanese forces couldn't hide in the jungle. What we walked through now was a young forest, no older than the destruction that had cleared it.

The ground told the rest of the story. Thousands of shallow depressions scarred the surface—shell craters from rounds that had exploded. Scattered among them were enormous, unexploded projectiles, some nearly a foot in diameter, fired from naval guns and still lying where they had landed. Presumably still live. We gave them a wide berth.

Just below the summit, Tim stopped abruptly. Partially hidden by vegetation was a small opening in the earth—a narrow gap, barely visible unless you knew to look for it.

At first, we thought it might be another bomb-shell hole. Tim bent closer and peered inside. Then he lowered himself onto his hands and knees.

"There's more in here," he said.

He went in first.

The crawl was miserable. Thick, sticky mud pulled at our clothes. The space narrowed quickly, forcing our shoulders sideways. Our legs dragged behind us as we pushed forward on our elbows, inch by inch. Light faded almost immediately, replaced by breathing and the scrape of bodies against earth.

When we finally switched on our flashlights, we found ourselves crouched inside a small chamber—about five feet high and ten feet across.

It had been lived in.

Broken stalactites and stalagmites had been cleared away to make space. A shallow sleeping hollow lay in one corner. Rice bowls sat where they had been set down. Sake bottles with Japanese characters were still visible. Fragments of Japanese military uniform cloth lay embedded in the mud.

Nothing had been disturbed.

The realization hit us both at the same time. This wasn't just another relic—it was a place untouched since the war, where Japanese soldiers had hidden while the hills below them were being torn apart.

Tim moved carefully, documenting everything, wrapping what could be preserved. These pieces would go into the museum—not as trophies, but as evidence. I stood quietly, imagining what it must have been like to wait in that darkness, listening as shells from the ships hammered the hillside below, each impact shuddering through the cave.

Near my boot lay broken fragments of stalactites, already detached and lying on the cave floor. Knowing my interest in geology, Tim nodded when I asked if I could keep one.

Today, that fragment still sits in my home. It took thousands of years for the cave to grow that mineral tube, and only seconds for it to be broken by a frightened soldier fighting to stay alive. I didn't take it as a souvenir. I took it as a reminder.

On many occasions during those years, I brought crew members to Banzai Cliff. Often, they were flight attendants—many of them young, many of them Japanese. Most had never heard of the Battle for Saipan.

We didn't go there to talk.

Standing on the edge of that precipice, with the ocean far below and the wind coming up the face of the rock, words felt unnecessary. Enemy or not, what had happened there transcended allegiance.

We stood. We listened. We bowed our heads.

I did not try to write about that place in narrative. A poem I wrote after standing there was later displayed in the museum on

Saipan while my friends were serving as park rangers. It appears in the Epilogue of this book.

Photo #40. Banzai Cliff, Saipan.

We usually left early the next day, with a 5:30 a.m. hotel pickup followed by a four-hour flight back to Narita. Some days we returned to Camp Narita; others, after several hours in the terminal, we headed back out—to Saipan, Guam, or Pusan—repeating the cycle until one final night in Narita before heading home at the end of the twelve-day trip.

I missed my family when I was gone. But I never wasted the time. I learned that living fully on the road—through routine, curiosity, and openness to the people and places around you—could turn distance into something that expanded life rather than shrinking it.

Learning Points:

- *War is grotesque and brutal, no matter how it is fought.*
- *A U.S. pilot is more than a person manipulating the controls of an airplane. Pilots are also emissaries for America to the far corners of the globe.*
- *The greatest souvenirs of travel are often the friendships and experiences that change us.*

Inside the Story *(Optional Reading)*

The Boeing 757

The Boeing 757 entered airline service in the early 1980s and represented a significant technological step forward from earlier jetliners such as the Boeing 727. Designed in the late 1970s, the aircraft incorporated far more automation and computerization than the generation of airplanes that preceded it.

One of the most important operational differences was crew size. The 727 required three pilots—a captain, a first officer, and a flight engineer who managed many of the airplane's mechanical systems. On the 757, those duties were largely handled by onboard computers, allowing the aircraft to be safely operated by two pilots instead of three.

The airplane was also far more efficient. A typical 757 could carry roughly one-third more passengers than a 727 while burning about one-third less fuel, dramatically reducing operating costs for airlines.

Despite the increased automation, the aircraft retained flight controls and handling characteristics that pilots generally found enjoyable to fly. Many pilots viewed the 757 as a well-balanced design—advanced enough to reduce workload, but still responsive and engaging compared to later generations of highly automated aircraft.

The History of Saipan

Saipan lies in the western Pacific Ocean about 125 miles north of Guam and sits along the edge of the Mariana Trench, the deepest known part of the world's oceans. Today Saipan is the capital of the Commonwealth of the Northern Mariana Islands, a U.S. territory.

For centuries before European contact, Saipan was inhabited by the Chamorro people, who had migrated through the Pacific from Southeast Asia. Their culture remains a strong presence throughout the Mariana Islands today.

Control of the island shifted several times over the past two centuries. Spain governed Saipan until the end of the Spanish–American War in 1898. Soon afterward, Spain sold the island to Germany, which administered it until the end of World War I. Following that conflict, the League of Nations placed Saipan under Japanese control as part of the South Pacific Mandate.

During World War II, Saipan became one of the most strategically important islands in the Pacific. In June 1944 U.S. forces launched an invasion to capture the island from Japan. After weeks of intense fighting, American forces secured Saipan in early July. The victory allowed the United States to construct airfields capable of launching long-range B-29 bomber missions directly against the Japanese home islands.

Today Saipan retains traces of that history alongside its modern role as a Pacific tourist destination, particularly for travelers from Japan and Korea. For airline crews flying the Pacific island routes, it was both a tropical layover and a place layered with historical significance.

CHAPTER 26

DUCK DUCK

"Reference the ELEPHANTS. Forget the ANTS!"
—Derived from Gustave Flaubert

AGE 48 · 2006

Most of my flying life has been spent in large jets—heavy airplanes, long runways, altitude measured in miles.

Every so often, I escaped that world and flew small airplanes with my friend Kim Frizzell—known to me as the Flying Scotsman.

Kim owned airplanes the way some people collect guitars, and through him I had access to more light aircraft than I could count. For years, we'd meet with no destination in mind—just two pilots and a key—content to see where the day took us.

One of Kim's side ventures involved a business using a light-sport airplane called the Flight Design CT. *(Inside the Story: The Flight Design CT.)* It was a modern little machine—two seats, composite skin, quick on the controls, honest in its feedback. We flew it often. Grass strips. Spot landings. Laughing at ourselves when one of us came up short or floated long. Flying like that stripped away pretense.

No schedules. No procedures thick enough to hide behind. Just hands, feet, judgment—playing in three dimensions.

This didn't feel like work.

This felt like flying in the purest form.

Photo #41. Kim's CT aircraft at 3,000 feet over Minnesota.

In 2006, Kim had an extra CT that would otherwise sit idle through a Minnesota winter. He offered it to me to use in Colorado. I had three teenagers at home who'd never flown in a small airplane, and I'd just had my flight instructor certificate reinstated.

It wasn't an offer I could reasonably refuse.

We agreed to fly the airplane out together from Minnesota to Colorado, one of us—neither ever admitted which—suggested we fly the entire trip at one hundred feet above the ground.

We both paused.

Then we smiled.

Seven hours in a light aircraft isn't trivial, and the low-altitude idea turned the delivery into more than transportation. It became an adventure—risky, no question, but over open country, with discipline, constant attention, and two experienced pilots sharing the workload, the risk was understood, controlled, and acceptable.

So, we launched early from Lakeville, climbed just high enough to clear the southern Twin Cities, then descended once the landscape opened up.

Cornfields rolled beneath us, uninterrupted, the ground rising and falling just enough to demand concentration.

At one hundred feet, nothing is abstract.

The pilot flying stayed busy—constant control inputs, riding gusts, matching terrain changes. The non-flying pilot handled the navigation, scanned for obstacles, and watched for birds. We swapped roles every thirty minutes and stopped often, not from fatigue alone but to keep the flight playful instead of grim.

That balance mattered. Two airline pilots, just flying for the joy of it.

We passed a wind farm west of the Missouri River—turbines towering overhead, blades sweeping air we had no intention of sharing. We gave them plenty of room.

Later, cresting a low ridgeline, we startled a herd of elk into motion. They scattered in a sudden, muscular wave, hooves churning dirt as we slipped past and vanished from their world just as quickly as we had entered it.

En route there was laughter. Easy talk. That quiet satisfaction pilots get when everything is working and nothing needs explaining.

By late afternoon, we reached Erie, Colorado. The flight had been worth every mile. Memorable. Not because it was daring, but because it required us to stay fully engaged for hours at a time—hands light on the controls, eyes always working, judgment never drifting.

This was the kind of flying that didn't let you coast or hide behind routine. It reminded me less of why I'd first fallen in love with flying than of why I'd stayed with it so long: when it's done right, flying still asks everything of you and gives you so much in return.

Over the next few months, that little airplane became a classroom. I taught all three of my kids the basics—how to feel the airplane, how to guide it into the air, how to bring it back again. They did well.

Sadly, none of them fell in love with flying, but I'd done my job as a parent and an instructor. I'd opened the door. The choice beyond that was theirs.

When spring returned, Kim needed his airplane back.

The return trip would be conventional—higher altitude, wider margins, a more relaxed cockpit. Fun had already been had.

Hours later, cruising at thirty-five hundred feet, the day settling down around us as we neared our destination, I was flying from the right seat. Kim sat quietly in the left seat, scanning with the practiced ease of someone who never stopped watching.

Then his voice sharpened.

"Ducks. Twelve o'clock high. Ducks."

I had been looking out the side window. My eyes snapped forward.

The windscreen filled.

Brown bodies. Green heads. Wings tucked—diving straight at us.

At our speed, a bird that size could shatter a windshield or destroy the propeller.

I pulled the power to idle and drove the stick forward.

The nose pitched down rapidly. The horizon vanished. The shoulder straps went tight as we came light in the seats, the airplane briefly unweighting us. Kim's hands floated off his knees, fingers splayed instinctively as the brief weightlessness stole their resting place. Then they dropped back down.

No one spoke.

Shapes tore overhead—close enough that I saw feathers flex, the color differences between drakes and hens.

I flinched—my chin tucking from instinct.

The altimeter unwound hard.

Then I eased back on the stick. The needle hesitated. Stopped. Began to climb.

A bead of sweat ran down between my shoulder blades. I became aware of my breathing inside the headset—loud, uneven, not yet under control.

For half a second, there was nothing more to do.

Just shared looks of astonishment.

Before we even had time to talk about the near-miss with a flock of three-pound birds, a dark, sweeping shadow crossed the cockpit.

Kim ducked first.

I followed.

A jet's glistening wing passed overhead. So close I saw individual rivets along the underside—too fast to track, too near to doubt.

The jet crossed perpendicular to our path and vanished.

No radio call.

No turbulence.

No acknowledgment.

My hands stayed on the controls, holding altitude by feel alone. The airplane responded as if nothing extraordinary had happened. But in the small space we shared, everything had changed.

Kim's head swiveled, tracking the jet as it streaked away.

"A Learjet." He said.

In seconds it was already far enough away to feel unreal—not because it had vanished, but because it had arrived without warning at all.

The cockpit was quiet.

We flew the rest of the way home on autopilot—not the airplane, but ourselves. Motions practiced, conversation absent, both of us still in a state of shock.

Only on the ground did the puzzle pieces finally assemble.

The ducks hadn't been reacting to us at all.

They were diving out of the way of the approaching Learjet.

That realization landed heavier than the event itself. Their instinct—ancient, unthinking, perfectly timed—had forced our escape. The brief descent didn't just save us by distance. It saved us by timing.

We never saw the Lear coming. The Lear's crew never saw us. Low sun. Small white airplane. A big sky that had suddenly become crowded.

Without the ducks, there would have been no warning. No cue. No chance.

We shut down, hangared the airplane, and stood there looking at each other longer than necessary before moving on.

Between us, we had accumulated tens of thousands of flight hours—most of them uneventful, many of them joyful, in everything from light airplanes to heavy jets. Encounters like this are vanishingly rare. This one stands alone—not because small airplanes are unsafe, but because timing and traffic can align in ways no amount of experience can prevent.

ANOTHER BULLET DODGED

Learning Points:

- *See-and-avoid works remarkably well—until one does not see what nature is masking.*
- *The most dangerous events often announce themselves indirectly.*
- *Sometimes random events occur for reasons that we cannot understand at the time.*
- *Aviation can be made remarkably safe. Life never can. If a wild cougar does not get you on a peaceful mountain hike, perhaps a flock of toothless Mallard ducks will on a casual day of visual flying.*

Inside the Story *(Optional Reading)*

The Flight Design CT

The Flight Design CT is a modern light-sport aircraft built primarily from carbon fiber composites rather than the wood, fabric, or aluminum structures common in earlier generations of airplanes. Carbon fiber is a woven material bonded with resin that can be molded into strong, aerodynamic shapes while remaining extremely light. This combination of strength and low weight allows the airplane to operate efficiently with a very small engine while still delivering excellent performance.

Power comes from a compact engine that burns ordinary automobile gasoline and consumes only about five gallons per hour—remarkably efficient for an airplane. Paired with the CT's advanced high-lift wing and favorable power-to-weight ratio, the design allows it to operate easily from short runways and small grass airfields where larger aircraft would never venture.

Unlike most traditional training airplanes that use a control yoke resembling a steering wheel, the CT uses center control sticks between the pilot's legs. Either the left or right seat pilot can fully fly the airplane because both seats have complete access to the flight controls, radios, and instruments. The stick provides direct control feel, making the airplane responsive and enjoyable to fly.

The airplane is also designed for exceptional visibility. Its high wing sits above the cabin, and a large bubble windscreen extends forward, while expansive side windows provide an unobstructed view in almost every direction. That visibility is ideal for flying under Visual Flight Rules (VFR), where pilots are responsible for seeing and avoiding other aircraft rather than relying on air traffic controllers to provide separation.

CHAPTER 27

THE DAY THE GROUND SHIFTED

"Happiness is not having what one wants, but appreciating what one has."
—Dalai Lama

AGE 28 & 50 · 1986 & 2008

Mergers are decided in boardrooms, justified by spreadsheets, and announced in press releases. But for pilots, whose careers are governed almost entirely by seniority, the consequences unfold slowly, sometimes for decades. *(Inside the Story: Deregulation and Mergers.)*

I was assigned to fly the very first widebody flight between two of the airline's hubs, post-merger of Republic-Northwest Airlines. At the time, I had no idea the flight would become a small preview of how difficult airline mergers can be. *(Inside the Story: Business Case for the Northwest Republic Merger.)*

The Minneapolis–Memphis route had always been Republic territory, flown by three DC-9s each morning. That day, one DC-10 would replace them all.

At least, that was the plan.

What followed felt less like a merger and more like two airlines discovering they spoke different languages.

The problems emerged before we ever reached the gate. Passengers wandered the concourses, staring up at dark flight monitors with no information. Republic and Northwest computer systems couldn't communicate with each other, and airline representatives couldn't help customers find their departing flights. As a last resort, gate agents made repeated public address announcements, calling destination cities out loud like a schoolyard roll call.

Throughout the airport, passengers stood still, clutching boarding passes, unsure which gate belonged to which airplane.

Eventually, we gathered most of our passengers and departed Minneapolis. The flight itself was uneventful. The illusion of normalcy lasted until we parked in Memphis.

We then waited.

The jetway would not rise high enough to reach the DC-10's door. It had been preset for DC-9s only—a limitation no one had thought to question, because this station had never handled a widebody airplane before.

Strike two.

Passengers sat. Crews waited. Mechanics tried to override sensors.

Time stretched.

When the door finally opened—nearly an hour after arrival—I went outside for the preflight walkaround while our passengers headed for baggage claim.

A ramp supervisor waved me over.

"How do I unload bags from one of these big boys?"

I showed him how to operate the electric cargo door and explained that the bags weren't stacked loose the way they were on a DC-9. On a widebody they were packed into aluminum containers—bins—that had to be pulled out with a transfer loader. I told him to drive the LD-3 loader to the airplane and pull the bins out.

In a southern accent, he said, "Ain't got one of them!"

He had worked the ramp for more than thirty years but had never seen a widebody airplane. He had no idea what I was talking about.

The station baggage manager was just as perplexed. Management had placed a DC-10 on the route, but no LD-3 container loaders had been positioned at the station. No trained personnel either. No plan existed to offload bags from a DC-10—because until that morning, no one at the station had ever seen one, or thought about the differences in its baggage system.

Inside the terminal, passengers gathered around a motionless carousel. Outside, their luggage sat motionless in the airplane's belly.

Not one bag came out.

Not one customer left the airport with their checked belongings.

Making matters worse, in 1986, most travelers checked their bags. Large rolling carry-on bags had not yet become part of everyday air travel.

Strike three.

An hour later, we flew back to Minneapolis—without our next set of passengers' luggage and still carrying every bag we had brought down with us. If bags couldn't be offloaded, it followed that bags couldn't be loaded either.

We were instructed not to tell the Minneapolis-bound passengers what had happened. Someone behind a desk believed this would reduce stress. Sadly, those passengers learned the truth the same way the Memphis-bound passengers had—standing at an empty carousel.

By the end of the day, one widebody airplane and one crew of eleven had delivered 570 people to their destinations with nothing but what they wore onboard or carried into the cabin.

Unfortunately, what happened in Memphis that day wasn't a one-time mistake. Episodes like this quickly produced a nickname among frustrated travelers for the newly merged airline.

North-worst.

That one day was an early preview of the merger itself.

The airplane worked fine.

The crew worked competently.

The problem lived in the spaces between two companies that had never truly been integrated.

For me, and for tens of thousands of other Northwest employees, failures like these made going to work painful. We were the face of the company, and every day we absorbed the frustration of customers who had every reason to be upset.

I was embarrassed, ashamed, and helpless to fix any of it. I had been with the airline only nine months when the Memphis fiasco occurred, but it did not take a twenty-year employee to know this was not normal. It was the first visible crack in a merger that would reshape my career—and much of my life—for decades to come.

One of the many aspects overlooked in this merger was corporate culture.

Republic was an airline where employees took care of one another, and executives interacted with frontline workers in a visible, respectful way. Northwest had better airplanes, broader routes, and higher pay—but its management culture treated employees as an inconvenience rather than an asset.

Republic felt like a company.

Northwest felt like an institution.

Republic's management knew your name.

Northwest's management referred to employees as numbers. *(Inside the Story: Corporate Culture.)*

Those cultural differences extended deep into the cockpit. Ironically, Northwest's management culture and cockpit culture were not the same thing. Employees often distrusted the former while respecting the latter. I was proud to work in a Northwest cockpit; there the airline was an industry leader in "Standard Operating Procedures" and safety.

A professional airline cockpit runs on a script. Standardized callouts and procedures—and the shared expectation that everyone will follow them—allow three pilots who may have never met before to function as a cohesive crew within minutes of introducing themselves.

Most trips begin exactly that way. We meet in the briefing room, shake hands, discuss the flight, and go to work. The consistency doesn't come from friendship or familiarity. It comes from everyone following the same script.

During the merger, parts of that script suddenly differed.

Northwest had largely embraced Crew Resource Management (CRM), emphasizing communication, standardized procedures, and shared responsibility in the cockpit. Some Republic pilots came from a more traditional captain-centered culture.

Neither approach was born of bad intent. But pilots who had never met before and come from a different airline were suddenly expected to function as a seamless crew while bringing different assumptions into the cockpit.

The merger wasn't just combining airplanes and routes.

It was combining habits, expectations, and professional identities.

Eventually, all those differences—culture, procedures, and competing ideas of fairness—collided in the one place pilots care about most: the seniority list.

When the merged seniority list was finally issued, I had already advanced to 747 second officer. The merger itself had happened two years earlier, but pilot integration had dragged on.

During that delay, my future career sat in limbo, while my present one progressed.

When the list arrived, it reset everything strictly by date of hire for second officers. Protections applied only to captains and first officers. *(Inside the Story: Pilot Seniority and Fleet Structure.)*

My job was fully unprotected after the merger.

The 747 widebody second officer position paid better than all Republic copilot positions and even better than some captains. Overnight, nearly two thousand Republic pilots became senior to me and eligible to move onto the 747.

Nothing I had done caused it, and nothing I could do would reverse it.

My advancement stopped, and a long slide backward began.

Reserve followed. Predictability disappeared. Days off were assigned; trips were forced.

The merger was no longer something discussed in conference rooms and arbitration hearings. It was deciding where I worked, when I slept, and how much control I had over my life.

I could have chased a different airplane or base to regain control.

I didn't.

We stayed where the family was settled in Minnesota, and I absorbed the hit. Stability at home mattered more than trying to outrun the list.

In the years that followed, the list moved slowly, and every advance felt provisional.

During that stretch I accepted a two-year remote assignment in Honolulu, flying the DC-10 as a copilot. When my contractual assignment ended in 1994, I was transferred to Boston on the DC-10.

Three weeks after arriving with my family of five, the base was closed.

We had barely unpacked.

With that, any chance of remaining a widebody DC-10 copilot disappeared. The DC-10 in Minneapolis and Detroit required more seniority than I had post-merger.

With no place left for me on the DC-10, I was displaced back to the 747 second officer position. It wasn't another demotion on the seniority list, but it was another step backward in a career that had already been reshuffled by the merger.

I had spent seven years in that non-flying engineer's seat before finally upgrading to the DC-10 as a copilot. Two years later, the recession and merger put me right back where I had started—sitting sideways, monitoring systems, and watching someone else fly the airplane.

On paper, it was a displacement.

To me, it felt like starting over.

In the airlines, seniority isn't part of your career.

It is your career. *(Inside the Story: Pilot Seniority and Why Airline Mergers Become So Contentious.)*

That was the moment it became clear the family could no longer move every time the airline, the economy, or another merger forced my hand.

Instead, we chose where we wanted to live. We stopped building our lives around the airline and started building them around the family. We planted roots in Colorado, and I became a commuter pilot for the first time in my career—something I had sworn I would never do.

I commuted in and out of Minneapolis to be a 747 second officer.

Airline commuting sounds glamorous until you do it. It means crossing the country as a passenger just to get to work, sleeping in crash pads, missing connections because of weather, and carrying the constant anxiety that any flight interruption might cost you your trip.

Thousands of airline pilots do it every day because seniority forces them to choose between career and geography.

Now I joined that shadow army.

The family lived in Colorado.

I waited for the list to move again.

Two decades later, when Northwest merged with Delta, I was a mid-seniority captain based in Minneapolis.

I was flying the 757 and holding the 12-day Asia trips I loved.

Photo #42. David standing inside the nacelle of a Boeing 757 engine.

After years of stagnation and bankruptcy recovery, the work had finally stabilized. I knew my schedule. I knew when I'd be home. I could plan.

Then the newly merged Delta seniority list erased that overnight.

Under the arbitrator's ratio formula, nearly fifteen hundred Delta pilots—many hired years after me—were placed ahead of me. Some Delta copilots became captains. Some Northwest captains were displaced to copilot.

I went from holding a good line to sitting reserve—eighteen days on call—on an airplane I had captained for over seven years. It wasn't just a schedule change—it was the erasure of familiarity, structure, and rhythm I had spent years building.

The Asia flying disappeared. Trips I had regularly flown were now senior work. Instead, I waited by the phone in a Minneapolis airport motel. After twenty-two years at the airline, I was back where I'd been early in my career—unable to plan my month, unable to predict my time, measuring life in standby days.

There were options on paper. I could have downgraded to copilot, but after absorbing a fifty percent pay cut during bankruptcy, another thirty percent cut wasn't realistic. Transferring bases didn't help; reserve was all I could hold anywhere on the 757 post-merger.

The only option that might have eased reserve life would have uprooted the family again—move back to Minnesota.

I didn't.

We'd already paid that price before.

We stayed where the kids were settled, and I commuted to reserve in Minneapolis, waiting each day for crew scheduling to call.

Twenty years earlier, the Republic merger had taught me something I did not fully understand at the time. Both groups felt wronged, and many carried that anger for years. I watched resentment harden into identity, and I did not want to become one of the captains who prematurely aged themselves through anger and bitterness.

I was not always successful at avoiding that during the Delta merger.

But I tried.

Most days, that was enough.

The Delta merger hurt me deeply—perhaps more in practical terms than the first one ever had. The seniority list did not end my career, but it ruptured my expectations of how that career would unfold. It took away flying I loved and returned me to reserve late in life.

I made the best of another difficult merger and worked to maintain a positive attitude. Honestly, the resentment never disappeared entirely. But over time, I found myself making friends from the other side of the list.

Eventually, it stopped mattering who had come from where. The pain was real, but it was not endlessly relitigated.

That mattered.

The anger faded into the background. The seniority consequences did not.

By the time I reached twenty-eight years at the airline, a 747-captain upgrade would normally have been routine. Historically, that seat went to pilots with far less time in service than I had accumulated. It was a predictable milestone—one Northwest pilots quietly measured themselves against as their careers matured.

After the Delta merger, that predictability vanished. *(Inside the Story: Business Case for the Northwest Delta Merger.)*

The integrated seniority list kept me junior in position far longer than was customary. The 747-upgrade window never opened before the fleet was finally retired.

I watched the airplane I had planned my career around slip out of reach—not because of performance or experience, but because the list no longer moved the way it once had.

There were ways to chase advancement—relocating again, retraining onto different aircraft, reshuffling what little leverage I had left.

I didn't.

By then, the kids were in college, my marriage had ended, and I was alone again. Stability mattered more than recovering lost trajectory.

Some ambitions have expiration dates.

This one reached its end—not with a decision, but with the quiet retirement of an airplane and the closing of a path I had expected would always be there.

Eventually, in my thirty-second year with the airline, I was awarded a captain position on the 777 widebody. On paper, it was the best airplane in the system and should have been the pinnacle of my career—the culmination of a life spent largely flying overseas.

The 777 itself was everything I had hoped for. The position surrounding it was not. I ended up as the most junior 777 captain in the system until the day I retired.

Year after year, the list barely moved. Retirement approached faster than seniority advanced. The mergers and seniority integrations that had shaped my career for decades kept me junior in position far longer than I had ever expected.

Even at this late stage of my career, I remained on call.

Trips didn't belong to me. Schedules didn't either. I waited by the phone.

I finished a thirty-five-year career still on reserve—not because I had chased pay or upgrades beyond what someone with three decades at the airline could reasonably expect, but because the list never caught up.

Life had instructed me in a reality that careers don't always unfold according to effort, experience, or plans. Sometimes they are redirected by decisions made far away, by people you'll never meet, for reasons you'll never control.

I couldn't control the mergers.

I couldn't control the list.

I could only decide how much of my life I was willing to surrender to them.

I didn't come out ahead in the way the job measures success.

I came out intact—and that mattered more.

ANOTHER BULLET DODGED

Learning Points:

- *Seniority governs airline careers more completely than performance, experience, or intent.*
- *Mergers alter careers incrementally, often long after the announcement fades.*
- *Endurance is a skill separate from ambition.*
- *Long-term exposure to resentment corrodes judgment and health.*

Inside the Story *(Optional Reading)*

Business Case for the Northwest-Republic Merger

In 1986, Northwest Airlines purchased Republic for $866 million in cash. From a business standpoint, the merger made sense. Northwest gained domestic feed, additional hubs, and a stronger position in the Midwest.

Strategically, it was defensible. What no spreadsheet could fully capture was how long its effects would echo—especially for the people whose careers would be reshaped, sometimes painfully. From the standpoint of corporate culture, however, the realities were far more complicated.

Today, a major airline may operate more than 900 airplanes and employ over 17,000 pilots. By comparison, the newly merged Northwest operated roughly 300 airplanes and employed about 5,000 pilots.

Yet in the mid-1980s, it was considered a large carrier. Systems were less sophisticated, staffing was leaner, and there was little room for mistakes. When leadership underestimated a problem, employees and passengers felt the consequences immediately.

From a conference room, the merger looked complete.

From the cockpit, it often felt like two airlines pretending to be one.

Passengers thought the merger was finished.

Employees knew otherwise.

Machines could be merged quickly. The people and systems that supported them took much longer.

Deregulation and Mergers

The Airline Deregulation Act of 1978 fundamentally reshaped the U.S. airline industry. Before deregulation, the federal government controlled routes and fares, limiting competition and keeping the industry relatively stable. Afterward, airlines gained the freedom to set prices, choose routes, and compete directly. The new environment rewarded efficiency, scale, and aggressive expansion, but it also exposed weaker carriers to sudden financial pressure.

Hub-and-spoke networks grew rapidly, new airlines entered the market, and competition intensified. Airlines sought greater efficiency, and mergers increasingly became a strategy for survival and growth.

In the years leading up to its 1986 merger with Republic Airlines, Northwest had built one of the strongest balance sheets in the industry. The airline owned all 133 of its aircraft outright, having paid cash as they came off the Boeing assembly line. It also held valuable real estate in downtown Tokyo, and a hotel near Narita Airport, and roughly two billion dollars in cash reserves. With no debt and a profitable international route system, Northwest was widely considered one of the most financially secure airlines in the United States.

Northwest was one of a small group of U.S. airlines holding extensive government-authorized international route authorities, alongside carriers such as Pan Am, TWA, and Braniff. Many of these routes faced little or no competition and generated strong profit margins.

Unlike some of its peers, Northwest paired this international network with a domestic system that fed passengers into overseas flights, creating a steady stream of high-value traffic.

After deregulation, many airline executives concluded that larger networks were essential for survival. While conventional strategy favored expansion into new geographic regions, Northwest took a different approach—acquiring competitors in overlapping markets. By consolidating operations at key hubs—particularly Minneapolis, Detroit, and Memphis—the airline strengthened its dominance and gained pricing power across many city pairs.

For passengers, mergers often appeared beneficial at first, promising more connections and broader route maps. Over time, however, reduced competition in concentrated markets frequently led to higher fares and fewer choices, as pricing power shifted to the remaining carriers.

Employees often faced the most difficult consequences. In seniority-based professions like airline piloting, careers are tied entirely to position on a company's seniority list. When airlines merge, those lists must be combined—a process that rarely satisfies both sides. Promotions, aircraft assignments, and long-term earnings can change overnight, creating tensions that can persist long after the merger itself is complete.

Corporate Culture

Corporate culture is difficult to define precisely, but employees recognize it immediately when they experience it.

Culture is reflected in how managers treat employees, how decisions are communicated, and whether people believe the organization values their contribution. Two companies may operate in the same industry and perform the same work yet feel entirely different from the inside.

Republic Airlines developed a reputation for a workplace culture where employees generally felt respected and supported. Management interacted with frontline workers in visible ways, and the company fostered a sense that employees and leadership were part of the same team. Northwest Airlines, by contrast, was widely perceived by many employees as having a more adversarial management culture. Labor groups often felt that executives viewed them less as partners in the operation and more as obstacles to be managed.

When companies with sharply different cultures merge, the financial and operational integration may occur quickly, but the human integration rarely does. Employees bring their expectations, loyalties, and identities from the original organization into the new one. If leadership underestimates these differences—or dismisses them as minor—the resulting tensions can linger for years.

In industries such as aviation, where safety, coordination, and trust among employees are essential, cultural differences can influence far more than morale. They shape how crews communicate, how conflicts are resolved, and how effectively teams function under pressure. For that reason, the cultural integration of two airlines is often more challenging than merging their fleets, route systems, and corporate structures.

Pilot Seniority and Fleet Structure

To understand why airline mergers become so contentious for pilots, it helps to understand how aircraft fleets shape pilot careers.

In most professions, experience alone leads to higher pay.

In airlines, career progression is tied to aircraft type and seat position. Larger airplanes generally pay more than smaller airplanes, and captains earn substantially more than copilots. Plus, airline pilots are paid hourly, not salary.

Because of this structure, most pilots try to progress through their careers by gradually moving to larger aircraft and eventually upgrading to captain. That progression often involves temporarily stepping back to a smaller airplane to obtain a captain position, then slowly moving upward again as captain on larger equipment. Over the course of a career, those decisions determine a pilot's earnings and quality of life.

Fleet composition therefore matters greatly in a merger. An airline operating many large airplanes offers more high-paying captain positions than an airline built around smaller aircraft. When two airlines combine, pilots naturally focus on how those fleets will translate into future opportunities. The types and numbers of aircraft entering a merger can significantly affect how careers unfold over the following decades.

Pilot Seniority and why Airline Mergers Become so Contentious

Unlike most professions, an airline pilot's career is governed almost entirely by seniority, based on date of hire. Pay, schedule, aircraft assignment, seat, base, vacation, and job security are all determined by a pilot's position on the seniority list.

During mergers, pilot seniority lists are integrated through binding arbitration. Arbitrators impose final, non-appealable decisions that shape careers for decades.

A single ruling can determine who upgrades, who moves, who commutes, and who spends years waiting.

If a pilot leaves one airline for another, that pilot starts over at the bottom of the list regardless of experience or accomplishment. Experience, safety record, and years flown don't transfer—only the hire date is relevant.

It is therefore unsurprising that pilots fight fiercely during mergers to protect their position on the seniority list. A single arbitrator's decision can alter careers, earnings, and quality of life for decades.

Business Case for the Northwest-Delta Merger

The Delta–Northwest merger ultimately produced a financially stable airline at a time when the industry desperately needed one.

After years of bankruptcies, contraction, and uncertainty, the combined company emerged stronger than either airline likely would have alone.

The airline survived.

The industry stabilized.

Those outcomes mattered—even if the costs were not shared equally.

CHAPTER 28

SOLAR FLARE

"A man's wealth is not measured by his bank account, but rather what he gives to his community."
—Ben Franklin

AGE 51-65 · 2008-2023

I had been on the roof most of the afternoon, absorbed in the quiet competence of a task I understood. The last section of flashing lay a few feet uphill from where I was kneeling, its metal surface warm under my palm. I had already secured the previous pieces and tightened the fasteners along the seam, and my attention narrowed to the familiar sequence that kept everything straight and square—the kind of detailed work that pushes everything else out of the way.

The wind picked up without announcing itself. At first, it only cooled the sweat on my back. Then it steadied, pressing instead of passing through. I noticed the temperature change, registered it, and kept working.

From below, the front door opened.

"Hey!"

Jillian's voice floated up, thin with distance.

I didn't answer. I finished the task, slid the tools into my belt, and reached for the next piece.

"David!"

Her voice was sharper now. I paused and finally stood, turning toward the west. The mountains were gone, swallowed by a dark, advancing shelf of clouds. The sunlight that had been bright and steady minutes earlier had flattened into a dull gray.

"I just saw lightning," she yelled. "You need to come down. Now."

There was no argument to make. I trusted her judgment without needing to see what she saw.

I lowered the metal flashing into place, secured it, tied down the remaining loose pieces, and gathered my tools. Each went back where it belonged. Nothing rushed. I moved deliberately toward the ladder, tested it with my foot, then turned and started down.

Halfway to the ground, a gust moved through the yard, the cottonwood branches above the roofline shaking hard enough to rustle against one another. I kept descending, eyes on the rungs, hands firm on the rails.

When I stepped off the last rung, I walked ten feet away from the house, angling toward the open yard and the cottonwood seven feet in front of me.

Lightning struck the tree.

The cottonwood was massive, its trunk wider than a man could reach around, its crown towering above the roofline where I'd been standing moments earlier. The strike didn't sound like thunder. It detonated. The concussive force lifted me off my feet and slammed me backward into the grass.

For a moment there was nothing—no sound, no movement, no sense of direction.

When I opened my eyes, I pushed myself upright, unsteady but conscious. My ears rang—not a tone, but a dense absence, as if the world had been packed with insulation. Jillian was running toward me from the house. Her mouth was moving, but I couldn't hear anything she said. The look on her face told me enough.

I stood, brushed grass from my arms, and took stock. I was breathing. Nothing burned. Nothing hurt in a way that suggested damage—except my hearing.

The yard was a mess. Bark and splintered wood were everywhere. The trunk of the cottonwood had split straight down the middle, peeled open like a failed seam. Smoke curled upward from the break, thin and gray against the darkening sky.

For the first time it occurred to me how close that strike had been to the roof where I'd been standing only moments earlier.

Inside the house, the lights were out.

Later, we would discover the televisions were all dead. The stereo. The router. Any sensitive electrical equipment connected by wires was fried. The strike had found the buried power line that ran past the tree to the front yard lights and followed it back into the house.

The tree hadn't survived.

The electronics hadn't survived.

I had.

ANOTHER BULLET DODGED

That evening, after the storm passed and the ringing in my ears began to fade, I stood in the dark living room, my hair still smelling faintly of wet wood and smoke.

Outside, the shattered cottonwood stood like a warning.

One I hadn't recognized until it was almost too late.

I kept replaying where I'd been standing. The height of the roof. The metal in my hands. The aluminum ladder resting on the gutter.

How close I had come—not abstractly, but physically.

Yet not every threat to survival arrives with noise. Sometimes it comes as a flash of light and a ringing in your ears. Sometimes it arrives in a letter, threatening the life you have already begun to build.

A year later, I stood at the edge of a very different kind of survival decision.

The old house was gone. We had torn it down completely. The foundation for the new one had already been poured and cured. The geometry of the future home was fixed in concrete.

I was standing on the lot when I unfolded the letter from my pilot union.

Northwest Airlines has entered Chapter 11 bankruptcy protection. *(Inside the Story: Bankruptcy and Airline Employees.)*

Those words had become familiar in the industry by then, but the number printed farther down the page stopped me cold.

A fifty-percent reduction in pay.

Effective immediately, with no defined end date. It wasn't negotiated. The company had asked the bankruptcy court to impose the cuts, and the judge approved them.

I didn't need a calculator.

I was the family's sole bread earner.

Mortgage. Construction loan. Monthly cash burn rate. The savings I had set aside for contingencies were never intended to supplement half of my salary. There was no financial buffer large enough to absorb the change.

I stood there longer than necessary, hands in my pockets, looking over the foundation. Framing would begin next. Materials were already ordered. Subcontractors were scheduled. Every downstream decision assumed continuity. There was no practical way to reverse course, no clean way to pause or unwind the project already underway.

Stopping would not have undone the risk—it would have locked it in place.

Continuing was the only way forward that didn't guarantee failure.

As the house neared completion, another requirement came into focus. Boulder County required renewable energy production before a certificate of occupancy would be issued.

That meant solar—a photovoltaic electrical system. *(Inside the Story: Photovoltaic Solar Power.)*

The solar bids arrived as we neared move-in.

Seventy-four thousand dollars.

Seventy-six.

Seventy-nine.

I read each one carefully, hoping I'd misunderstood the scope or misread a line item. That type of expense was simply not in the budget.

Like it or not. Afford it or not. It was mandatory.

That night, I sat at the computer and started researching alternatives. One article on solar PV led to another. Technical diagrams. Forum discussions. Installation photos posted by homeowners rather than companies. The systems weren't mysterious. They required planning, structure, wiring, and attention to detail—things I understood from a lifetime of building and maintaining complex systems.

What they did not offer was any assurance the plan would hold together once tools touched the roof. But it was an opportunity to regain some control—and with that, get back within budget.

However, before any distributor would sell to me, I needed to be a legitimate corporate entity. The next morning, I formed an LLC. The process was almost absurdly simple. A few forms, a filing fee, and suddenly there was a company name attached to what had been an idea the night before.

Forming the company didn't feel entrepreneurial. It felt defensive. I wasn't chasing an opportunity—I was trying to keep the walls from closing in.

In January of 2008, Affordable Alternative Energy, LLC officially sprang into existence—less a startup than a financial lifeline.

A week later, I wrote a check for the equipment. My own money. Paid in full. No distributor offered credit to a company without history. When I sealed the envelope, I knew exactly what it represented. Not investment capital. Not the beginning of a company. Just the price of finding out whether I could make this work myself.

I mailed it anyway.

The system went together. It worked.

Then neighbors asked if I would install systems for them. I agreed before fully appreciating what that commitment meant. After building the third system, something came into focus: a way out of my financial hole.

Soon, all three of our children would be in college at the same time. With my airline income cut in half, the math simply didn't work. The tuition savings we had once set aside had been repurposed years earlier during other financial pressures. Building this solar experiment into a real company wasn't part of a grand career plan—it was the only path I could see that might rebuild the income needed to meet those obligations.

I put together a business plan, accessed the last of our remaining savings, and spent a lot of sleepless nights trying to chart a path back to financial stability.

Work arrived unevenly at first, then steadily. I sold systems, ordered equipment, coordinated subcontractors, and climbed roofs. Cash flowed out before it flowed back in. Equipment was paid for in advance. Customers paid later.

From the beginning, there were lines I refused to cross. If we said we would be there on a certain day, we showed up. If we designed and contracted a system a certain way, that was exactly what we built—even when it cost more than expected. If we bid a job at a certain price, that was the price the customer paid, regardless of what surprises surfaced along the way.

Those rules limited growth at times, but they also limited regret.

During the first decade, the company evolved from a one-man operation into a real small business. We added vehicles, insurance, payroll systems, written policies, and a formal training program. New hires learned not only how to install solar systems, but how to do the work safely. Roofs, weather, and high-voltage DC power are unforgiving teachers. I had learned one of those lessons the hard way; my employees would not.

By 2019, I was still flying full time for Delta, the airline Northwest had become after the merger, while also running the solar company full time. There were no off days—only days with different responsibilities.

When COVID shut the world down in 2020, municipal building permits stopped. City offices closed indefinitely. Phones went unanswered. Without permits, we were legally unable to work. Crews sat idle while payroll dates continued to arrive on schedule.

For several months, the business was completely shut down.

The Paycheck Protection Program wasn't luck, and it wasn't skill on my part. It was a political decision that arrived just in time to keep my employees from losing their jobs for reasons entirely outside their control.

Without it, I would have been forced to lay off people who had done nothing wrong and had nowhere else to go.

When municipalities finally resumed permitting and work restarted, I didn't need to rehire or retrain. The crews were already there. That continuity allowed us to take on more complex work as trust and experience accumulated.

Years later, we completed what became our most visible project—a large photovoltaic installation on the roof of Concourse C at Denver International Airport.

Photo #43. The roof of concourse C at DIA (Denver International Airport).

It wasn't the largest system we ever built, but it was the most complex and the most public. Aircraft moved continuously beneath us, and the operational exposure was absolute. Any mistake would have gone largely unnoticed by the traveling public, but it would not have gone unnoticed within the industry. A failure there would have damaged our credibility and constrained the company's ability to grow.

It was managed with calm professionalism by two brothers, Casey and Clay Cole, who had been with the company for years. I stayed deliberately in the background, dealing with a pile of red tape and administrative paperwork while letting them lead. The system came together exactly as designed.

Watching that happen made it clear the company no longer depended on my constant presence.

With my sixty-fifth birthday approaching, I wanted a lower-stress life. I had already completed a thirty-five-year airline career and fourteen demanding years building and running my own company. The goals I had set back in 2008—paying for my children's college educations and building a business with staying power—had been met and exceeded.

I had hoped that one or more of my children might want to take over the company. I offered them that opportunity freely, just as I had taught them to fly and shown them aviation as a possible future. They chose different paths, and I respected that choice.

On January 4th, 2023, I sold the majority of the company to the Cole brothers, retaining a small ownership stake but removing myself entirely from day-to-day operations.

I unseated myself on purpose.

That had always been the goal.

Learning Points:

- *Creating and owning a business is among life's most rewarding endeavors, second only to parenting. It is also among the most stressful, rivaled only by illness or loss of a loved one.*
- *If you don't love the work you are performing, it is hard to love life.*
- *A good business owner views his employees as the reason for the company's success.*
- *Risk changes form, but it never disappears.*
- *The moments that altered the direction of my life didn't arrive with plans or warnings—they arrived as problems that had to be solved.*
- *A business is more than a product or service. It educates customers, creates opportunity, employs neighbors, and strengthens the communities it serves.*
- *Character is revealed when business decisions pit profit against principle. Financial rewards are fleeting; the consequences of doing what is right—or wrong—can last a lifetime.*

Inside the Story *(Optional Reading)*

Bankruptcy and Airline Employees

When an airline enters Chapter 11 bankruptcy protection, the goal is not liquidation but financial reorganization. The company continues operating while it attempts to restructure debt, reduce costs, and renegotiate obligations to remain viable. In the airline industry, where fixed costs are enormous—aircraft leases, fuel contracts, airport facilities, and labor agreements—bankruptcy has often been used as a tool to reset the economic structure of the company.

During the early 2000s, many U.S. airlines turned to bankruptcy courts for that purpose. Judges overseeing these cases had the authority to allow management to modify or reject existing labor contracts if the company could demonstrate that such changes were necessary for survival. As a result, large pay reductions, changes to work rules, and reductions in benefits were frequently imposed on airline employees.

For workers, the experience could feel very different from the corporate explanation of "reorganization." Pay cuts could arrive quickly and remain in place for years, while uncertainty about the company's future created persistent anxiety about job security. Even when airlines eventually emerged from bankruptcy, the compensation and working conditions employees had before the filing were often permanently altered.

Photovoltaic Solar Power

Residential solar electric systems use photovoltaic (PV) panels to convert sunlight directly into electricity. Each panel contains semiconductor cells—typically made from silicon—that generate electrical current when exposed to sunlight. The direct current produced by the panels is routed through an inverter, which converts it into alternating current compatible with household electrical systems.

A typical home solar installation includes several major components: the PV panels themselves, mounting hardware attached to the roof structure, electrical wiring and safety disconnects, and one or more inverters that condition the power for use inside the home. In many systems, excess electricity produced during sunny periods can be fed back into the utility grid through a process called net metering, allowing the homeowner to receive credit for the power supplied.

In the past, the economics of residential solar installations were heavily influenced by incentives. Government and utility renewable-energy programs were often used to encourage homeowners to adopt solar power by offsetting the initial installation costs. Today, the cost of installing a PV system has declined enough that many typical residential systems can recover their installation cost in roughly fifteen years even without credits or rebates. Because most solar systems are expected to operate for thirty to forty years, they can provide decades of electricity after the initial investment has been recovered.

Chapter 29

SHITMATES

Part 1 — Failures

"I learned to always take on things I'd never done before. Growth and comfort do not coexist."
—Ginni Rometty

Age 54 · 2012

3/26/12 — Day 1

The Dash-8's engines powered back and the airplane settled onto final approach for Guaymas. The landing was smooth enough that no one commented—the kind that doesn't announce itself. By the time we rolled up to the small terminal, my mind had already shifted into sailing mode.

Immigration and customs took minutes. Stamps. A nod. I stepped outside.

No one was there.

It was a small airport. One curb. One door. There wasn't anywhere to miss each other.

The dry Sonoran Desert heat pressed in. I waited.

Twenty minutes passed.

I called the boat captain. He answered immediately, as if he'd been expecting the call.

"The dune buggy won't start," he said casually. "Just grab a taxi to the marina and I'll see you there."

There was no apology—just instructions delivered as if this had been the plan all along. I slipped the phone back into my pocket and flagged a taxi.

The van rattled when the door shut. The driver was a genial, middle-aged Mexican man, a little overweight, who spoke perfect English and explained that we'd have to drive slowly until the engine warmed up. He wasn't kidding. I suspected I could have walked faster.

A few minutes later he pulled into a gas station, pointed to the gauge, and asked if I could cover a little fuel. One gallon went into the tank—just enough, apparently, to get us to the marina and not much farther.

When we pulled back onto the road, blue smoke curled behind us. The engine hesitated, then caught, and we lurched forward again. With no air-conditioning, we drove with the windows down while dust and exhaust drifted through the cabin. Slowly, unevenly, we made our way to the marina.

At the marina I met the crew: Bob, the captain, and Keith, who worked for him back in Arizona. Keith was eager and alert and admitted immediately that he'd never sailed before. I had sailed many times, but only day sailing—never for weeks at a time.

Our route was ambitious: a forty-one-foot Beneteau from San Carlos, Sonora, down the west coast to Panama, through the canal, then up the Gulf of Mexico to Texas. The scale of it was obvious to all of us, and the excitement on the dock was real, even if each of us was feeling it for our own reasons.

I wasn't there for adventure alone.

Parts of my life back home had begun to feel unsteady, and I was hoping a few weeks at sea might help me sort out what land no longer could.

Photo #44. The Beneteau 41' we sailed, pictured here in the San Carlos marina with Mount Tetakawi in the background.

The dune buggy push-started easily—no tools, no discussion—as if that were its normal starting procedure. Hmm. We drove off to complete the Mexican government paperwork and then returned to the boat.

The boat sat quietly in her slip. Halyards slapped softly against the mast. The cockpit smelled of diesel, salt, sunblock, and old canvas that had seen too many seasons.

We loaded supplies—food, alcohol, and the dinghy. Bob said the boat was in tip-top shape, stocked with plenty of tools and spare parts.

I didn't inspect it. I wasn't the captain.

At 1500 hours we pushed off.

Leaving the marina safely required manual control and the use of the small motor. Once clear of the harbor, the sails went up and the autopilot took the load. The helm settled into the herky-jerky rhythm of machine steering—whining, correcting, hunting with each small adjustment.

The shoreline slid slowly aft as we adjusted to the new arrangement. A few minutes later Bob reached down and pulled the engine fuel shutoff handle. The T-handle came away in his hand, detached, a frayed cable dangling from it like something that should not have come loose so easily. For a moment he just stared at it. We all did.

The engine kept running.

Bob disappeared below and reached the secondary fuel shutoff valve in the engine compartment. Closing that valve should have stopped the diesel relatively quickly.

It didn't.

The steady thumping from the engine compartment continued the same.

A few minutes later Bob poked his head back up through the hatch.

"Don't know why she's still running," he said. "Better than not. We'll deal with it later."

Not long after, a warning alarm began sounding from the helm pedestal—high, insistent, cutting straight through the cockpit and into your chest.

"What's that?" someone asked.

"Autopilot disconnect warning," Bob yelled from below. "Someone steer."

I took the helm. The wheel felt heavy, the boat more alive, the motion sharper as the swells rolled under us.

Bob and Keith opened the console. Inside was a loose mass of wires—none of them bundled or labeled the way you'd expect. They talked back and forth as they worked—what it might be, what to try next, what probably wasn't the problem—testing one idea, rechecking it, then moving on to another.

The alarm had begun sounding only twenty minutes into the voyage. Fifteen more minutes passed before they finally silenced it by disconnecting the control box entirely.

Sometime after that—no one checked a watch—the engine finally quit on its own. Bob noticed it and shrugged.

We had been at sea for barely an hour when, with little explanation, Bob slipped below deck, pale and quiet, and lay down. Keith stayed with the wiring, tools spread at his feet, troubleshooting everything he could. I remained at the helm as the sun crept across the sky and the swells lengthened as we moved farther offshore.

I too was suffering from mild seasickness. That left the boat effectively short-handed.

Still, we were able to rig for a downwind sail with the jib poled out to port, stretched wide to catch the wind coming from directly behind us. With the mainsail eased to starboard, the boat settled into a steady downwind run. *(Inside the Story: Sailboat Headsails and Downwind Control.)*

Nearly three hours into the passage a sharp concussive bang erupted forward of the cockpit—the kind that snaps your head up before thought arrives.

Bob came up yelling, "What did you do to my boat!"—before he looked forward.

With an angry gesture he took the helm and sent Keith and me forward to investigate. The jib pole fittings had snapped. Parts were bent in places where nothing should have moved, metal deformed under load. Lines were pulled tight and out of alignment. The jib sail flapped freely in the breeze.

But nothing was torn.

We worked the pole and sail free, stowed the damaged gear, and went back to our positions in the cockpit.

By late afternoon, three systems had failed.

The boat kept moving.

Darkness came without ceremony. The autopilot still wasn't working. We ran two-man watches, always keeping two people in the cockpit. Every two hours, one of us rotated below, but the watch itself never broke—one at the helm, the other keeping watch and making sure the first didn't drift off.

The swells were long and heavy. Each one lifted the bow, dropped it, then lifted it again, over and over, like an amusement-park ride trying to tumble your gyros. The wheel never stayed where you set it. Steering took constant pressure and small corrections. Standing for hours at the helm burned my lower back. My hands were cold and wet as the temperature dropped rapidly.

Below deck was worse. The motion was amplified, the air stale. My stomach rolled the moment I lay down. My berth was tempting, but the boat's constant movement made it useless. I spent most of my off-watch time half-curled on the cockpit floor, bracing against the molded fiberglass bench, damp and cold, waiting for my turn back at the helm where at least the horizon stayed in sight.

3/27/12 — Day 2

By morning the seasickness had faded, but the cold hadn't. My clothes were layered and damp, and my hands felt thick and slow to respond. So did my brain.

The sea eased as the sun climbed. We continued steering manually through the morning while the rising sun slowly dried the dew that had coated the boat and us. Eventually the wool hat and foul-weather gear came off.

Only then did I have room to think about why I had come. I needed distance from a life that had stopped working, and I needed this trip to work.

Photo #45. Me wearing four layers of clothing just before sunup.

Midday, a pod of humpback whales surfaced off the starboard side—six adults and a calf. One animal held position between the calf and the boat with a calm that felt deliberate. They moved, breathed, rolled once, then slipped back beneath the surface. The water closed quietly over them.

Late in the afternoon the autopilot repair was finished. Course control passed back to the machine, the wheel went light again, and no one celebrated.

We continued south.

Learning Point:

- *Often people hold the mechanical quality of their equipment in a much higher regard than it deserves.*

Inside the Story *(Optional Reading)*

Sailboat Headsails and Downwind Control

Most sailing boats carry a triangular sail ahead of the mast called a jib, or headsail. Positioned in front of the mainsail, the jib helps direct airflow and contributes significantly to the boat's forward drive. Together, the two sails work as a coordinated aerodynamic system that turns wind into motion.

When sailing downwind with the mainsail on one side and the jib on the other, the jib can lose its shape or fold inward as the boat rolls and the wind shifts. To hold it steady and fully exposed to the wind, sailors sometimes use a spar called a whisker pole, or jib pole. One end attaches near the mast; the other holds the outer corner of the jib outward, keeping the sail spread and drawing properly.

This arrangement helps the boat remain balanced and maintain speed while running downwind. If the pole or its fittings fail, the jib loses that support and begins to flap or collapse. The crew must then reconfigure the sail plan or continue under reduced sail.

Chapter 29

SHITMATES

Part 2 — Entitlement

Age 54 · 2012

3/28/12 — Day 3

By the third day we were clear of the Sea of Cortez and easing into the Pacific. The motion had changed—longer swells now, slower, and heavier, lifting the boat and setting her back down again with no rhythm I could ever quite anticipate. Sleep was still shallow and fragmented. My hands stayed cold even when the air warmed.

Through the evening haze, Mazatlán appeared ahead of us as a low smear of lights, eighteen nautical miles off the bow. At our speed, we'd be in within three hours.

The captain announced we should clean up. "Once we're docked, we'll go ashore for dinner." *(Inside the Story: Sailboat Heads.)*

Nearing the marina, the engine surprised us and started without complaint. Keith and I dropped the sails, rigged the fenders, and took our positions on the port side with lines coiled in our hands, ready to step off onto the dock. A mild side current nudged us toward the fueling berth. Bob corrected smoothly.

Nothing went wrong.

We slid in cleanly at 2215.

That small success felt earned—out of proportion to what it was, but earned all the same.

The fuel dock was closed. So, we tied up anyway, first in line for morning fueling.

Once ashore, the city felt oddly muted. Too quiet for a coastal town that size. We wandered longer than we should have before finding a restaurant that was technically open. The food was forgettable.

By the time we walked back toward the marina, my legs felt heavy and my patience thin.

3/29/12 — Day 4

It was after midnight when we passed one last bar that still had its lights on.

Inside, it was nearly empty. A few older patrons settling tabs. One woman sitting alone near the wall.

She stood to leave, hesitated, then sat back down.

Keith noticed.

He was thirty—alert in the way men get when a long night suddenly offers an unexpected opportunity. Bob and I exchanged a glance and nudged him in her direction. After a few drinks of liquid courage, Keith joined her table. Eventually, she came back with him and sat with us.

She was Canadian, traveling alone through Mexico. Capable and unafraid, though finding her alone in a nearly empty bar at midnight in Mazatlán struck me as unusual.

I was too tired to think much about it.

With fatigue taking command, I suggested we all head back to the boat for a drink. It seemed like the only move that might give Keith the night he was hoping for.

Back on the boat, the four of us sat in the salon and shared a single shot of tequila. It felt ceremonial and unnecessary to me, but it loosened whatever still felt tentative between the two of them.

Once the glasses were empty, I went straight to my berth.

Sleep came fast and hard.

I woke early to a sharp concussive engine backfiring somewhere in the marina. The sound echoed off concrete and water, announcing the start of a new day like a mechanical rooster.

Below deck, Bob was still face down in his berth, fully dressed, passed out.

Keith's bunk was empty.

I climbed topside for air and found Keith pacing—unsteady, visibly furious.

Keith was still half drunk and vibrating with anger.

"I'm done," he said. "I'm leaving. I'm packing right now."

He didn't pack.

Instead, he talked.

He circled the same grievance again and again—denied, robbed, humiliated—each pass rougher than the last. Alcohol had stripped away whatever filter remained.

"That asshole made her choose," he shouted again.

I didn't interrupt him. I didn't correct the language or challenge the framing. I just kept him talking.

Partly because I wanted to understand.

Partly because if Keith left the boat, I wasn't staying alone with Bob.

Finally, we went ashore for coffee. Steam rose from the cups into the cool morning air.

Steam still rose from Keith too.

The words kept coming. It became crystal clear that our fragile crew camaraderie was at risk. Keith viewed the situation as black and white.

Piece by piece, the story took full shape.

Bob hadn't gone to his berth after the tequila shot.

He stayed topside, elbowing into conversation not intended for him.

Hour after hour. He refilled glasses. He told stories—about boats he'd owned, races he'd driven, people he knew, places he'd been. Each story landed like a marker pushed across the table. Every time the moment drifted toward privacy, he inserted himself again.

The age difference between him and Keith stopped being incidental. Bob leaned into it—experience versus youth—forcing the comparison into the open. He spoke longer. Louder. As if the outcome were already decided.

At some point, he began talking about women in general—what they wanted, what they responded to—as if she weren't sitting there at all.

Keith tried to keep up.

He had youth and looks.

That was all he had.

Against ownership, authority, stories, and time—it wasn't a fair fight.

It wasn't meant to be.

Sometime near dawn, she left the boat and disappeared into the morning.

Keith felt robbed.

He saw it as sabotage.

As betrayal.

By the time Keith and I returned to the dock, the fuel station had opened. Bob was already there fueling the boat, short and irritable. He snapped at us for being late. I let it pass.

Keith went below to stay out of Bob's sight while I readied the boat to shove off.

Once we cleared the marina and began motoring toward a municipal mooring down the coast, Keith reappeared in the cockpit. That was when I opened the conversation.

"Bob, we need to talk about last night."

Keith unloaded everything in one long, furious stream. Bob listened without interrupting. When Keith finished, I asked Bob to respond.

He didn't deny much.

Then he said it—flatly, without irony or embarrassment.

"This is my boat. Any woman who comes on this boat, I get first.

Once I'm done, either of you clowns can have what's left."

The words landed and sat there.

For a moment, no one spoke.

I stopped trying to mediate.

"We're not pirates," I said. "We're not sailing together under arcane rules like that."

Bob launched into a rambling defense—ownership, authority, entitlement. My boat. My rules. It sounded rehearsed, brittle, and deeply small.

In the end, we reached an uneasy agreement and stopped talking. When the sails were up or the engine running, the captain commanded. When the boat was secured, we were equals—no hierarchy, no bullshit, no competition.

Keith agreed to stay.

I agreed to continue.

The agreement kept the trip alive. It did not settle everything.

We tied up to a municipal mooring ball down the coast and spent the day in town. By the time we returned to the boat that night, there was plenty left to say, but none of us had the will to ride that horse again.

We slept.

Learning Point:

- *People often present a polished version of themselves in normal life. Isolation, fatigue, alcohol, and confinement strip that away. What remains is often closer to the truth.*

Inside the Story *(Optional Reading)*

Sailboat Heads

On most sailboats, the bathroom is referred to as the head, a term dating back to the earliest days of sailing ships when the crew's toilet was located near the bow, or "head," of the vessel. Modern recreational sailboats retain the name even though the facilities are usually located within the cabin.

Because space on a sailboat is extremely limited, the head is typically designed as a compact wet-room. The toilet, sink, and shower share the same small enclosure, often molded from fiberglass to simplify construction and waterproofing. When the shower is used, the entire compartment becomes wet, with drainage directed to a small sump or bilge pump system.

The compact layout is efficient but offers very little room to move. In many smaller cruising boats, the space is barely large enough for an adult to stand and turn, making simple tasks awkward. Functionality rather than comfort defines the design, reflecting the constant trade-offs required when living within the confined space of a small sailing vessel.

CHAPTER 29

SHITMATES

PART 3 — THE FOOL

AGE 54 · 2012

3/30/12 — Day 5

As we prepared the boat to depart Mazatlán, the fog arrived with dawn, creeping in low and deliberate, flattening the marina until distance disappeared. The far edge of the anchorage faded first, then masts, then hulls. Sound carried oddly—water against pilings, an engine coughing somewhere unseen—while shape and direction dissolved.

There was no reason to rush—no tide window, no schedule pressure, nothing waiting on the other side of blind movement.

I assumed we would wait.

I was wrong.

Bob came up from below already dressed, already irritated. He glanced at the fog, then at the boat, then at us.

"Stow the dinghy," he said. "We're leaving."

For a moment I thought I'd misheard him. The visibility was measured in feet, not miles. I could barely see the next mooring ball. I waited for the follow-on sentence—the joke, the qualifier, the reconsideration.

None came.

The engine started. Keith began hauling the dinghy aboard. Lines were cast off. The boat eased forward into a gray wall that erased everything beyond the bow.

"What are we doing?" I asked.

No answer.

We motored out.

Then accelerated to five knots.

Not a cautious crawl, but a committed pace.

The fog thickened as we moved, the air wet and opaque, swallowing the sound of our own wake. The anchorage behind us vanished as if it never existed.

I knew this was wrong before I could fully put the danger into words. It wasn't vague unease—it was training, pattern recognition, and signals I had learned to trust, all firing at once.

Years of managing threats and errors had trained me to speak up. But years spent working with people and their egos had also shown me that, when someone is already defensive, a direct challenge can make them dig in deeper.

Bob had already made this personal. Pushing hard after he had issued an order would only turn it into a contest. So I tried a softer approach—measured, neutral, giving him a chance to reach the right conclusion himself.

"I'd be fine waiting for this to lift."

Nothing.

I looked to Keith. He had no frame of reference for what this meant—fog, traffic, closure rates. To him it was just weather. To Bob, I knew, it was a choice.

I tried one more time—direct now, no hedging.

"We shouldn't be motoring in this fog in a busy harbor."

"I know what's best on my boat," Bob snapped. "You don't know your place."

Bob poured coffee and sat relaxed in the back of the cockpit. Keith joined him. They talked casually, as if this were any other departure. The contrast between their posture and the conditions was surreal.

I stopped trying to persuade him. It was clear I had no influence over the decision. All that was left was to take action in the only ways I could.

We had no collision avoidance radar.

No AIS, the electronic system that lets boats identify themselves to one another.

No meaningful way to see or be seen beyond luck and reaction time. And "See and avoid" only works if you can see.

We couldn't.

I went below and switched on the navigation lights—something that should have already been done. Then I moved forward to the bow with a handheld white light, knowing it wouldn't help me see much, but hoping it might help someone else see us a second earlier.

The fog felt textured, like moving through wet wool.

Sound arrived before shape—and sometimes without any form at all.

Engines somewhere. Water slapping metal. Voices drifting through the gray with no body attached to them.

Bob ordered the mainsail hoisted, chasing wind that wasn't there. In theory, a bit of sail can steady the rolling motion of a boat under power, but there wasn't enough breeze for that to matter. Whatever the intention, it did nothing to change the situation—we were still running blind in thick harbor fog.

I stayed at the bow, scanning the nothing ahead of us, heart rate up, jaw tight. I was trapped up there—watching a dangerously bad decision play out with no authority to stop it.

Anger sat just under the surface, held in place by the same discipline that kept my eyes forward. Every sense narrowed.

Then something appeared.

At first, it was just a darker blur inside the gray. My brain rejected it, then recalculated.

I pointed and jumped up and down.

"Rock, rock!" I yelled. "Rock dead ahead!"

No response.

I glanced back. Bob looked up from his coffee, barely interested, and never put the cup down.

The shape grew, changed form, resolved.

It wasn't a rock.

It was the stern of a commercial fishing vessel.

"Boat, boat!" I shouted. "Boat—five hundred feet!"

The thing materialized all at once, stationary and massive, steel where we were small and fiberglass. I could see crewmen on the aft deck, smoking, watching us with open confusion. Their faces registered the same question mine did: What the hell are you doing?

Bob finally turned the wheel, swinging us to port.

At five knots we were closing at about six hundred feet per minute. Less than a minute to impact.

We cleared the vessel. The fog closed back in behind us, swallowing its outline as if it had never been there.

We passed three hundred feet off the trawler's stern, close enough to smell diesel, close enough to understand exactly how small we were. *(Inside the Story: Closure Rates.)*

If the trawler had been moving toward us instead of anchored, the time to impact would have been cut in half. If I hadn't been on the bow, we likely would not have seen it in time.

"That was reckless," I said. "That endangered all of us for no reason."

Bob didn't even look at me.

"I saw the boat," he said. "I turned. We were never in danger. Get me a beer."

That was the moment it settled.

He hadn't learned anything. He hadn't even registered the risk. What he had seen was a challenge—to his authority, his judgment, his self-image.

We got very lucky that morning. I didn't believe luck was something we could keep spending all the way to Texas.

The fog finally broke thirty minutes later. Sunlight burned through and revealed a perfectly calm morning. Blue sky. Open water. No urgency. No reason to have rushed.

We could have waited.

We didn't.

ANOTHER BULLET DODGED

We continued south.

Learning Point:

- *Owning a boat can make someone a captain in name. It does not make them one in practice.*
- *Leadership is learned, judgment is earned, and without both, authority is just ownership pretending to be command.*

Inside the Story *(Optional Reading)*

Closure Rates

Closure rate describes how quickly the distance between two moving objects decreases. When two vessels move toward one another, their speeds combine to determine how rapidly the separation disappears.

At sea, the numbers involved may sound small. A sailboat moving at six knots is traveling only about seven miles per hour, but at that speed the boat still covers roughly six hundred feet per minute. In low visibility, an object five hundred feet ahead leaves less than a minute to recognize the hazard and react.

If both vessels are moving toward each other, the closure rate doubles and the available reaction time is cut in half. Even modest speeds can therefore create surprisingly little margin, especially in restricted visibility such as fog.

The opposite illusion exists in high-altitude flight—events can appear to unfold slowly even though aircraft may pass one another with closure rates exceeding one thousand miles per hour. The difference is not the speed, but the distance available to see the other object. When that distance is measured in miles, the brain has time to process the motion. When it is measured in hundreds of feet, the same closure develops almost instantly.

Chapter 29

SHITMATES

Part 4 — Wildlife

Age 54 · 2012

3/30/12 — continued. Day 5

After the near miss with the fishing trawler and our exit from the waters around Mazatlán, the sea was magnificently alive.

First, we sailed through a scattered field of sea turtles. As far as the eye could see, shells dotted the surface, each about a hundred feet apart, gently rising and falling with the swells while the animals themselves remained mostly submerged. Only the rounded hump of each shell showed above the waterline.

Nearly all of them appeared to be the same size—roughly two feet across. No smaller shells. No larger ones anywhere in sight. I guessed it was some sort of exclusive midlife club out for a sunny float. Whatever the explanation, it was mesmerizing, and we sailed through carefully, leaving them undisturbed.

A few minutes later, we were strafed by a Staffel—the German word for squadron—of twelve to fourteen gray pelicans.

They approached high out of the sun and swooped in single file like dive bombers making a run on a WWII aircraft carrier. As they closed in, they altered their wing geometry, transitioning from a high-speed delta shape into a broad low-speed glide. Not one of them flapped a feather.

They had elegantly converted stored altitude into effortless glide flight.

One by one, they passed low over our boat, each clearly eyeing us during their precise reconnaissance.

Then, as quietly as they had arrived, they climbed back into the sky in a modified wedge formation and disappeared.

With the birds gone, the ocean returned to its quiet routine. The remainder of the day unfolded under inconsistent winds, resulting in a mix of motoring and sailing.

By late afternoon we had put 101 nautical miles between us and Mazatlán when the captain decided to anchor near a group of small, craggy islands—Isla Isabel—a protected bird breeding refuge.

That night, thankfully, we would not stand watch in shifts.

Instead, we all slept, rocked gently by the rhythmic bobbing of the boat, and enjoyed a full, uninterrupted night's rest.

3/31/12 — Day 6

We woke to a gentle rolling motion and the sound of fishing pangas—small, nondescript, rickety Mexican fishing boats—motoring briskly around us.

We also discovered that the bird sanctuary was home to tens of thousands of birds, all seemingly squawking in deafening unison. These F'ing birds were everywhere one looked. In this case, F stood for frigate bird.

The frigate is a beautiful, slender bird—long-winged and angular, built more like a glider than a flapper. Trailing straight behind it is a narrow, feathered, stinger-like appendage. I wasn't watching them as a birder. I was watching them as an aviator. Every pass overhead looked like a demonstration of design and control.

Through binoculars I noticed an astonishing aerodynamic trick hidden in that odd little tail. The stinger could be splayed outward at roughly forty-five degrees to both sides, acting like dive speed brakes. Deflected to one side, it worked like a turn augmenter, tightening the bird's turning radius.

Magnificent flying.

As the frigates drifted off to continue their patrol of the island, we resumed our own far less elegant progress.

The morning passed quietly. I read, wrote, and watched the sky.

Mid-level stratus streaked the atmosphere—often a sign of an approaching upper-level weather system. It gave us hope that wind might finally arrive. We were growing tired of motoring.

A short while later we passed the Islas Tres Marías and finally caught some breeze. We raised every sail and trimmed for peak efficiency, scooting along at seven knots.

The joy didn't last.

Two hours later the air went dead still again. The sails sagged uselessly and the halyards began banging against the mast.

I turned to Keith and said sarcastically, "This is a sailing trip… right?"

He shrugged and went back to his book, *Sailing for Dummies.*

We had been dragging fishing lines for days without success. Around 1700 hours, discouraged and ready to reel them in, our luck finally changed. Keith caught the first fish of the journey—a small skipjack, but enough to feed three.

Keith clearly had no idea what to do next, and I was of little help. Once on deck, the two-foot-long fish thrashed violently, beating its tail against the deck and launching itself nearly a foot into the air, seemingly as determined to return to the water as it was to avoid Keith's grasp. I handed him my safety knife, hoping he could end the sideshow.

Unfortunately, that only escalated things.

The scene devolved into a B-rated horror film—or a dark comedy. The captain looked over and said, "Do something, you idiots. The fish is suffering." Way out of character for Bob, this moment of empathy—for something other than himself—was almost impressive. He handed Keith a metal winch handle and said, "Put the fish out of its misery."

Keith proceeded to whack the poor creature repeatedly. He must have hit it a dozen times, but the fish simply refused to die, continuing to flop and jump and spread blood everywhere.

Every blow appeared to offend the fish more than injure it.

When the drama finally ended, the deck looked like a crime scene—blood splattered across the cockpit, the sides of the boat, the stern—and us.

It was horrific. And embarrassing.

We had made a mess of the boat, and because of our ineptness the fish had suffered. We genuinely felt bad about that.

Still, the animal did not die in vain. Fresh fish tacos were a welcome change from canned and jarred food. We honored the life that had been given and agreed we would do better next time.

4/1/12 — Day 7

The nighttime safety practice of keeping two men on watch has real merit—it functions much like a buddy system. But with only a three-man crew it carries a steep cost. Each person gets scheduled rack time every four hours, and only for two hours at a stretch. After a few nights the routine leaves everyone exhausted—sometimes worse.

Keith and I shared the final watch before dawn, miserable and counting minutes until sunrise. Shortly after first light, a pod of dolphins appeared off the starboard side, jumping and frolicking in the low morning sun. I like to think the performance was for us—to revive our weary minds—but more likely they were herding fish, or a few juveniles were simply horsing around. Either way, it was a wonderful way to start the day.

During the night we had edged closer to shore, and now in sunlight the Mexican coastline south of Puerto Vallarta came into full view. It was as dramatic and beautiful as any coastline I had seen in Northern California—rugged, barren cliffs in the foreground with tall, densely wooded mountains rising behind them in rich contrast.

After a brief fuel stop at Barra de Navidad we motored back out. Once clear of the coastal topography we finally encountered the first steady winds since leaving Mazatlán three days earlier. We set the sails, trimmed for eight knots, and took up a 140-degree heading toward Ixtapa.

Learning Points:

- *Marine life encountered during coastal sailing is a vivid reminder of nature's abundance.*
- *Periods of natural beauty and calm are not distractions from a journey; they are essential to sustaining it.*
- *Rest, when available, is a strategic resource and should be taken without hesitation.*
- *Even deeply flawed people are not one-dimensional; moments of empathy can emerge where least expected.*

Chapter 29

SHITMATES

Part 5 — Borrowed Peace

Age 54 · 2012

4/2/12 — Day 8

The coastline thirty-five nautical miles north of Ixtapa began to soften and mellow. The rugged mountain spine that had dominated Mexico for most of our journey pushed inland, giving way to rolling hills and a gentler shoreline.

By nightfall, I had retreated to the bow, as far from the cockpit as I could get without leaving the boat altogether. The sea slid past beneath me, dark and indifferent. I felt isolated in a way that had nothing to do with distance—this was the isolation of being trapped in someone else's bad decisions.

The motion of the boat was steady, hypnotic, but my chest felt heavy, compressed. I stared into the darkness and felt the accumulated weight of the trip settling on me—the small humiliations, the constant vigilance, the exhaustion of never knowing when the next outburst would come. What had begun as a long-awaited adventure now felt hollow. The joy had slipped away quietly, replaced by something harder to name.

My thoughts drifted beyond the boat—to the end of my marriage to Jillian, and then to the quieter unraveling of my relationship with Joanne. Two different losses layered close together, each leaving its own empty space. Sitting there in the dark, it all felt connected—like this trip was simply the latest thing I'd failed to hold together.

It was a tough night.

That was when they appeared.

I had been gazing down into the frothing water just off the bow when three full-sized dolphins materialized out of the darkness, illuminated by a bright five-eighths moon. They slipped effortlessly into our bow wake and began to frolic.

They swam a graceful ballet, crisscrossing in front of the boat for at least ten minutes. I clipped my safety line to the railing and leaned out as far as it would allow, watching and silently communicating with my three new travel mates.

Their joyful play lifted my spirits almost instantly.

As if on cue, our boat happened to be passing through a region dense with microscopic phosphorescent plankton. When disturbed, the tiny organisms flared to life with a yellow-green glow.

The black water suddenly came alive.

Every movement the dolphins made ignited streaks of light. Their bodies carved luminous arcs through the sea, each turn leaving a glowing wake that lingered in the darkness like contrails behind a jet. For moments at a time, each animal seemed wrapped in a living halo of light.

When the first three departed, five more dolphins arrived to take their place.

A few behaved like brothers—pushing, shoving, jumping, and showing off.

At one point two of them rolled onto their sides and swam parallel to the bow, so close I could see the detail in their eyes. But it wasn't just eye contact. There was an unmistakable sense of awareness—of being noticed, assessed, included. For a moment it felt like a shared exchange, not between man and animal, but between two intelligences meeting in motion.

Then, just as suddenly, they peeled away and vanished into the night.

Maybe it meant nothing beyond play and motion.

Maybe it was simply coincidence and chemistry.

But that night, it felt like connection.

They had come to cheer me up.

It worked.

4/3/12 — Day 9

We passed Ixtapa and finally anchored around 0100 in the bay off Zihuatanejo—nicknamed Z-what—in the state of Guerrero.

We motored slowly among other boats, searching for a spot that would allow our boat to swing freely at anchor without encroaching on our neighbors.

Until now, we had always tied up to docks or mooring balls. This would be our first time deploying the anchor on Bob's boat.

Below deck at the bow sat the anchor locker—a small compartment housing hundreds of feet of heavy chain.

Keith and I worked to deploy the anchor, but at the critical moment the chain jammed. We struggled to pass the metal clevis bolt through the deck eyelet that guided the anchor chain out.

It was immediately clear the clevis bolt was larger than the eyelet hole.

A simple rule applies to most mechanical problems: never pull hard on something that's snagged without first understanding why.

Given our already-fragile relationship with Bob, neither Keith nor I wanted to risk damaging his boat.

This caution did not sit well with the captain.

From the helm he shouted, visibly agitated, "Launch the damn thing you idiots!"

We couldn't. The clevis was stuck below the eyelet leaving the chain completely trapped down below.

Bob idled the engine, stormed forward, shoved us aside, and began shouting profanity. Rather than helping or explaining, he took over—determined to demonstrate how he alone could "get 'er done."

Bob yanked hard on the chain. Something gave way below, and the anchor finally dropped. The sudden release sent the chain rattling through the deck hardware—as if it had been waiting all along for brute force instead of understanding.

Faulty equipment once again became a referendum on our intelligence.

What followed was another tirade.

"You two disgust me," he barked. "Get out of my way and get me a beer. Fetching me a beer is the height of your talents."

I was burning mad—but I held my tongue. There are moments when responding only pours fuel on the fire, and this was clearly one of them.

We finished securing the boat in silence.

Later, after Keith had gone below, I approached Bob.

"We need to talk."

I resisted the urge to vent. Anger would have gone nowhere.

Instead, I chose my words carefully.

"As a captain myself," I said, "I understand your frustration. But belittling us isn't helping us become a high-functioning crew. We need some training so we can meet your expectations."

To my surprise, he didn't explode. He listened, jaw tight, eyes hard. After a long pause, he muttered that he'd show us how he wanted it done the next light. It wasn't an apology. It wasn't even agreement. But it was something—and I took it.

Still, I suspected the next critical moment wasn't far off.

Morning revealed a magnificent, well-protected bay—the kind sailors instantly relax into. Calm water. Good holding. A place where the boat—and we—could rest. Beyond it sat Zihuatanejo itself, an old-style Mexican town with no high-rises and no strip malls—just low buildings tracing a stone walking path along the beach.

Bob suggested Bloody Marys to start the day off right, and we sat in the sun with drinks in hand making small talk. In his own way, it felt like a peace offering for the night before.

After an hour Keith and I were feeling no pain. Unfortunately, that was also when he called on us to launch the dinghy.

In my head I replayed the previous night's anchor fiasco and Bob's tongue-lashing. I immediately wished we had put the dinghy in the water before consuming several ounces of alcohol.

Thankfully—and somewhat miraculously—we launched it without incident.

We headed ashore, wandered through town, found a beachfront café with Wi-Fi, good food, and friendly staff, and spent hours eating, drinking, and working on our computers.

Photo #46. Beach café in Zihuatanejo looking out at the bay.

Later we each went our separate ways. The time alone felt restorative. As I walked around, I was struck by how friendly the local people were—and how attractive they looked.

That evening, Bob dinghied Keith and me to the pier. We hopped on the city bus for 85 cents and rode the 25 minutes to Ixtapa. The driver kept an open change tube by his seat, handing coins back to anyone who didn't have exact fare. No fuss. No suspicion. It struck me as oddly reassuring.

Where Z-what was intimate and charming, Ixtapa was corporate and congested—high-rise hotels and strip malls blocking the view of the beach. Keith instantly loved the vibe of Ixtapa. I couldn't wait to depart.

On a side street we came upon a broken-down bus that had stranded a college marching band. Instead of sulking, they unloaded their instruments and began playing in the street. Drums, brass, woodwinds—music filled the air as steam poured from the engine.

Watching them, I felt something I'd noticed again and again in Mexico—a quiet ability to turn setbacks into celebration.

4/4/12 — Day 10

The next morning, I treated myself to a beachside massage.

Face down on a table in the sand, waves rolling nearby, a cool breeze drifting through the tent, I slipped into a state of deep calm.

Children laughed.

Tropical flowers scented the air.

Carne asada sizzled on nearby grills.

The tide slid slowly in and out.

But in that moment, I hoped this pocket of peace might linger long enough to give me the patience required to continue tolerating my Napoleonic captain.

Because my patience was wearing thin.

Learning Points:

- *New, big, and modern is not always better than old, small, and quaint.*
- *Often the best discoveries when traveling are the places where few people travel.*
- *Calm moments reset the mind, but they don't cure dysfunctional leadership.*
- *The real danger isn't conflict—it's being led by someone who mistakes intimidation for authority.*

CHAPTER 29

SHITMATES

PART 6 — RELATIONSHIPS

AGE 54 · 2012

4/5/12 — Day 11

At 0425 we were sailing downwind on a course for Acapulco, with the jib billowing out ahead of the bow.

With the wind squarely behind us, this should have been a textbook spinnaker run. But it wasn't. The fittings that attached the spinnaker to the mast had failed on day one when the jib pole broke. Without those fittings, we were hamstrung—forced to limp along using the jib alone for downwind sailing.

Bob and I were working together in the pit, and as usual, the tension between us felt like an anchor dragging along the seabed.

I genuinely wanted to find some balance—something that would let us function as a crew, even if enjoying the voyage together wasn't in the cards. At a minimum, getting along would make the journey safer and more tolerable for everyone.

I persisted in engaging him.

I searched for that elusive Rosetta Stone—a way to communicate with Bob without triggering his defensiveness. Somehow, with each attempt, I still managed to push the wrong buttons.

Bob was a relic at sea, operating with an authoritarian leadership style straight out of another era. In many ways, he reminded me of some of the airline captains I flew with in the 1980s. *(Inside the Story: Captain Leadership Styles.)*

Like those old timers, Bob had unshakable confidence and a gift for improvisation. He could jury-rig almost anything and keep broken machinery functioning—a useful trait on a long ocean passage.

What he lacked, however, was any interest in leading or teaching. Rather than developing his crew, he preferred to demonstrate how much he knew and how much he could accomplish single-handedly. Encouragement was rare. More often, Keith and I were reminded that we were, in his words, a "useless bag of bones."

That approach did nothing to build camaraderie.

The tragedy was that Keith and I each brought useful skills to the voyage.

Bob never seemed interested in using either of them.

Collaboration was off the table.

Respect was optional.

As the days passed, his behavior toward me grew increasingly defensive and rude. Asking for input seemed beyond his emotional reach. It felt as though Keith and I were little more than unwanted appendages—something Bob was stuck with.

I naively hoped for dialogue.

Bob wanted edicts.

Eventually, I gave up and chose silence. It wasn't worth provoking him unless the issue involved safety or survival. Avoidance reduced conflict, but it surely did nothing to build a functioning crew.

His disdain created a corrosive environment—one where mistakes became more likely, not less.

By the afternoon of the eleventh day, something finally changed.

Not the captain's attitude toward me, nor the sporadic breeze, but the temperature shifted. For the first time on the voyage, it was genuinely warm. Shirts came off. Long pants were stowed.

Out came Bob's frilly straw hat.

It was something to behold.

Totally ridiculous on an adult male—but he wore it proudly. As I had already learned, confidence was never Bob's weak point.

In daylight, with good visibility and little traffic around us, we considered a single-person watch sufficient. With the sun shining and a slight breeze pushing us along at four knots, Bob stood watch on deck while Keith and I slept below.

I was jolted awake by what sounded like a hull slamming against ours on the starboard side.

Then came shouting.

My first thought was pirates.

I poked my head through the companionway and froze. Armed men were boarding the boat—automatic weapons in hand.

My heart leapt into my throat. For a split second I couldn't make sense of what I was seeing.

A small boat alongside.

Shouting from above.

Men with guns

My mind raced through the impossible explanations.

Drug runners?

Hijackers?

A hostile boat takeover?

I had no weapons. What the hell could I do?

Then I saw the uniforms. It was the Mexican Navy—their equivalent of the Coast Guard—conducting an at-sea inspection.

Even with nothing to hide, having armed soldiers moving through your boat is unnerving no matter how innocent you are.

They explained that they had been calling us repeatedly on the radio. With no one visible topside and no response to their calls, they moved to intercept us, assuming we might be smuggling drugs or money.

Instead, they found our captain asleep on deck beneath a ridiculous frilly straw hat, while the rest of us were out cold below—hardly the picture of hardened smugglers.

Photo #47. The Mexican Navy/Coast Guard alongside our boat.

They still searched the boat thoroughly and examined our paperwork, ensuring our story checked out.

Contrary to the stereotype of corrupt officials shaking down gringos, these men were professional and businesslike. Despite the language gap—our poor Spanish and their limited English—the inspection unfolded quietly and without drama.

I couldn't help but wonder if Bob's ridiculous hat had played some small role in defusing the situation.

Armed boarding parties and fragile egos make a dangerous combination.

We got lucky… again.

ANOTHER BULLET DODGED

Learning Points:

- *Authoritarian leadership suppresses information flow and increases operational risk.*
- *Safety depends not only on skill and equipment, but also on trust, communication, and emotional maturity.*
- *Wise people are curious about what others know and understand.*
- *Diminishing others is the tyrant's tool of choice to maintain control.*

Inside the Story *(Optional Reading)*

Captain Leadership Styles

Leadership styles in aviation and maritime operations have evolved significantly over time. Earlier generations of captains often operated under an authoritarian model in which the captain held near-total control and decision-making authority. Questioning the captain was discouraged, and crew input was limited, regardless of experience or situational awareness.

Over time, accident investigations and human factors research revealed that this model introduced risk. Critical information was sometimes not communicated, and errors went unchallenged. In response, modern professional operations adopted a more collaborative approach known as Crew Resource Management (CRM). Under this model, all members of the crew are expected to contribute information, challenge decisions when necessary, and work together to maintain situational awareness.

While there is no single correct leadership style, the most effective captains balance authority with openness to input. They maintain command responsibility while encouraging communication from the entire crew. The shift from authoritarian control to collaborative leadership has been a significant factor in improving safety in both aviation and maritime environments.

Aviation eventually learned that silence kills.

Bob was still operating under the old rules.

CHAPTER 29

SHITMATES

PART 7 — SINKING

AGE 54 · 2012

4/6/12 — Day 12

We sailed through the night of the 5th and into the morning of the 6th on a 120-degree heading. By 0900 we rounded the bend and entered Acapulco Bay.

The harbor was vast and crowded, ringed by mountains and humanity. It bore little resemblance to the Acapulco of my childhood imagination—the romantic images of cliff divers and small exotic hotels. Instead, massive concrete towers lined the shoreline, with dense neighborhoods stacked behind them like cans on a grocery store shelf.

I was ready to dismiss the place entirely when something unexpected caught my eye.

Whales.

Large whales moved slowly through the bay, surfacing and sounding as if the city barely existed. For a moment, it felt like the humans were the intruders and the whales still controlled the harbor.

We tied up to a mooring ball, and secured the boat. We had another of the captain's infamous Bloody Marys and gave in to exhaustion. The next thing I knew, it was mid-afternoon, and we had slept straight through.

4/7/12 — Day 13

The next morning, we dinghied ashore during Semana Santa. The beach was packed—every square foot of sand occupied.

We hired a local handler named Nacho Camacho to help us get around town and source supplies. His cousin, Macho Camacho, watched the dinghy. In Mexico, you either pay now or you pay later. We paid now.

4/8/12 — Day 14

Bob's girlfriend, Doris, was due to arrive from Phoenix later that day.

Her impending arrival introduced a new variable. Bob might become even more insufferable, performing for an audience, or he might suddenly remember how to behave like a functioning adult.

Time would tell, though I doubted it would take long.

For the first time on our voyage appearances mattered. The boat was scrubbed. We all shaved and showered. Laundry was done. The floating bachelor flophouse was transformed in anticipation of her arrival.

Bob left for the airport to pick up his girlfriend, leaving Keith and me ashore to guard the dinghy—the same dinghy he had barked instructions about earlier: it wouldn't idle, it would stall above half throttle, and it had only half a tank of fuel. That was the extent of the briefing. The message was clear—we weren't to go touring. Stay put and be ready when they returned from the airport.

In Bob's world that translated to one thing: don't screw this up.

So, we waited.

Unable to joyride, we sat on the dinghy at the beach for hours.

When Bob returned with Doris, her luggage was the first clue this was a new relationship—a massive, rigid suitcase, completely inappropriate for life aboard a small sailboat where bags need to be soft and collapsible to fit into tight lockers. The second clue was Bob himself. During the entire ride on the little dinghy, he and Doris kissed and pawed at each other, seemingly oblivious to the rest of us crammed in beside them. It was difficult to ignore.

We had previously all agreed that once Doris was aboard, we would be leaving Acapulco Bay and heading south that afternoon.

Instead, Bob motored us on a leisurely tour of Acapulco Bay and then anchored one bay south in Puerto Marquez.

A token move.

Not a departure.

Just enough motion to pretend he hadn't broken his word.

Trust was already a big issue on this boat; this deception only shone a brighter light on Bob's character.

Then came the directive: Keith and I were to leave the boat so Bob and Doris could have privacy.

Not a request. An order.

With no plan—just get out.

We were in an unfamiliar bay, with no town in sight, at night, and only half a tank of gas in the dinghy.

We argued.

He didn't care.

Then we left.

The sun had already set when Keith and I pushed off in the dinghy. The bay was nearly black. The dinghy had no navigation lights. No handheld spotlight. No way to spot obstacles or find our way.

Our options were limited.

We motored slowly toward a single dim light on shore, hoping it would lead to something—anything—better than blind darkness. The ride in was quiet, both of us scanning the shoreline, neither saying what we were thinking: that this was a bad plan.

As we got closer, the light resolved into a crowded beach still full of loud, drunken holiday revelers.

Leaving the dinghy there would have guaranteed it would disappear. Instead, we hid the dinghy behind the remains of a decaying concrete boardwalk—an old marina long since abandoned, now reduced to broken slabs and rotting pilings. Leaving it there still felt like a gamble, but far safer than the crowded beach.

From there we walked along a dark pathway until we reached a row of abandoned seaside restaurants and small shops. Each sat recessed into its own concrete alcove, forming a series of shallow horseshoes facing the water—once a lively place to eat and drink, now shuttered and slowly decaying.

That's where we met them—two strangers. A young Mexican woman who spoke excellent English and her companion, drunk, loud, and unpredictable. Every instinct I had said this was not a place to linger. But they offered us each a beer, and since every place along the row had long since closed down, we accepted.

The young woman was well dressed, educated, and Keith's age. The two of them hit it off right away. Once again, I could see that I was about to be the fifth wheel.

When her companion began retching, she told Keith he was just a friend from the preschool where she taught, back home in Mexico City.

Then Señorita Schoolteacher announced that she needed to get el barfo back to his hotel room, and then she would be free to kick up her heels for Semana Santa. I instantly saw what was about to happen. And right on cue, Keith fell into the role of white knight in shining armor and offered to help bring the drunk man to their hotel.

I objected.

Then gently argued.

Then insisted we stay together and not venture far from the dinghy. In fighter aviation there is a simple rule: the wingman stays with the lead. Separation is where trouble begins. *(I know we are not fighter pilots but go with me here.)*

Standing there in the dark, that rule kept repeating in my head.

"Stay together."

Keith waved me off.

He assured me he would be fine and that he would call me later.

As they turned to leave, I called after him, half joking and half serious:

"I hope you still have both kidneys in the morning."

He was thirty years old, driven by optimism, hormones, and the belief that nothing bad ever really happens—especially to him.

I watched them disappear into the darkness, hoping—irrationally—that he might turn around.

He didn't.

I was alone.

The fear didn't hit all at once.

At first, it was irritation.

Then unease.

Then the unmistakable realization that I had been abandoned in a place I didn't trust, in a country where I barely spoke the language and in the pitch dark.

The beach noise felt different now—closer, harsher. The darkness pressed in, and the broken concrete structures behind me felt like places someone could step out from without warning.

I decided to leave.

I found the dinghy still where we had left it, half hidden behind the broken concrete. The relief lasted about three seconds.

Getting back to the sailboat should have been simple.

It wasn't.

Launching the dinghy alone was immediately harder than I expected. With two people, it's awkward. Alone, it's a four-handed job with only two hands.

I untied the boat and shoved it toward the water. The surf pushed it right back into me, slamming the inflatable tube against my leg.

I tried again. Same result.

I waded deeper—knees, thighs, waist—timing my pushes between waves, using momentum instead of strength. Finally, I got the dinghy just past the worst of the break.

Now I had to get in. I scrambled over the tube and immediately swung the outboard engine down into the water—the way I had overheard Bob instruct Keith earlier.

I pulled the starter cord.

Nothing.

A wave shoved the boat shoreward. I yanked the motor back up just in time to keep the prop from smashing into the rocks, jumped back into the water, and dragged the dinghy out into deeper water.

This dance repeated itself, wave after wave.

On a fourth attempt, as I reached for the choke, the metal choke lever slipped loose from its mount and came away in my hand. It hadn't broken—it had detached. Like so many other pieces of Bob's machinery, it now required repair.

I stared at the pieces in my hand for a split second, getting more pissed, then jumped back in the water, shoved the boat back onto the sand and wedged it between rocks.

Crouched over the engine in the dark, I worked to reattach the lever by feel, acutely aware of how exposed I was. Every sound felt amplified—laughter, footsteps, voices drifting too close.

A lone gringo with mechanical trouble felt like easy prey.

Fear and anger tangled together—fear of the place, anger at Bob for putting us here, and disappointment in Keith for leaving me.

Eventually, the linkage was reattached.

I shoved the dinghy back into the water again, dragged it past the break, climbed in, swung the motor down, and pulled.

This time, the engine caught.

I didn't wait. I pointed the bow into the bay and crept forward at half throttle. I dared not open it more—and risk a stall.

The bay was pitch black. Just darkness and the sound of water sliding past the hull.

No moon yet. No anchor light on our sailboat either—because of course there wasn't an operable one. Bob treated basic safety like optional paperwork, and now somewhere out there in the black water was our boat… but I had nothing to steer toward.

The night sky and ocean were so dark that they melted as one. With no bearing markers visible, left, right, up, and down all bore the same empty sense of space-leading nowhere.

Minutes passed.

Then I noticed water in the dinghy.

At first, it was barely visible—a thin sheen across the floor.

Then it began to slosh.

Each roll of the boat pushed the water from one side to the other. The level crept upward—covering the soles of my deck shoes, then the laces.

And it was still rising.

I couldn't let go of the throttle to investigate—the engine wouldn't idle without stalling. I couldn't bail; Bob's boat had no bailer. All I could do was keep moving and hope that an inflatable could not truly sink.

I motored for nearly thirty minutes, scanning the darkness, searching for anything familiar. The water crept higher—now above my ankles. I kept the engine at what I believed was a safe half throttle as I searched for the mother ship.

As the water rose around my feet, fear began to override caution. I eased the throttle higher, pushing toward the upper edge of what I thought the little engine could handle. I wanted more speed—anything that might get me back to the boat sooner.

I knew I was pressing my luck.

But fear doesn't negotiate.

The engine coughed and sputtered, then died.

Silence.

Moments earlier my biggest concern had been getting mugged on shore. Now I was sitting in a sinking dinghy in the middle of a black bay, trying to figure out how not to go under.

I forced myself to slow down.

Panic wouldn't help.

Balancing in the stern, I braced myself and yanked hard on the starter cord, careful not to sway the boat enough to tip it.

Once. Twice. On the third pull, the engine restarted.

I kept it at half power and scanned again.

Finally, I spotted a powerboat with party lights glowing faintly in the distance. I remembered anchoring near it earlier. I turned the dinghy and aimed for it.

When I finally found our sailboat and nudged alongside, relief hit me so hard I had to grip the gunwales to steady myself.

Bob appeared above me. For the first time during our voyage together, I was honestly relieved to see him.

"Where's Keith?" he asked.

Then he looked down.

"And why are you sitting in a bathtub?"

It was hard to get any words out. My teeth were clenched so tightly my jaw ached. My shoulders were up around my ears, my hands still shaking—my body had not yet gotten the message that I was safe.

As I bailed water from the dinghy, I discovered the cause of the flooding: the drain plug was the wrong size and had worked itself loose. Perhaps I had dislodged it while working in the dark to reattach the engine's choke.

Of course, Bob blamed Keith and me, then walked away in disgust, muttering, "Knuckleheads."

Another marginal piece of Bob's equipment. Another quiet failure. Another risk that never should have existed.

I was trying hard not to let the poison of Bob's life leak into mine.

But in that moment, I wanted to throttle him.

I was furious at Bob for sending us ashore in the darkness in his shitty dinghy—and at Keith for abandoning me in a godforsaken place.

Both had placed me in harm's way.
Unnecessarily.

ANOTHER BULLET DODGED

4/9/12 — Day 15

In the morning I acknowledged to myself that I was not beholden to this jerk, other than my agreement to help him get his boat through the Panama Canal. After this latest life-threatening experience—precipitated by his callousness—I couldn't care less about being part of his crew or getting to Panama or beyond. His treatment of me needed to end. I had had my fill. I began to consider my options.

Keith returned—kidneys intact.

4/10/12 — Day 16

The next day blurred into heat, engine vibration, and forced cooperation. My mind raced with options. Quitting is not in my nature, but real fear for my well-being kept pushing into my consciousness.

The sea was calm, but the boat didn't feel safer.

That evening I looked at Bob and Keith and, with as little emotion as possible, declared, "At our next port of call, I'm jumping ship!"

Bob stepped close, invading my space, staring at me in silence with his icy cold dark eyes—waiting, I think, for an apology or retreat.

I didn't give him either.

"I'm done," I said calmly. "Sailing with you is neither fun nor safe."

He said nothing.

I smiled—not out of triumph, but relief—and walked away.

4/11/12 — Day 17

At Huatulco, with the sun just above the horizon, we all stood in the salon looking at each other. Again, Bob stood too close to me for it to be an accident.

We said no words.

My hands stayed at my side, unsure how to react to his subtle aggression.

Bob offered his hand. "No hard feelings," he said.

I shook it. Not because I wanted to—but because refusing would have made me as big a prick as he was.

I had plenty to say. None of it would have made any difference. So I said nothing. Blowing off steam would have been just noise.

Bob's life was no longer my problem.

Keith and I shared a sincere goodbye. I wished him luck. There was more we could have said, but it didn't need saying.

I picked up my duffel bag and threw it over my shoulder.

I stepped off Bob's boat for the last time.

ANOTHER BULLET DODGED

I didn't get to transit the Panama Canal. To this day, that saddens me.

But I survived.

Learning Points:

- *Fear escalates when responsibility and support are absent.*
- *Equipment failures matter, but leadership failures are far more dangerous.*
- *Leaving an unsafe system is not quitting—it is survival.*
- *A fragile, damaged ego can cause one to lash out at others when threatened.*

CHAPTER 30

DEPARTURE

"Life is like riding a bicycle. To keep your balance, you must keep moving."
—Albert Einstein

AGE 55-62 · 2013-2020

Since moving to Colorado in 1994, I had commuted to my work domicile—the city where I was based as a pilot. It was an airline life built around departures.

For over two decades, my workday began long before I ever stepped into my cockpit. Extra flights. Extra hotel nights. Extra alarms. By the time I arrived at work, much of what I had to give was already spent.

The original reason for living in Colorado had been simple: stability. Airline careers move people—often. I didn't want that life for my children. Planting my family in one place spared them from being uprooted every few years as my job inevitably shifted. It worked. They grew up with continuity. But by 2013, they were grown and gone. Jillian and I had divorced three years earlier. The reason for staying in Boulder had expired.

If I wanted my work life to improve—less stress, less fatigue, more joy, and more time off—I needed to stop commuting.

By then, the old Northwest career path—including the expected move into a Detroit-based 747 captain's seat—had disappeared. Bankruptcy, the Delta merger, and the increase in the mandatory retirement age had reshuffled the deck. Seniority no longer delivered what it once promised.

At my adjusted position, the highest and best remaining options was a captain position on the Airbus A330 based in New York or Detroit.

I had spent most of my career flying Boeings. For the previous twelve years, I had been a captain on the Boeing 757 and 767. I knew those airplanes. I trusted them. I didn't want to learn a new system late in my career by transferring to an Airbus.

Remaining on the 75/76 was the practical choice.

The advantage of the 75/76 was flexibility. Multiple domiciles. Great destinations. And no retraining required to change bases. I could move and keep flying the airplane I knew.

I just had to decide where to land.

New York offered great flying but too much city. Detroit and Minneapolis felt like returning to a chapter I had already finished. Atlanta had the best trips in the system, but humidity had never been my friend—and five years after the merger, the old Northwest–Delta divisions were still visible.

That narrowed the list to Salt Lake City, Seattle, and Los Angeles.

I dismissed LA right out of the blocks because the beach communities I liked weren't affordable to me yet. In 2013, I, along with all the other Delta pilots, was still operating under the huge pay cuts forced onto the pilots during the 2006 bankruptcy. I still had college tuition payments to make, and financial responsibilities that extended beyond me. Even with the kids grown, my decisions were not yet entirely my own.

Seattle was tempting, but the downtown density had grown beyond what I wanted. That left Salt Lake City.

Salt Lake was an hour flight from my family in Colorado. The geography, climate, and outdoor activities felt familiar. The scale felt right. Most importantly, I could live downtown without a car. Light rail connected the airport to the city. I could walk to what mattered. Uber to the rest.

I bought a three-bedroom condo on the 20th floor of the American Towers at Main and Broadway. In April 2013, I moved to Salt Lake City.

When I arrived, I knew no one. It was a clean reset: a new work domicile, a new city to live in, and a place that supported the outdoor life I valued. That combination had not come together since my years in Hawaii two decades earlier.

The condo unit had been vacant for a year, but thankfully it needed little work. After years of renovation projects, it was a rare luxury to move into a place that didn't require tearing something apart first.

And, for the first time in my life, I was furnishing a home entirely on my own—no roommates, no wife, no family, no compromises. I took my time. Bought what I liked. Set up the space clean, modern, comfortable. Most importantly, it was 100 percent the way I wanted to live.

Furnishing the place had an unexpected side benefit: shopping turned out to be a great way to learn the city.

For two years, I lived an urban life without a car. I took the train to work. I walked everywhere else. The city grew familiar. It fit. I was happy both at home and at work.

In 2015, Bryn Morris, a Delta flight attendant, entered my life, and what began as a new phase quietly became the life I would build from then on.

Not long after, she moved in—and promptly began redecorating what I had just finished furnishing. She was far better at it than I was, so the place improved immediately, even if it was no longer entirely my own. I did at least get two full years in a space that was completely mine, which in the grand history of male homeownership may qualify as a respectable run.

We eventually moved into one of the penthouses in the same building, originally designed for Utah entrepreneur and mountaineer Dick Bass to use as a downtown entertaining space. As a corner unit on the twenty-fifth floor, it was the perfect canvas for my ninth renovation project. I could see the bones of the space—how walls could move and rooms could change—but Bryn had the instinct for how it should feel once people lived in it. Together, we turned it into a home.

Photo #48. Bryn during our 2016 renovation, tearing off linen wall coverings.

When I first moved to Salt Lake City, I assumed it would be my final airline move before mandatory retirement in 2023. However, working in the airline industry for 30+ years had taught me that plans for the future weren't worth the paper they were written on.

In 2018, Bryn and I moved again—this time to Los Angeles—so I could fly the Boeing 777 as the final airplane of my career and, just as importantly, avoid commuting again.

To understand how that final chapter unfolded, you must go back one year. In April 2017, I was awarded the Los Angeles captain position on the triple-seven. After everything that had come before—the mergers, the displacements, the years of reserve and commuting—it felt like the final shape of my airline career had at last come into view.

The award, however, did not mean immediate movement. A full year passed before Delta sent me to training. In April 2018, I spent the entire month in Miami in the simulator, preparing for the final checkride that would place the FAA Boeing 777 type rating on my certificate.

Then, two days before my final triple-seven checkride, Delta announced a cutback and displaced me off the 777. Just like that, the position that had taken thirty-two years at the airline to reach—and another year to begin training for—vanished before I ever flew the airplane in regular passenger service.

By then, Bryn and I had already committed fully to Los Angeles. I had purchased a home there for what was supposed to be my June 2018 start on the 777. My Salt Lake City condo had already been rented out. Movers were scheduled for late May. The next chapter of life was no longer theoretical. The move itself had become unstoppable—too many commitments had already been made to reverse cleanly—but the career plan attached to it collapsed instantly.

Yet, like so many of the industry's peculiar rules, Delta still required me to take the checkride, knowing full well that even if I passed, I would not actually fly the airplane I was qualifying to command.

I did the checkride. I passed. I received the 777 type rating—and then had to set it aside.

In May, I was back flying the 767 as a captain in Salt Lake City. The 767 was familiar and reliable—but it wasn't where I expected to be after completing 777 training and preparing to finish my career at the pinnacle of the airline.

In June, I moved to Los Angeles and continued flying the 767 there, living in the house I had purchased for a job that no longer existed.

The shifts were constant—professional, geographic, and mental. Train for one airplane. Qualify. Lose it. Move anyway. Re-anchor. Then wait.

In July, Delta reversed course. The airline discovered it had cut one triple-seven captain too many. I was reassigned to the Los Angeles 777 captain position and sent back to complete the remaining training: initial operating experience (IOE), the final step before being cleared to fly the airplane in regular passenger service.

A few weeks later, I was finally flying the airplane I had been displaced from just months earlier—this time as the most junior 777 captain in the entire system.

The triple was now the queen of the fleet, and flying her was the culmination of a long career. The airplane was superb. She handled like a high-performance sports car, not the seven-hundred-thousand-pound behemoth that she was.

What I had once imagined as an arrival became another reminder that nothing in that system ever fully settled. I stayed in Los Angeles, flew the airplane, and let go of the idea that time would ever return the seniority the merger had taken.

Under normal circumstances, the triple-seven offered better schedules, but as the most junior captain, I was placed on reserve status in LA, just as I had been numerous times earlier in my career—no fixed schedule, always on call, ready to report on short notice when Delta needed a pilot.

Being three miles from the airport in the wonderful little beach town of Playa del Rey changed reserve completely for me. There was no commuting and no cheap motel rooms waiting for the phone to ring. If they needed me, I could be at the airport in minutes. If they didn't, I was already where I wanted to be. With the kids grown and out of college, the unpredictability that once meant missing birthdays and school events no longer carried the same weight.

When the airline didn't call, I rode my bike along the beach trail each morning, worked on another renovation project, and most afternoons watched the sun settle into the Pacific. Living at the beach in Los Angeles—phone nearby, toes in the sand—softened the waiting.

Amazingly, the airline rarely called.

It was a good life. For the first time since Hawaii in the '90s, everything aligned perfectly. I was content.

Then it stopped.

By late spring of 2020, the airport terminals were quiet in a way I had not seen since 9/11. Flights disappeared from schedules overnight. Borders closed. Airplanes sat idle. Pilots had no work to perform. *(Inside the Story: COVID-19 and the Airline Industry.)*

I hadn't touched a yoke since late January 2020.

That amount of time without flying told us all we needed to know about what was coming.

By June, attempting to stem the flow of red ink, Delta announced the immediate retirement of the entire 777 fleet. Regardless of how the pandemic unfolded, I would never return to that triple-seven cockpit.

In July, I was informed that if I did not accept early retirement, I would be reassigned to Seattle and forced to retrain on the Airbus A330.

The message was unambiguous.

I didn't want to hang up my spurs, but I didn't have another forced relocation left in me.

I didn't have the desire to start over on a new airplane.

After thirty-five years, the handwriting was on the wall: my airline rollercoaster career would end here.

I accepted the severance package and retired at age sixty-two and a half. *(Inside the Story: Airline Pilot Retirement.)*

Retirement arrived without transition. There was no final year to prepare. No last flight with family onboard. No water cannon salute. No gate ceremony.

Just silence.

On September 1, 2020, along with 1,900 other senior Delta pilots, my career ended—with an email instructing me to FedEx my company ID back to the airline.

No call.

No handshake.

No goodbye.

No gold watch.

Just an email.

At 12:01 a.m., I was no longer a professional pilot. After forty-two years, the flight was over. *(Inside the Story: Airline Pilot's Last Days.)*

One small piece of good news, I never contracted the virus. Like most people, I know people who did, and some who did not survive it.

Perspective matters.

But COVID still took something precious from me—my first love—earlier than I ever imagined.

Retirement also took my next love—living by the ocean. The sea was—and is—my happy place. It settles me and brings a sense of balance to my daily life. But with Bryn still based in Salt

Lake City and my flying career over, returning to Utah simplified what remained.

The choice was not really about geography. The beach and our condo had been wonderful, but Bryn mattered more than any place. I was not about to spend the next chapter of my life asking the person I loved to keep living out of a suitcase. Leaving the beach life in Los Angeles was difficult, but it was the right choice.

I can still visit the beach and fly small airplanes.

Both are enjoyable.

It is not the same.

I spent decades trying not to define myself by my profession. That proved difficult when the profession had defined my days for most of my adult life. And honestly, it was such a cool job. The command experience—the responsibility, the precision, the quiet authority—gave me a sense of meaning that is hard to replace.

Flying was never just a job. For forty-two years, it had given structure to my days, purpose to my decisions, and a sense of belonging that never wavered. When it stopped, something essential went quiet with it.

Retirement has its own gifts. Control over my days. Time without alarms. A life no longer governed by schedules—only freedom.

It is good.

It is not the same.

Perhaps the strangest aspect of retirement, for someone like me, is knowing I accomplished my goal—and that it is now over. After a lifetime pursuing that five-year-old boy's dream, it is hard to accept that it was achieved, lived, and is now a thing of the past.

While living that dream, I was often focused on what came next rather than where I was. Another airplane. Another seat. Another chapter. For that reason, I sometimes drove myself hard, impatient to reach every goal. Now, looking back over my shoulder, it feels as though it all came and went in a flash.

Career Summary

Over thirty-five years at the airline, time was measured less by calendars than by airplanes, seats, and bases.

I flew six airplanes, in three seats, across eight cities—and moved bases far more than is enjoyable.

Minneapolis.

Detroit.

Minneapolis.

New York.

Minneapolis.

Honolulu.

Boston.

Minneapolis.

Detroit.

Minneapolis.

Detroit.

Minneapolis.

Detroit.

Minneapolis.

Salt Lake City.

Los Angeles.

Salt Lake City.

Los Angeles.

Seattle.

Nineteen assignments in all.
Some lasted years.
One lasted only three weeks.
Sometimes the move was my choice.
More often, it wasn't.
I started as a second officer on the Boeing 727.
Then the DC-10. Then the 747.

Eventually, I became a copilot on the DC-10.
More transfers followed.
New schedules.
New cities.
New routines that rarely lasted long.
Ten and a half years in, I upgraded to captain on the 727.
From there, the airplanes changed but the pattern didn't.
The 757.
The 767.
The 777, on paper only.
Back to the 767.
Finally, the 777.
Bases continued to come and go.
Each time life began to settle, a bid closed.
A base disappeared.
An airplane retired.
A merger intervened.
A recession arrived.
The needs of the service always came first.
Homes were temporary.
Friendships were provisional.
Furniture stayed light.

For pilots, that sequence tells a story of time: progress, setbacks, and survival within a seniority-driven system that never stops moving.

For everyone else, it means this: stability was always conditional.

Along the way, I experienced one strike, two separate periods of pay cuts, three industry-wide disruptions, four recessions, five CEOs, six contract negotiations, a hostile leveraged buyout, and a bankruptcy.

I never had to start over at another airline.
I never lost my profession.
I never lost my seat permanently.
I never stopped flying.
By airline standards, that was more than a good career.
It was a fortunate one.

ANOTHER BULLET DODGED

Final Flight

My last flight was a routine leg from Shanghai to Los Angeles on January 29, 2020. At the time, I had only read brief reports about a new virus circulating in China.

At the gate, three passengers waiting to board displayed obvious signs of illness. I did not allow them onto the airplane. I will never know what they were suffering from. In retrospect, it hardly mattered. The world was already changing in ways none of us yet understood.

Aviation was on a collision course with something no checklist could solve.

At the time, I had no idea it would be my last flight.

I never touched the controls of a commercial airplane again.

Final Thoughts

To the captains I flew with before my upgrade—thank you. You taught me, mostly without words, what leadership looked like under pressure. Some showed me exactly what I never wanted to become. Most showed me what professionalism meant.

I carried those lessons with me every day I sat in the left seat.

To the first officers who shared the cockpit with me for twenty-four years—thank you. You brought competence, judgment, humor, and perspective into a workspace that demanded all of it. I learned from you constantly. My job as captain was easier—and better—because of you.

To my parents, thank you for never discouraging a five-year-old's improbable dream. You treated it as something possible long before it was.

To Bryn—thank you for making life after flying something I look forward to. You arrived at a moment when the future needed reinvention, and you made that transition not just bearable, but joyful.

To my ex-wife, thanks for always running the household in my absence and taking such good care of our children.

To my children: I know it felt like I was gone a lot. I missed things I wish I hadn't. Please know that I loved flying, but coming home to you was always the best part of every trip. You were the reason home meant more to me than any airplane ever could.

And to the unknown Eastern Air Lines DC-7 captain who once invited a wide-eyed five-year-old boy into his cockpit—I hope I did you proud. I tried to pass that gift forward every chance I got.

Throughout my career, I carried a Polaroid instant camera in my flight bag. It wasn't company-issued. No one asked me to do it. I simply felt compelled to do it. It started when I became a captain and never stopped.

Whenever time allowed, I invited children up to the cockpit. I let them sit in a pilot's seat. I handed them a hat. I pointed out the instruments, flashed colored lights and rang alarm bells. Sometimes they asked questions. Sometimes they were too overwhelmed to speak.

I took a picture every time.

The camera whirred. The film slid out. I shook it once, gently, and handed it to them while it developed. Parents stood back. Kids watched the image appear in their hands, the flight deck slowly coming into focus behind them.

Before cell phones, before cameras were everywhere, that picture mattered. I gave it to them and sent them back with something new to think about.

In my era, children could no longer remain in the cockpit during taxi and takeoff. Those days were gone. But the thrill of stepping into that magical front room while the airplane was still at the gate—well, that never faded.

I like to think that somewhere, on desks in pilots' home offices, are framed photos of children sitting in a cockpit, wearing a pilot's hat that was too big, smiling at a future they could not yet imagine.

No matter how many thousands of hours I logged, the magic never faded.

Every time I raised the airplane's nose fifteen degrees skyward, that five-year-old boy—the one who first stepped into a cockpit and never wanted to leave—was still there, quietly amazed, deeply grateful, and smiling.

Learning Points:

- *Life is a journey—enjoy the odyssey!*
- *Planning provides direction, but flexibility is essential when plans inevitably change.*

- *Keep learning, growing, and pursuing new goals until the end.*
- *A successful life may be one that ends with goals still left to pursue.*
- *Be more inquisitive and less judgmental.*

Photo #49. David in front of a Boeing 777 engine, months before Delta retired the airplane and the pilot.

Inside the Story *(Optional Reading)*

COVID-19 and the Airline Industry

The COVID-19 pandemic caused an immediate and severe collapse in long-haul international travel, the segment of the airline industry that supports widebody aircraft such as the Boeing 777. As countries closed borders and imposed entry restrictions, international routes were among the first to disappear from airline schedules.

Commercial aviation has significant fixed expenses, including aircraft ownership or lease payments, maintenance, airport facilities, and labor. When passenger demand drops sharply, those costs remain largely unchanged, making it difficult for airlines to sustain operations without the substantial revenue those operations were planned around.

For airlines like Delta, widebody fleets are among the most expensive assets to operate and maintain. These aircraft are designed for high passenger loads and long-distance routes, both of which vanished almost overnight when the pandemic was declared. With demand effectively gone, many of these airplanes became economically unsustainable to keep in service.

In response, airlines grounded large portions of their fleets, reduced schedules, and sought ways to conserve cash. Many aircraft were placed into long-term storage, while others were retired earlier than planned. At Delta, this included the retirement of entire aircraft types, including the 777, as the company moved to simplify operations and reduce costs.

These decisions were not tied to a short-term recovery timeline; they reflected an expectation that international travel would remain depressed for an extended period.

For pilots, the impact was immediate and personal. Aircraft retirements, base closures, and reduced flying hours forced difficult choices—relocation, retraining on different aircraft, or early retirement. Workforce reductions, early retirements, and furloughs became widespread as airlines adjusted to the sudden and uncertain decline in travel demand. Senior pilots, in particular, often faced the decision of whether to start over on a new airplane late in their careers or leave the profession earlier than planned.

Airline Pilot Retirement

Airline pilot retirement is unique among professions because it is both mandatory and predictable. Federal regulations require pilots flying for U.S. airlines to retire at age sixty-five, regardless of experience, skill level, or desire to continue working. Unlike many careers, there is no option to extend employment beyond that age in commercial airline operations.

Most pilots spend decades working toward positions that combine seniority, aircraft type, and schedule control. By the final years of a career, many have reached the peak of their profession—flying the largest aircraft, earning their highest pay, and holding the most favorable schedules. Retirement, therefore, often represents not a gradual winding down, but an abrupt end to a long-developed professional identity.

The transition can be challenging. Airline pilots are accustomed to environments that demand constant decision-making, procedural discipline, and responsibility for safety. Moving from that structured, high-consequence role into retirement often involves a significant shift in daily purpose and identity.

For that reason, many pilots approach retirement with a mix of anticipation and reluctance. While it offers freedom from schedules and obligations, it also marks the end of a career that, for many, has defined their sense of purpose for much of their adult lives.

Airline Pilot's Last Days

The end of an airline pilot's career is typically a structured and anticipated event. In the final year before mandatory retirement, pilots often enjoy the benefits of top seniority. Senior pilots commonly select meaningful final trips, often flying with family members on board, and coordinate their last flight as a symbolic milestone.

Traditionally, the final flight itself carries ceremonial significance. It may conclude with a water cannon salute from airport fire crews, followed by a small gathering at the gate with colleagues, friends, and family. These rituals serve as a formal acknowledgment of a long career and provide a sense of closure for both the pilot and those they worked with.

Under normal circumstances, this final phase allows time for reflection, preparation, and emotional transition. The structure of the process helps mark the end of a career that, for many pilots, has spanned decades and defined a central part of their identity.

When that last year is removed, the transition can feel abrupt and incomplete. The absence of a final flight, a farewell, or even a clear endpoint can leave the conclusion of a career feeling unresolved.

EPILOGUE
FIELD NOTES

These pieces weren't written to be poetry. They were written when life caught me off guard—on a bus, on a layover, in the middle of a life that no longer fit the way it once had.

I wrote them the way you jot something down on the back of a flight release or a hotel notepad—not to impress anyone, not to explain myself, but to capture what felt true before it slipped away.

SILVER WINGS

DBW 2002

We float through the skies, on silver wings,
Faster and safer than the Wrights once dreamed.
Trusting our lives to countless hands and things,
Pilots, mechanics, steady and unseen.

How familiar, flight has become,
Millions flying, trusting what will come.
As the miracle fades, from modern air travel,
Old fears and anxieties, slowly unravel.

But now, Airports and airways strain at the seam,
Traffic controllers, ready to scream.
People rushing, pushing, chasing a routine,
Too busy to notice, the miracle of the machine.

Jet travel has shrunk our little blue ball,
At 500 knots, the jet airplane does haul.
The farthest horizons pass in the blink of an eye.
Thanks to two brothers, who dared to try.

As cities and towns drift from sight,
Savor the serenity of this special flight.
Let earthly worries release and flow.
The Zen awaits, as the world drifts below.

We float through the skies, on silver wings,
Rarely reflecting on this marvelous scene.
Forgetting the wonder these journeys can bring.
At 33,000 feet, life is so serene!

CITY BUS

DBW 2000

I rode the city bus,
To Santa Monica today.
The number 7 Pico's,
In a place called LA

Packed tightly together,
Smooshed like sardines.
Shoulder to shoulder,
Swaying as the bus would lean.

In a city not known,
for brotherly Love,
I saw far more,
Than a push and shove.

I spent the time,
By looking at the faces.
I gazed into their eyes.
Seeing people, not their races.

I saw strangers exuding,
Warmth and compassion.
It almost seemed,
Kindness was in fashion.

Like the young white male,
Who helped an elderly black man,
I watched humans of all types,
Just lending a hand.

Then came a Hispanic lady,
Who bounded aboard,
Passing out hugs and kisses,
For the driver, and others she adored.

Or the punkster,
Who looked rough and tough,
Who offered his seat
And got up off his duff.

I witnessed humanity at its best—
simple, mundane, and plain.
Right here on this local city bus,
Average people, acting very sane!

So, thank you Los Angeles,
And to all on the Pico's #7 that day.
For I experienced hope for humanity,
Now and in the future, I must say!

RELATIONSHIP GARDEN

DBW 2011

We need to tend to it daily.
It needs to be hydrated often with love.
Nurtured regularly, to stimulate growth.

Till gently with compassion—
Break up hardness with tender care.

Plant seedlings of communication often.
Oxygenate to foster development.
Encourage all that push through.

Don't trample when they're fragile.
Weed carefully, so as not to damage new growth.
Protect it from outside predators—

A garden doesn't die all at once.
Neglect is the enemy.
It withers while you're busy elsewhere.

What survives is what was tended to.

OLD DOG NEW TRICKS
DBW 2003

Automation, auto switching, autoland.
Cockpit, Flight Deck, what the heck.
I want to bury my head in the sand!

A pilot once was a leader and doer.
Now with computers and high-tech,
a keyboard do I peck.

It used to be the captain was in command.
Today three autopilots steal the show.
Couple and engage—the rulebooks demand.

The machine quietly does its work.
I'm simply watching for the gremlins that lurk.
Often it feels less like a perk.

I miss my trusty Seven-Two-Seven!
She always demanded a pilot's best.
Offering a momentary pass through heaven.

Once upon a time, the pit had five.
Then four, three, two.
If I predict one, will you call it jive?

Soon the machine will do it all.
Stories will be told of the pilots of old.
What we once did, some may recall.

Alas... 'tis no nobler to admit the truth.
Aviators are antiques, with outdated techniques.
With pride and despair, I bow out—with couth.

So, farewell to the job I loved and knew.
The memories are rich,
of the years when I really flew!

EPILOGUE

PARADE of SOLDIERS

DBW 2010

For weeks and months we deal with snow.
Slush-covered runways, and temperatures so very low.
Winter's fury, coupled with a hefty blow.
Weather so foul, perhaps we shouldn't go?

Centerline lights... but markings obscured.
Vis so low, my vision is blurred.
Above this mess, blue skies endure.
The magic of meteorology, a mystery for sure.

Every winter, it's the same old game.
Delays & cancellations, but Mother Nature is to blame.
A Minnesota winter is like a shrew to tame.
At best, beyond what forecasts proclaim.

But then one day, the snow is all gone.
The rains begin, greening up the lawn.
A sign of relief, as spring prances in like a fawn.
Yet we aviators know, what's waiting just beyond.

Soon winter yields its power and might.
To towering thunderstorms, that will blast us at night.
Storms so massive, they climb out of sight.
And energy so great, they could smash us in flight.

Thus begins the summer drama as we fly.
Lines of monsters, refusing to let us by.
Blocking our way and goading us to try.
Like a parade of soldiers, marching in the sky.

So, farewell to peace & tranquility as we cruise.
Calm has been replaced by pyrotechnics on the loose.
Behemoths so powerful, man can only muse.
But left or right, a pilot must choose.

For the next 5 months, this dance will go on.
Battling Gaia, as she flexes her brawn.
Yet around the corner, the T-storms will be gone.
A moment's rest, before the next new dawn.

And so, the cycle begins anew.
Another day, another problem, for the pilot to chew.
Choose as he will, Mother Nature will still do.
Tests and challenges, reminding who's who.

BANZAI CLIFF

DBW 2004

I have laid my feet upon hallowed grounds.
I have walked amongst the dead on many a battlefield.
I have felt the stirring of souls long lost.
I have wept from the horrors of our past.

Today I stand upon sacred land in the Central Pacific.
Today I gaze unto the sea, atop the cliffs of Saipan.
Today I stand in the footsteps of dead Japanese soldiers and civilians.
Today my eyes see what they could not have seen.

I stand on this precipice, in 2004, alongside two Japanese companions.
I struggle to understand the events of decades past.
I live in a world so very different from 1944.
I cannot begin to make sense of what happened here.

We do not discuss war, or of being enemies.
We do not speak of Victors, or Vanquished.
We do not speak.
We listen. We feel. We bow our heads in respect.

Yesterday we were mortal enemies, fighting a bloody war.
Yesterday, in my father's time, Japan was the Villain.
Yesterday, 5,005 American Soldiers died taking this tiny island.
Yesterday, 20,000 Nippon jumped to their deaths from these cliffs.
Yesterday, war touched everyone's life.

Today, Japan is a vital partner and friend of the U.S.
Today, Japan is a mighty economic force… in my time.
Today, the concept of World War seems remote and distant.
Today, we search for the meaning of this carnage.

Sixty years ago, thousands committed suicide on Saipan.
Sixty years ago, boys were dying in foreign lands by the droves.
Sixty years ago, blood flowed from the pores of the Earth.
Sixty years ago, God turned his back on his children.

I dedicate my thoughts, this hot August day, to the fallen.
I honor the Americans and Japanese who died for their country.
I pay homage to those who died in the way.
I pray for the souls of those who sent these boys to die in faraway lands.

Walking through downtown Portland on a layover with three young flight attendants, I watched them recoil from a homeless man we passed. They saw the dirt and the smell. I found myself wondering what he wished they could see and wrote this.

McGRIFF

DBW 2001

My name is McGriff.
And if I thought it would make any diff.
I could dye my hair orange, purple, or green if.
Your heart I could have in a jiff!

Your presence has awakened this drunk and his fif'.
Beauty so fine, yu have left me breathless & stiff.
I pray you perceive the real McGriff.
Though you may only see raff-riff.

I may not be pretty, nor very spiffed.
And I sure hope you don't get a big whiff.
A shower and a shave will make a big diff.
Then you might recognize the true McGriff.

Do not run or act too miffed.
From a sad lonely man, hoping for a liff.
A smile and a nod perhaps—if,
Your heart has room for old McGriff.

Alas, I shall leave O so swiff.
For I am not looking for a tiff.
I'll return to my hovel by the cliff.
Dreaming you remember… meeting McGriff!

GOD

DBW 2001

Is there really a God?
Thy creator, who giveth thee life.

Life begins at conception.
Yet our being begins at birth!

At birth our struggle begins,
to understand life.

And life is the search
for answers about God.

Yet God stays elusive and cloaked,
till death takes life.

Only in death,
Thou answerest life!

AFTER THE CHOCKS

DBW 2020

The engines are quiet now.
The checklists are done.

I loved flying not because it was easy,
but because it demanded everything—
attention, humility, judgment.

Up there, excuses didn't matter.
The airplane didn't care who you were.
Only what you did.
And whether you understood
the consequences of your choices.

Some days I was skilled.
Some days I was lucky.
Most days, I needed both.

Aviation taught me this:
you don't survive by avoiding risk.
You survive by respecting it.

By knowing when to push.
And when to stop.

When the final chocks go in,
the flights are over.

What you carry with you afterward—
the people you protected,
the mistakes you owned,
the professionalism you showed when no one was watching—

That's what stays after the engines go quiet.

ABOUT THE AUTHOR

David B. Waldman retired from a thirty-five-year airline career after flying six aircraft types, serving as captain on four of them, and accumulating thousands of hours around the world.

He now lives in Salt Lake City, Utah, with his partner Bryn, where he continues to remodel homes, hike, ski, and pursue whatever challenge seems interesting at the moment.

His three children are all grown, and becoming a grandfather has given him a new appreciation for how quickly life moves and how precious ordinary moments can be.

He remains endlessly curious about people, places, and the strange ways life can change course without warning.

Another Bullet Dodged is his third book.

A FRIEND'S PERSPECTIVE

Few people live life to the fullest. David Waldman is one of them.

After five years as David's friend and neighbor—and after reading about all the escapades described in this book—I have gained an understanding of his unique approach to life. Whereas most of us face new challenges with caution and an eye toward safety, David says, "Why not?"

As a result, throughout his entire life David has predictably gotten himself into unusual predicaments. But then, through some kind of magical, almost miraculous turn of events, he has been able to extricate himself from untoward consequences each and every time. Hence, "Another Bullet Dodged"!

The reader will find his recounting of each of his individual ventures both engaging and entertaining, often humorous, and frequently educational. In addition to his engaging narrative style of writing, he also includes informative segments regarding aviation, sailing, and more widely applicable and useful life principles. His passion for life clearly shines through.

After reflecting on his decisions and experiences, and how they apply to us, we may each change a little and determine to live a life that is a little fuller.

Enjoy!

Charles H. McLeskey, M.D.
Friend and neighbor

Made in the USA
Coppell, TX
20 August 2026

86903807R00233